A Beginner's Guide to Developing Documentum® Desktop Applications

A Beginner's Guide to Developing Documentum® Desktop Applications

---

*Techniques and Solutions Using Visual Basic®
and the DFC*

M. Scott Roth

iUniverse, Inc.
New York Lincoln Shanghai

A Beginner's Guide to Developing Documentum® Desktop Applications
Techniques and Solutions Using Visual Basic® and the DFC

Copyright © 2005 by Michael S. Roth

All rights reserved. No part of this book may be used or reproduced by any means, graphic, electronic, or mechanical, including photocopying, recording, taping or by any information storage retrieval system without the written permission of the publisher except in the case of brief quotations embodied in critical articles and reviews.

iUniverse books may be ordered through booksellers or by contacting:

iUniverse
2021 Pine Lake Road, Suite 100
Lincoln, NE 68512
www.iuniverse.com
1-800-Authors (1-800-288-4677)

ISBN: 0-595-33968-9

Printed in the United States of America

Disclaimer

The author has made every effort to ensure that the information in this book is complete, and accurate. This information is provided "as is". The author makes no warranty concerning the information, and shall have no liability with respect to loss or damages arising from its use.

Trademarks

All terms and product names mentioned in this book that are known to be trademarks, registered trademarks, or service marks have been properly spelled, capitalized, and notated. The use of a term or name in this book should not be regarded as affecting the validity of any trademark, registered trademark, or service mark.

Documentum, Documentum Desktop, Documentum Application Builder, Documentum Server, Workspace, Docbase and Content Server are either trademarks or registered trademarks of Documentum, a division of EMC Corporation, in the United States and other countries.

Windows, Visual Basic, Visual Studio and IntelliSense are either trademarks or registered trademarks of Microsoft Corp. in the United States and other countries.

Java is a registered trademark of Sun Microsystems, Inc. in the United States and other countries.

Verity, TOPIC and KeyView are registered trademarks of Verity, Inc. in the United States and other countries.

Oracle is a registered trademark of Oracle, Corp. in the United States and other countries.

*I thankfully dedicate this book, as with all of my labors,
to the glory of God.*

*I also dedicate this book to my loving wife, Rachael,
who has tolerated me sitting at this keyboard
every night. I love you.*

*And to my daughter, Kristin,
who is my treasure.*

Micah 6:8
Joshua 24:15

Contents

PREFACE XVII
   ABOUT THE AUTHOR XVIII
   CONTACT INFORMATION XVIII
   REFERENCES XVIII
1. INTRODUCTION 1
   1.1 WHO SHOULD READ THIS BOOK? 2
   1.2 ORGANIZATION OF THIS BOOK 2
   1.3 SOURCE CODE 3
   1.4 CONVENTIONS USED IN THIS BOOK 4
      1.4.1 Typographic *4*
      1.4.2 Variables And Source Code *4*
      1.4.3 Class And Interface Nomenclature *5*
   1.5 A BRIEF INTRODUCTION TO THE DOCUMENTUM FOUNDATION CLASSES 5
      1.5.1 Docbase Classes *7*
      1.5.2 Service Classes *8*
      1.5.3 Documentum Desktop Classes *9*
   1.6 OVERVIEW OF A DOCUMENTUM DESKTOP APPLICATION 10
   1.7 INTERFACE INHERITANCE AND TYPE CASTING IN VISUAL BASIC 12
2 GETTING STARTED WITH APPLICATIONS AND COMPONENTS 15
   2.1 BUILDING A STANDALONE APPLICATION 16
      2.1.1 Setting Up A Standalone Application Project *16*
      2.1.2 Application Skeleton Code *20*

  2.1.3 Debugging And Testing The Application 23

  2.1.4 Packaging And Deploying the Application 23

 2.2 BUILDING A COMPONENT 24

  2.2.1 A Word About COM And Documentum Components 24

  2.2.2 Setting Up A Component Project 25

  2.2.3 Component Skeleton Code 31

  2.2.4 Debugging And Testing The Component 36

  2.2.5 Packaging A Component 42

  2.2.6 Adding A Component To A DocApp 44

 2.3 MODIFYING THE DOCUMENTUM DESKTOP MENU 48

  2.3.1 A Word About Menus 48

  2.3.2 Adding A Global Component To The Menu 48

  2.3.3 Adding A Type-Specific Component To The Menu 51

  2.3.4 Adding An Executable Application To The Menu 51

 2.4 MODIFYING DOCUMENTUM DESKTOP COMPONENTS 52

 2.5 TROUBLESHOOTING COMPONENT DELIVERY 54

 2.6 CHAPTER SUMMARY 55

3 WORKING WITH QUERIES AND COLLECTIONS 56

 3.1 HOW TO QUERY THE DOCBASE 57

  3.1.1 Using Run Query 57

  3.1.2 Using The Query Manager 58

  3.1.3 Using The IDfQuery Class 64

 3.2 TYPES OF QUERIES 66

  3.2.1 SQL Pass-Through Queries 66

  3.2.2 Cached Queries 68

  3.2.3 Full-Text Queries 71

 3.3 HOW TO PROCESS COLLECTIONS 82

3.3.1 Basic Collection Processing *82*
3.3.2 Tracing For Open Collections *85*
3.3.3 Calculating The Size Of Collections *86*
3.3.4 Recursive Processing Of Collections *88*
3.3.5 Processing Collections With Unknown Content *91*
3.4 Useful Queries 93
3.4.1 Full-Text Queries *94*
3.4.2 Full-Text Index Queries *96*
3.4.3 Registered Table Queries *97*
3.4.4 Virtual Document Queries *100*
3.4.5 Workflow Queries *101*
3.4.6 Inbox Queries *104*
3.4.7 Object Queries *105*
3.4.8 Content, Cabinet, and Folder Queries *106*
3.4.9 Setting Up Indexes *108*
3.5 Chapter Summary 108

4 IMPLEMENTING CORE DOCUMENT MANAGEMENT FUNCTIONS 110
4.1 Implementing Library Functions With The DFC 111
4.1.1 Creating Objects *111*
4.1.2 Deleting Objects *114*
4.1.3 Copying Objects *120*
4.1.4 Checking Out And Editing Objects *124*
4.1.5 Viewing Objects *126*
4.1.6 Canceling A Checkout *127*
4.1.7 Checking In Objects *128*
4.2 Implementing Library Functions With DFC Operation Classes 129
4.2.1 Overview Of Using Operations *132*

- 4.2.2 Creating And Viewing Objects *133*
- 4.2.3 Deleting Objects *133*
- 4.2.4 Copying Objects *134*
- 4.2.5 Checking Out And Editing Objects *135*
- 4.2.6 Canceling Checkout Of Objects *137*
- 4.2.7 Checking In Objects *138*
- 4.2.8 Implementing An Operation Monitor *139*
- 4.2.9 Processing An Operation Abort *141*
- 4.3 CHAPTER SUMMARY 143

5 PROVEN SOLUTIONS FOR COMMON TASKS 145
- 5.1 LOGIN USING THE DFC 146
- 5.2 LOGIN USING THE LOGIN MANAGER 147
- 5.3 PASSING A SESSION TO A FORM 151
- 5.4 SESSION LOCKING 153
- 5.5 A NON-BLOCKING VISUAL BASIC SLEEP() FUNCTION 156
- 5.6 RUNNING DOCUMENTUM COMPONENTS 157
- 5.7 ERROR TRAPPING 160
- 5.8 TRACING 162
  - 5.8.1 Client-Side Tracing *162*
  - 5.8.2 Server-Side Tracing *171*
  - 5.8.3 Custom Tracing *174*
- 5.9 AUDITING 176
- 5.10 USING THE PROGRESS SENTINEL 180
- 5.11 USING THE REGISTRY 182
  - 5.11.1 Accessing The Registry *183*
  - 5.11.2 Accessing Checked Out Files *183*
  - 5.11.3 Enumerating Subkeys *185*

5.12 CREATING A DOCUMENTUM RESOURCE LOCATOR 190

5.13 SENDING E-MAIL FROM A DOCUMENTUM DESKTOP APPLICATION 192

5.14 FINDING THE FOLDER PATH FROM AN OBJECT ID 194

5.15 CREATING DOCBASE PATHS 197

5.16 WORKING WITH THE INBOX 201

5.17 DUMPING AND LOADING THE DOCBASE 204

   5.17.1 Dump *204*

   5.17.2 Load *211*

5.18 IMPLEMENTING A SIMPLE SEARCH FORM 216

   5.18.1 The Form *216*

   5.18.2 The Code *218*

   5.18.3 The Results *225*

5.19 CHAPTER SUMMARY 225

6 WORKING WITH SCREEN CONTROLS 226

6.1 DOCUMENTUM VALIDATION CONTROLS 227

   6.1.1 Referencing Validation Controls In Your Visual Basic Project *228*

   6.1.2 Example Of Documentum Validation Controls *228*

6.2 DOCBASE-AWARE CONTROLS 234

   6.2.1 Referencing Docbase-Aware Controls In Your Visual Basic Project *235*

   6.2.2 Example Of Docbase-Aware Controls *236*

   6.2.3 The Documentum Open Dialog *241*

6.3 VISUAL BASIC CONTROLS 245

   6.3.1 Referencing Microsoft Controls In Your Project *245*

   6.3.2 Example Of Emulating Validation And Docbase-Aware Controls *246*

6.4 THE OBJECT SELECTOR FORM 261

   6.4.1 The Form *261*

   6.4.2 The Code *263*

    6.4.3 Using The Form *276*

  6.5 CHAPTER SUMMARY 277

7 TIPS, TOOLS AND HANDY INFORMATION 278

  7.1 THE DOCUMENTUM API 278

    7.1.1 dmAPIExec() *279*

    7.1.2 dmAPIGet() *279*

    7.1.3 dmAPISet() *280*

  7.2 THE DOCUMENTUM API FROM THE DFC 280

    7.2.1 apiExec() *280*

    7.2.2 apiGet() *281*

    7.2.3 apiSet() *281*

  7.3 THE INTERACTIVE MESSAGE TESTER 282

  7.4 THE IAPI32 AND IDQL32 COMMAND LINE UTILITIES 283

  7.5 SAMSON 283

  7.6 RESETTING THE DOCUMENTUM DESKTOP 283

  7.7 CLEARING THE CLIENT-SIDE CACHES 284

  7.8 ANATOMY OF THE DMCL.INI FILE 284

    7.8.1 Backup DocBroker *285*

    7.8.2 Client-Side Cache Size *285*

    7.8.3 Local Path *285*

    7.8.4 Batch Hint Size *285*

    7.8.5 Compression *286*

    7.8.6 Cached Queries *286*

    7.8.7 Tracing *286*

  7.9 ANATOMY OF THE R_OBJECT_ID 287

  7.10 OBJECT TYPE IDENTIFIERS 287

  7.11 ATTRIBUTE DATA TYPES 291

7.12 Computed Attributes	292
7.13 Format Types	294
7.14 Object Permissions	309
7.15 Registered Table Permissions	310
7.16 Verity KeyView File Filters	311
7.17 Menu Command State Flags	312
7.18 Uninstalling DocApps	315
7.19 Server Error Files	316
7.20 Anatomy Of The server.ini File	320
7.20.1 Enforce a Four Digit Year	320
7.20.2 Client Session Timeout Period	321
7.20.3 Concurrent Sessions	321
7.20.4 Login Ticket Timeout Period	321
7.20.5 Mail Notification	321
7.20.6 User Authentication Case	322
7.20.7 Workflow Agent Sleep Interval	322
7.21 Chapter Summary	322

8 PUTTING IT ALL TOGETHER IN A SAMPLE APPLICATION 323

8.1 dmSpy	323
8.1.1 The Form	326
8.1.2 The Code	328
8.1.3 Using dmSpy	357
8.2 Chapter Summary	357

AFTERWORD 359

INDEX 365

Preface

When I began writing this book it wasn't supposed to be a book, it was a project to organize a manila folder into some sort of usable and manageable collection. The folder contained Documentum® tech support notes, chapters from books, source code listings, Internet posts, tips, tricks, and best practices I had collected or developed over the years. Two things happened that changed the purpose and audience for this project. First, I started a job with a staff of experienced programmers that had never programmed in Documentum. My peers didn't need insight about general programming; they needed insight about programming in Documentum. I planned to give them guidance and jump-start their Documentum programming experience by documenting my own experiences. The organization of this material was a first step.

The second thing that happened was the Internet buzz regarding the lack of third-party Documentum training, books, tutorials, and documentation reached another all-time high. People were clamoring for the kind of information I had in my folder and in my head! With these two things in mind, I decided to broaden the audience for this project, and write this book for you, the beginning Documentum programmer.

This book focuses on the basic building blocks of Documentum development and is largely a product of my personal experiences. This book strives to be both a hands-on guide to developing applications and solutions for Documentum, as well as a guide to best practices. It demonstrates how to start a Documentum project, issue and process queries, and use screen controls. Along the way, it touches on some other common building blocks and best practices. For instance, it demonstrates how to implement basic document management functionality (e.g., checkin, checkout) using custom code as well as Documentum operation classes. It recommends best practices for session management, and tips for tracing and debugging applications and components. It also provides quick access to some of the most frequently referenced Documentum definitions and constants (e.g., object permission values).

About The Author

Scott Roth is a Senior Software Engineer and a Microsoft Certified Solution Developer (MCSD) with Science Applications International Corporation (SAIC). He has been developing Documentum solutions for the Federal Government and commercial industry since 1998. Mr. Roth's experience includes Documentum 3.1, EDMS 98, Documentum 4i, Documentum 5, RightSite, the WDK, peripheral products, and numerous customization jobs. He has also spoken twice at *Momentum*, Documentum's user conference, on the topic of managing digital assets with Documentum.

Mr. Roth is a frequent contributor to the `www.dmdeveloper.com` website, as well as the `groups.yahoo.com` Documentum discussion forums. In 1999, he developed Db-Documentum, a Perl module that interfaces with the Documentum API. This module allows Documentum applications to be written in Perl. Db-Documentum is available free from the Comprehensive Perl Archive Network (CPAN): `http://www.cpan.org/modules/by-authors/id/M/MS/MSROTH/`.

Contact Information

I have created a website for this book at: `http://www.dm-book.com`. The website contains many useful bits of information including: all the source code in the book, corrections, a sample chapter, reviews, utilities and other articles, contact information, and an opportunity to order more books.

The easiest way to contact me is through the website. However, if you prefer to email me directly, my email address is: `Scott@dm-book.com`.

Please contact me and let me know what you think of this book. Ask me a question, provide a correction, give me a tip, a trick, a best practice; or tell me I'm out of my mind! I look forward to hearing from you.

References

The information, the code, and the best practices contained in this book came from my personal experience with Documentum. However, to refresh my memory and verify certain aspects of the Documentum, I frequently access the publications and references list below. I encourage you to take advantage of them also.

Documentum Publications
- *Developing DFC Applications*
- *Developing Documentum Applications*
- *Documentum 5 Architecture: A Technical Overview*
- *Documentum Application Performance and Tuning*
- *Documentum Content Server Administrator's Guide*

- *Documentum Content Server API Reference Manual*
- *Documentum Content Server DQL Reference Manual*
- *Documentum Content Server Fundamentals*
- *Documentum Content Server Object Reference Manual*
- *Documentum Desktop Development Kit Development Guide*
- *Documentum Foundation Classes API Specification*
- *Documentum Foundation Classes Development Guide*
- *Using DFC in Documentum Applications*

Documentum Resources
- Documentum technical support notes
  (The Documentum tech support site is a great place to find information from Documentum engineers not necessarily included in any of their publications.)
- Documentum training classes
- Documentum online "webinars"
- Momentum training sessions
- Documentum professional services consultants

Internet Resources
- dm_developer (dm_developer is the Internet's premier Documentum discussion site and source for free advice, articles, and tools.)
  `http://www.dmdeveloper.com`)
- Documentum developer website
  `http://developer.documentum.com`)
- Documentum discussion groups at Yahoo!
  (`http://groups.yahoo.com`)
- Microsoft Developers Network website
  (`http://msdn.microsoft.com`)

Introduction

One problem with developing custom Documentum applications is knowing where to begin. My purpose for writing this book was to de-mystify this process. I say "de-mystify" because to a beginner—even one that has taken the introductory Documentum training courses—producing a custom Documentum application is a bit of a mystery. How do you approach the problem? Are there templates? Do I write a standalone application, or a component? What's a component anyway? What and where are the Documentum Foundation Classes (DFC)? Do I have to learn the API? Where is the Documentum Desktop®, all I see is Microsoft Explorer? How do I login to the server and establish a session? Once logged in, how do I establish a client? What's this query and collection stuff? How do I bind Docbase™ data to a screen control? To the uninitiated, building a custom Documentum component or application can be a mind-boggling experience. There is no course, book, or other material that continues where the introductory courses end, to guide a developer into his first application. That's where this book comes in.

This book strives to bridge numerous sources and consolidate the best that they have to offer into a concise reference. It contains everything a beginning Documentum developer needs to know to get started building components and applications. It draws from Documentum training, Documentum reference books, personal experience, and Internet discussions to provide the best material available. It provides approaches to particular problems. It provides templates and skeleton code. It begins with developing the framework for both an application and a component. It continues by walking the reader through some basic concepts: queries, collections, operations, screen controls, etc. It covers many common techniques like establishing a session, debugging, and using library functions. In addition, this book addresses many of the questions I hear most frequently asked on the Internet and among my colleagues. This book provides beginning

Documentum developers not only the basics they need to be productive quickly, but also solutions, techniques, and best practices for common tasks and problems.

The Documentum developer community has formed a support network—both physical and virtual—for the free exchange of ideas and solutions. There are many Documentum Users' Groups (see `http://www.documentum.com/user_groups` for a list of groups near you), and a host of websites and newsgroups (you can find a list of these in the *Preface*) devoted to Documentum development. You will discover that most developers are willing to help you, and you can benefit greatly from their experience.

So, where do you go from here? If you want to learn about the component and application frameworks, go to Chapter 2. If you want to learn about queries, collections, core functionality, or screen controls, go to their respective chapters (3, 4, and 6). If you want to learn a few techniques for solving common problems, go to Chapter 5. Chapter 7 is full of miscellaneous information. If all you are interested in is the sample application, you'll find it in Chapter 8. The remainder of this chapter provides an overview of the DFC, Documentum applications in general, and Microsoft Visual Basic® and interface inheritance.

1.1 Who Should Read This Book?

This book was written for experienced software developers who are new to Documentum development. I assume a degree of proficiency with Visual Basic and the Microsoft Visual Studio® IDE, a familiarity with Documentum and the DFC, and knowledge of basic object-oriented programming concepts. You won't find any wizard-like techniques in the code examples or that I have exploited some little-known nuance of Visual Basic or the DFC to implement a solution. The examples are all simple, straightforward, and clearly illustrate the technique or best practice under discussion.

Readers should know how to install and use the Documentum Desktop® and Documentum Application Builder®, and be familiar with the Documentum's architecture, philosophy, and operation. You will find the subjects discussed in this book are not esoteric or overly technical in nature, but rather, are exceedingly practical.

1.2 Organization Of This Book

This book is organized into eight chapters that can be read sequentially or randomly:

- Chapter 1, *Introduction*, provides overviews of Documentum applications and Documentum application development, the DFC, and some object-oriented programming concepts unique to Visual Basic and the DFC.

- Chapter 2, *Getting Started with Applications and Components*, covers setting up the Visual Basic environment to create both applications and components, setting up and using test harnesses to test components, and use of the Documentum Desktop menu system.

- Chapter 3, *Working with Queries and Collections*, covers several techniques for querying the Docbase and processing the results (collections). It examines and demonstrates three types of queries: SQL pass-through, cached, and full-text. This chapter also contains a collection of useful queries.

- Chapter 4, *Implementing Core Document Management Functions*, demonstrates how to write seven custom document management functions (library services). It then demonstrates how to implement these same functions using the Documentum Operation classes.

- Chapter 5, *Proven Solutions for Common Tasks*, provides a collection of proven solutions for tasks commonly encountered by Documentum programmers. These tasks include: logging in, error trapping, tracing, auditing, using the registry, Dump and Load, and creating custom search forms, and others.

- Chapter 6, *Working with Screen Controls*, examines three classes of screen controls: Documentum validation controls, Docbase-aware controls, and Microsoft ActiveX® controls. This chapter concludes with the creation of the Object Selector form, a self-contained form for navigating the Docbase and selecting objects.

- Chapter 7, *Tips, Tools and Handy Information*, contains an eclectic assortment of information, most of which does not involve programming.

- Chapter 8, *Putting It All Together in a Sample Application*, walks you through constructing the *dmSpy* application. *dmSpy* is a programmer/administrator utility for examining objects in the Docbase. The application uses the techniques and information covered in the previous chapters to implement its functionality.

1.3 Source Code

The working examples of source code in this book are denoted with a **Source Code** label. These examples can be found in the `dm_book_src_1-0.zip` file available for download from: `http://www.dm-book.com`. Each example has been developed as a standalone application and can be run independently of any other example in the book. Therefore, each example contains a login subroutine, and where needed, a subroutine to select a random object from the Docbase to operate on. Any code that could cause damage or loss of data to your Docbase has been disabled in these examples.

All of the examples used in this book were developed using Microsoft Visual Studio 6 and Documentum Desktop 5.1. To use them, you will need a machine configured similarly.

1.4 Conventions Used In This Book

I use three categories of conventions in this book: typographic, variables and source code, and class nomenclature. Each of these is discussed in the following sections.

1.4.1 Typographic

Table 1.1 contains examples and explanations of the typographic constructs and conventions used in this book.

Table 1.1—Typographic Conventions

Typographic Construct	Purpose
`Courier font with gray background`	Denotes blocks of source code.
`Courier font`	Within the context of paragraphs, denotes source code elements, object properties and attributes, and commands. As a standalone paragraph, it denotes sample statements and inputs.
`Courier font with Italics and ()`	Within the context of paragraphs, denotes method names, subroutine names, and function names.
Arial font	Within the context of paragraphs, denotes forms, menus, and screen elements.
Boxed text	Denotes output or file contents.

1.4.2 Variables And Source Code

The code snippets in this book assume the following variables are global and defined outside the scope of each code snippet:

```
Dim cx As DfClientX
Dim client As IDfClient
Dim session As IDfSession
```

```
Set cx = New DfClientX
Set client = cx.getlocalClient
Set session = client.newSession()
```

In addition, the examples frequently contain hard-coded object Ids. I hard-coded them to simplify the examples and make the source code more concise.

In order to keep the code examples a reasonable length, and to keep them focused, most of them omit error trapping and session locking code. However, the full-length examples in this book (e.g., the Object Selector form and *dmSpy*) do contain these elements.

1.4.3 Class And Interface Nomenclature

There are three primary types of classes discussed in this book: DFC classes, DFC interfaces, and Desktop classes. DFC classes are identified by a `Df` prefix, as in DfClientX. DFC interfaces are identified by an `IDf` prefix, as in IDfClient. Finally, Desktop classes (i.e., classes only available in the Desktop libraries, and not the DFC proper) are identified by a `Dc` prefix, as in DcReport. This is an important distinction to make, because any class beginning with `Dc` will not be available in all programming environments (e.g., Java®).

Once any of these classes are instantiated, I refer to them as objects, regardless of whether they were DFC or Desktop class. In addition, I also refer to interfaces as classes. I realize this blurs the object-oriented distinction that the terms *class* and *interface* were designed to imply. Yet, both Visual Basic and Documentum tend to blur this distinction themselves, especially when it comes to inheriting interfaces (more on that later). For simplicity, any type of template, class or interface, is referred to as a class, and any instantiation of them is referred to as an object.

1.5 *A Brief Introduction To The Documentum Foundation Classes*

The Documentum Foundation Classes (DFC) comprise Documentum's hierarchical class library, which provides access to the functions and capabilities of the Documentum client and server. The DFC is an object-oriented library that sits on top of the Documentum Client Library (DMCL), the server's command-oriented API library. The DFC is actually written in Java, but a Component Object Model (COM) wrapper around the library makes it accessible from Visual Basic. However, there are some quirks with this arrangement as discussed later in this chapter.

Figure 1.1 depicts the conceptual architecture of a Documentum application and the Documentum libraries. The application layer denotes any Documentum client that uses the DFC—custom application, Documentum application, or component. The DFC High-level Classes layer contains high-level DFC classes; such as the Documentum Operation classes. This layer can also include custom developed classes. Classes in this layer contain a high-degree of specialized functionality. The DFC Mid-level Classes layer contains mid-level DFC classes; such as the Workflow and Virtual Document classes. Classes in this layer tend to provide services and contain more generalized functionality than the High-level classes. The DFC Core Classes layer contains the lower-level, core DFC classes, such as DfSysObject. Classes in this layer are the building blocks of all the others. These classes provide basic data access and control. Finally, the DMCL layer contains the command-oriented functions that actually implement the methods of the DFC.

Applications can use classes from any layer in the architecture and frequently mix them. The purpose of Figure 1.1 is simply to illustrate how the classes of the DFC can exhibit a hierarchy in their complexity and interaction. However, the classes in the DFC are not usually referred to as high-level, mid-level, and core. As you will see later in this section, a more natural way to categorize DFC classes is Docbase (classes that represent objects in the Docbase), Services (classes that implement services), and Desktop (classes that are unique to the Documentum Desktop).

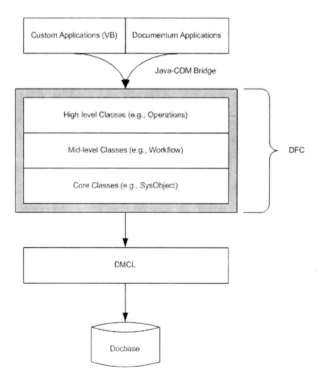

Figure 1.1—Documentum Application Architecture

Remember, everything in Documentum is considered an object. That's not to say that all of your code will be truly object-oriented. All Documentum objects (i.e., things in the Docbase) have properties, methods and a type. Properties are known attributes or characteristics about an object. Methods are functions or subroutines that the object can perform. Each object has a type identifying the template which created it, and where it fits in the hierarchy of objects. All objects of a given type share common, core properties and methods. Not all Docbase objects are represented in the DFC. In these cases, the objects are referenced using their supertypes.

1.5.1 Docbase Classes

A large part of the DFC mirrors the object types and structure found in the Documentum Server®. For example, the IDfSysObject class mirrors its server counterpart, `dm_sysobject`. Figure 1.2 depicts a subset of this structure.

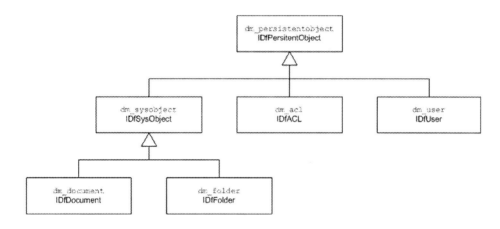

Figure 1.2—Example of Relationship Between DFC Objects and Docbase Objects

All objects that live in the Docbase inherit from the `dm_persistentobject` type. However, you cannot instantiate or query a `dm_persistentobject`. This object type is an abstract class that establishes a core set of properties inherited by all typed, persistent objects in the Docbase. Similarly, the IDfPersistentObject class defines an analogous set of properties and methods for representing `dm_persistentobjects` in the DFC. Like with the `dm_persistentobject` object, you cannot create an IDfPersistentObject directly.

The IDfPersistentObject class provides setter and getter methods for all attribute types; methods to save, fetch, and destroy the object; methods to relate the object to other objects; methods to validate attribute values against the data dictionary; and direct access to the DMCL. Because IDfPersistentObject is the supertype of all typed, persistent objects in the DFC, most of the objects you will work with will inherit these capabilities from IDfPersistentObject.

The IDfSysObject class corresponds to the `dm_sysobject` type in the Docbase. The `dm_sysobject` is a persistent object *with content*. A few of the most important features of `dm_sysobjects` are: they can have content, they can be checked in and out, they reside in a folder structure, they can be versioned, and they can be subject to access control. The IDfSysObject class exposes methods and properties to implement these features in the DFC. Every object in the Docbase that has content is a `dm_sysobject` or a subtype of it. The most common subtype of `dm_sysobject` is `dm_document` (IDfDocument in the DFC), which is Documentum's generic representation of a document in the Docbase. Consistent with its Docbase counterpart, the IDfDocument class does not expose any additional methods or properties beyond those inherited from IDfSysObject.

Table 1.2 contains a few of the most common Docbase classes found in the DFC. In Visual Basic, these classes are contained in the `DFCLib` type library.

Table 1.2—DFC Docbase Classes

DFC Class	Docbase Object
IDfACL	dm_acl, an access control list
IDfActivity	dm_activity, a workflow activity
IDfDocument	dm_document, a document
IDfFolder	dm_folder, a folder
IDfFormat	dm_format, a format object
IDfGroup	dm_group, a user group
IDfPersistentObject	dm_persistentobject, an abstract, persistent object type
IDfProcess	dm_process, a workflow template
IDfSysObject	dm_sysobject, a content object type
IDfUser	dm_user, a user
IDfWorkflow	dm_workflow, a workflow (run-time version of dm_process)
IDfWorkItem	dmi_workitem, a workflow task

1.5.2 Service Classes

The second category of classes in the DFC is one that provides services, for example, IDfQuery, IDfOperation, and IDfSession. These classes do not have a hierarchical inheritance tree like the Docbase classes discussed previously. Instead, these classes live in a relatively flat library and are manufactured by the DfClientX factory class, or are returned by other classes' methods. These classes represent services and objects that are useful to developers, but do not necessarily represent real Docbase objects.

Table 1.3 contains a few of the most common service classes found in the DFC. In Visual Basic, these classes are also contained in the `DFCLib` type library.

Table 1.3—DFC Service Classes

DFC Class	Purpose
DfClientX	Provides factory methods for many DFC objects, and access to the DFC from COM (i.e., Visual Basic).
IDfCollection	Encapsulates a collection object
IDfDocbaseMap	Encapsulates information about a Docbase and the DocBroker
IDfException	Implements exception handling
IDfFile	Encapsulates a file system file
IDfId	Encapsulates the ID data type
IDfList	Implements a simple list of objects
IDfLoginInfo	Encapsulates login information
IDfOperation (and all of its specialized subtypes)	Encapsulates the Documentum-provided library operations
IDfProperties	Encapsulates property information for an object
IDfQuery	Implements a query
IDfQueryMgr	Encapsulates complex and cross-Docbase queries
IDfSession	Encapsulates a session
IDfTime	Encapsulates the TIME data type
IDfTypedObject	Encapsulates typed objects (i.e., just about anything in the Docbase)
IDfValueAssistance	Implements the value assistance for an object
IDfVirtualDocument	Encapsulates a virtual document

1.5.3 Documentum Desktop Classes

Finally, there is a set of classes that are unique to the Documentum Desktop. These classes provide specialized services to the client, for example, DcLoginManager, DcReport, and DcRunQuery. These classes make developing Desktop applications a little easier by encapsulating common activities into classes that contain standardized user interface elements. In Visual Basic, these classes can look like part of the DFC because, after they are referenced in the project settings, they appear in Visual Basic's IntelliSense®. However, they are actually separate. Notice that these classes all start with a Dc or IDc prefix instead of Df or IDf.

Table 1.4 contains a few of the most common Documentum Desktop classes. In Visual Basic, these classes are contained in libraries and components that begin with a Dc prefix.

Table 1.4—Documentum Desktop Classes

DFC Class	Purpose
DcComponentDispatcher	Encapsulates initializing, running, and de-initializing Documentum COM components
DcItems	Implements a container to pass items among COM components
DcLoginManager	Encapsulates the login process
DcReport	Implements exception and error handling
DcRunQuery	Encapsulates a basic query mechanism, including a UI to display the results
The Docbase validation and Docbase-aware screen controls	Encapsulates numerous screen controls that have built-in awareness of the Docbase.

1.6 Overview Of A Documentum Desktop Application

This section is a preview of Chapter 2, *Getting Started with Applications and Components*. In it, I give you an overview of the structure and flow of a generic Documentum Desktop application. You will find more detail in Chapter 2.

Documentum applications usually begin by acquiring references to local client objects. The local client objects are DfClientX and IDfClient.

```
Dim cx As DfClientX
Dim client As IDfClient

' set up factory class
Set cx = New DfClientX

' get local DFC clients
Set client = cx.getLocalClient
```

Once instantiated, these objects load all the necessary client-side Documentum libraries. The DfClientX object acts as a factory and can manufacture most of the DFC objects you will use. The IDfClient object contains everything necessary to implement the client side of the Docbase connection.

The next step is to establish a session between the application and the server. There are several ways this can be accomplished. One approach is to use an IDfLoginInfo object. Another approach is to use the

DcLoginManager. Both of these approaches are discussed in detail in Chapter 5, *Proven Solutions to Common Tasks*. The result of either approach is an IDfSession object, which encapsulates the connection between the application and the Documentum Server.

```
Dim li As IDfLoginInfo
Dim session As IDfSession

' manufacture a li object
Set li = cx.getLoginInfo

' set li properties
li.setUser ("user")
li.setPassword ("password")
li.setDomain ("domain")

' login and get session object
Set session = client.newSession("docbase", li)
```

Obtaining a valid session (IDfSession object) is necessary since nearly every class and method in the DFC requires a reference to a valid session object.

Once a session is established with the Documentum Server, your application can begin its custom processing. Most likely, your application will create or access objects in the Docbase. Most methods that return objects from the Docbase will return them as IDfPersistentObjects. Remember, the IDfPersistentObject is the abstract supertype of all directly accessible objects in the Docbase. You almost always *cast* this object to its specific subtype (e.g., IDfSysObject if it is a dm_sysobject). You will want to read the section, *Interface Inheritance and Type Casting in Visual Basic*, later in this chapter for more information about casting.

```
Dim sobj As IDfSysObject

' create a new document object and cast it to an IDfSysObject
Set sobj = session.newObject("dm_document")

' set some attributes
sobj.setContentType ("crtext")
sobj.setObjectName ("my object")

' set content
sobj.setFile ("c:\my_text_file.txt")
```

```
' save it
sobj.save
```

If your application needs DFC objects such as a query object (IDfQuery), Id object (IDfId), or operation object (IDfOperation), they can be manufactured by the DfClientX object. For example:

```
Dim q As IDfQuery
Dim id As IDfId
Dim opObj As IDfCheckinOperation

' manufacture query object
Set q = cx.getQuery

' manufacture an id object
Set id = cx.getId("0900218d80053e47")

' manufacture an operation object
Set opObj = cx.getOperation("Checkin")
```

Other service-type objects, such as IDfCollection, are returned as results of methods.

```
Dim col As IDfCollection
q.setDQL "select * from dm_document where folder('/Temp')"

' execute query and return results in collection object
Set col = q.execute(session, DF_READ_QUERY)
```

When your application quits, it should disconnect from the Docbase and close its session.

```
session.disconnect
```

In general, this is how all Documentum Desktop applications function—both components and applications. Of course, the magic is in the details of what happens between the login and the disconnect. Starting with Chapter 2, *Getting Started with Applications and Components*, I'll begin to draw back the curtains and reveal some of that magic.

1.7 Interface Inheritance And Type Casting In Visual Basic

The DFC prior to version 5.1 relied upon Microsoft's virtual machine to implement the bridge between the Java code in which it was written, and the COM objects in Visual Basic, which used it. A shortcoming of Microsoft's virtual machine was it did not implement interface inheritance for COM objects. The result was that you could not inherit methods and properties from DFC supertype interface classes to subtype interface classes. There was a work-around, but it required you to use twice as many variables, one for the supertype and one for the subtype, and call methods on both objects.

For example, consider the hierarchy of DFC classes (really interfaces) depicted in Figure 1.3.

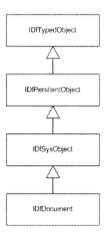

Figure 1.3—The IDfDocument Interface Hierarchy

In Java, if you instantiate an IDfDocument object, it inherits all of the properties and methods of the classes in its hierarchy. For example, the *save()* method is defined in the IDfPersistentObject interface, and the *setTitle()* method is defined in the IDfSysObject interface. When an IDfDocument is instantiated, it inherits both the *save()* method and the *setTitle()* method because they are methods of classes in its hierarchy. To illustrate, consider the following Java snippet:

```
IDfDocument dObj = null;

dObj = (IDfDocument) session.newObject("dm_document");
dObj.setTitle("Test Object 1");
dObj.save();
```

In this code a new IDfDocument object, dObj, is instantiated by assigning it to the result of the *session.newObject()* method. The *session.newObject()* method returns an IDfPersistentObject, which is cast to the appropriate subtype, in this case, IDfDocument. The remainder of the code sets the title of the object using *setTitle()* inherited from IDfSysObject, and saves it using *save()* inherited from IDfPersistentObject.

In Visual Basic, with the DFC prior to version 5.1, the same code is a little more awkward because of the necessary work-around.

```
Dim sObj as IDfSysObject
Dim pObj as IDfPersistentObject

Set pObj = session.newObject("dm_document")
Set sObj = pObj
sObj.setTitle("Test Object 1")
pObj.save
```

In this code a new IDfPersistentObject object, pObj, is instantiated by assigning it to the result of the *session.newObject()* method. The IDfPersistentObject must be cast to the appropriate subtype, in this case, IDfSysObject. The cast is achieved by using the Set operation: Set sObj = pObj. Notice that in the remainder of the code, both objects are required: title is set using *setTitle()* on the IDfSysObject, and the save is executed using *save()* on the IDfPersistentObject.

This type of casting only works if the two classes involved are compatible (i.e., in a supertype-to-subtype relationship or a peer-to-peer relationship). The disadvantage to this methodology and a frequent point of confusion is that sObj has access to only the methods defined in the IDfSysObject class and none of the methods defined in IDfPersistentObject. Therefore, the *setTitle()* method is invoked from the sObj and the *save()* method from the pObj, even though both variables reference the same object.

Having said all of that, if you are using DFC 5.1 or later, you don't need to worry about casting. Starting with DFC version 5.1, Documentum wrote their own Java-COM bridge based upon Sun's virtual machine. The Documentum implementation of the Java-COM bridge fully implements interface inheritance and obviates the need for the work-around. For example, the following code snippet is now valid in Visual Basic:

```
Dim dObj as IDfDocument

Set dObj = session.newObject("dm_document")
dObj.setTitle("Test Object 1")
dObj.save
```

In some respects, the casting done here is even better than that in Java. With the new Java-COM bridge, there is no need to explicitly cast types; it is smart enough to do it for you. Notice that the IDfPersistentObject returned by *session.newObject()* is automatically cast to an IDfDocument object based upon the declaration of dObj. Very nice.

The examples in the remainder of this book assume you are using at least DFC 5.1 and are taking advantage of the Documentum Java-COM bridge.

Getting Started With Applications And Components

There are two types of Documentum applications discussed in this book: standalone applications and components. Standalone applications are programs that run in their own process space and are usually contained in `.EXE` files. Users can access these applications from the **Start** menu or a desktop icon.

Components are Microsoft COM objects that must be loaded into a running program's process space to function (e.g., Microsoft Explorer). These applications are usually contained in `.DLL` files and "launched" from the parent process. The Documentum Desktop is comprised mostly of a collection of components that load themselves into the Microsoft Explorer process space. Therefore, the Documentum Desktop serves as a model and framework for developing additional client applications and components.

In this chapter, I discuss how to set up Visual Basic projects for both standalone applications and components, and provide skeleton code for each. I also discuss debugging and testing techniques, modifying Documentum stock components, and how to modify the Documentum Desktop menu to launch applications and components. This chapter does not concentrate on the *why* of doing things the way they are done, but rather the *how* of doing them. The goal of this chapter is to create the infrastructure in which the rest of the techniques in this book can be implemented. If you are really interested in the *why* of creating applications or components in this manner, I encourage you to see Documentum's publications on the subject, most notably *Developing Documentum Desktop Client Components*.

The procedures outlined in the following sections assume you have the Documentum Desktop installed on the same computer with Visual Basic. This is necessary in order to access the DFC type libraries and components from Visual Basic.

2.1 Building A Standalone Application

This chapter starts with the standalone application since it is a little simpler to understand and implement than the component. You would choose to write a standalone application if you are not using the Documentum Desktop as your primary interface with the Docbase. For example, your application may allow users to see only a certain part of the Docbase, or certain types of objects, or present the Docbase in a particular manner, or implement a business process via its UI. These are types of customizations easier to implement in a standalone application than in the Documentum Desktop using components.

The general procedure to create a standalone application is:

- Create a new Standard EXE project in Visual Basic
- Create a module
- Add login logic to the module
- Have the module load a form and pass the session Id to the form
- Add all the logic the form needs to operate
- Test and debug the application
- Package and deploy the application

2.1.1 Setting Up A Standalone Application Project

The steps to set up a new Visual Basic project for developing a Documentum Desktop standalone application are as follows:

1. Create a folder on your hard drive with the name of your application to hold the application files.
2. Start Visual Basic.
3. On the **New Project** dialog, choose **Standard EXE**, and click **Open**.
4. From the **Project** menu, choose **Properties**.
5. The **Project Properties** dialog box, similar to the one shown in Figure 2.1 should be visible. On the **General** tab, enter a **Project Name**. (In this example, `MyProject`.)

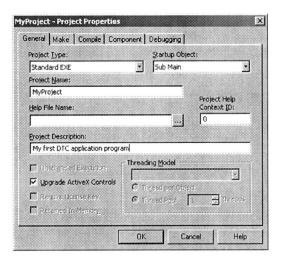

Figure 2.1—Project Properties—General Tab

6. Enter a description of your project in the **Project Description** field.
7. Change the **Startup Object** to be `Sub Main`.
8. Click the **Make** tab. The **Make** tab should look similar to Figure 2.2.
9. On the **Make** tab, select **Auto Increment** for the **Version Number**. This ensures that each build of your application has a new version number to help you track revisions.
10. Enter a title in the **Title** field. (In this example, `MyProject`.)

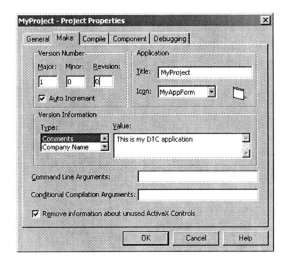

Figure 2.2—Project Properties—Make Tab

11. You may also want to enter information in the **Version Information** fields. This information is then available from Microsoft Explorer.
12. Click the **Compile** tab. The **Compile** tab should look similar to Figure 2.3.

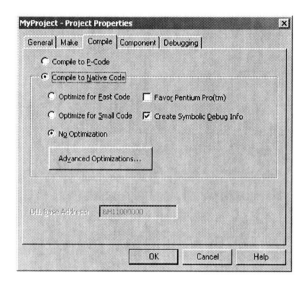

Figure 2.3—Project Properties—Compile Tab

13. Select **Compile to Native Code**, the **No Optimization**, and the **Create Symbolic Debug Information** options.
14. Click **OK**.
15. Select **References** from the **Project** menu. The **References** dialog box, similar to the one shown in Figure 2.4 should be visible.

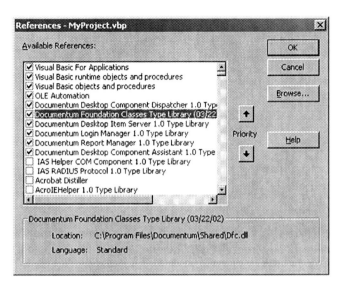

Figure 2.4—References Dialog Box

16. Add the following references to your project:
    - Documentum Foundation Class Type Library
    - Documentum Item Server Type Library
    - Documentum Login Manager Type Library
    - Documentum Report Manager Type Library
    - Documentum VB Component Development Assistant
    - Documentum Component Dispatcher Type Library
17. Click **OK**.
18. Click on `Form1` in the **Project Explorer** window of the Visual Basic IDE. Name the form in the **Properties** window below the **Project Explorer**. (For this example, name it `MyAppForm`.)
19. Right-click in the **Project Explorer** window, and add a **Module** to your project. Give it a name in the **Properties** window below the **Project Explorer**. (For this example, name it `MyAppCode`.) Your project should look like the one shown in Figure 2.5.

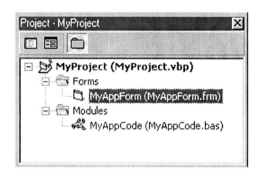

Figure 2.5—Project Explorer Window for MyProject

20. Open the `MyAppCode` module you just created, and create an empty subroutine named `Main`.
21. From the **File** menu, choose **Save Project** and save your project to the folder you created in step 1.

You are now ready to begin writing your application.

2.1.2 Application Skeleton Code

The following source code implements a skeleton Documentum Desktop standalone application. This code omits most of error checking and other processing that is necessary to implement a robust standalone application. Its intent is to provide the minimum framework necessary for implementing the topics discussed in the remaining chapters of this book. The application itself doesn't do anything useful. The rest of this section assumes you created your project as described above and have one code module named `MyAppCode`, and one form named `MyAppForm`.

The `Main()` subroutine in the `MyAppCode` module executes first when the application is launched because we configured it to do so in step 7. The `Main()` subroutine handles logging into the Docbase, and loading the `MyAppForm` form.

Source Code A working example of this source code can be found in the "`Chapter2/Application`" directory of the source code archive.

```
' MyAppCode module

Option Explicit

' DCTM globals
Public loginMgr As New DcLoginManager

Sub Main()
    Dim sessionId As String
    Dim frm As New MyAppForm

    ' if no session, login
    If (sessionId = "") Then
        ' use login manager to login
        sessionId = loginMgr.Connect("", "", "", "", 0)
    End If

    ' if no session, error out
    If (sessionId = "") Then
        MsgBox "Could not Login.", vbCritical, "Could Not Log In"
        Set loginMgr = Nothing
        End
    End If

    ' pass sessionId to form
    ' assumes form has public string variable named sessionId
    frm.sessionId = sessionId

    ' show form
    frm.Show

    Set frm = Nothing

End Sub
```

The `Main()` subroutine obtains a Docbase session using the Login Manager, and passes the session Id to the form by assigning it to a public variable in the form. The Login Manager is discussed in Chapter 5,

Proven Solutions to Common Tasks. For now, just know that it manages the login process by displaying a login UI, authenticating the user, and returning a session Id.

The skeleton code for the application's form is next. It is important to notice that it contains a `Public` variable named `sessionId`, which is set from the `Main()` subroutine when the form is loaded. Also, notice that the form contains its own local instances of the DfClientX, IDfClient, and IDfSession, the DFC client objects. Though not technically necessary, all forms in your application should follow this best practice: the session Id is passed in as a `String` variable, and each form contains local DFC client objects.

By declaring the DfClientX, IDfClient, and IDfSession objects global to the form, every subroutine and function on the form can access them—and probably will. It is important to note that instances of the DfClientX, IDfClient, and IDfSession are instantiated in the `Form_Load()` subroutine. Instantiating these variables in the `Form_Load()` subroutine ensures that they are instantiated as soon as the form is loaded, and nothing can use them before then.

```
' MyAppForm form

Option Explicit

' public var set from Main
Public sessionId As String

' private vars used globally in this form
Private cx As DfClientX
Private client As IDfClient
Private sessionObj As IDfSession

Private Sub Form_Load()

    ' setup dfc client objects
    Set cx = New DfClientX
    Set client = cx.getLocalClient
    Set sessionObj = client.findSession(sessionId)

    ' your code here . . .

End Sub
```

2.1.3 Debugging And Testing The Application

For the most part, debugging and testing standalone Documentum Desktop applications is no different than debugging and testing any other Visual Basic application: you can set breakpoints, output debug statements to the **Immediate** window, and observe variables in the **Watch** window. You can also start and stop your application using the Visual Basic debugging VCR buttons and step into, or over subroutines.

2.1.4 Packaging And Deploying the Application

After writing, debugging, and testing your application, you may want to revisit step 13 in Section 2.1.1, *Setting up a Standalone Application Project*, to disable debugging, and choose **Optimize for Fast Code**. Once you have recompiled, the easiest way to deploy your application is to use the Package & Deployment Wizard that comes as part of the Microsoft Visual Studio. I am not going to detail the use of the Packaging & Deployment Wizard, but I do want to make one point about the configuration of your deployment file.

During the process of creating a deployment file, the wizard will ask you to identify the .DLL files referenced by your application that you would like to bundle in the deployment file. To avoid any licensing or legal issues with redistribution of Documentum binaries, I suggest that you unselect DFC.TLB and any .DLL that starts with Dc, or has Documentum in its path, as shown in Figure 2.6.

The output of the Package & Deployment Wizard is a .CAB file, a setup.exe program, and a setup.LST file. These files are all that are necessary to install your application on an end-user's workstation. Note that since you explicitly omitted key Documentum files from the package, this .CAB file will only deploy to workstations that already have the Documentum Desktop installed.

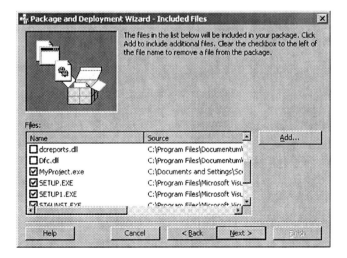

Figure 2.6—Package & Deployment Wizard—Unselect Documentum .DLLs

2.2 Building A Component

Now that you have seen what goes into a standalone application, let's look at Documentum Desktop components. You might consider building a component if you want to specialize the Documentum Desktop or extend its functionality. For example, you might create a custom properties dialog, implement a business rule with a custom UI, or launch a workflow. The distinction is: the Documentum Desktop will be your primary interface with the Docbase and the component will change or augment its basic functionality. As you will see, building a component is a little more involved than building a standalone application; however, there are many similarities. For instance, the Docbase login process is the same, there is a central entry point to the code that loads the component's form, and the session Id is passed to the form as a string. Like the standalone application skeleton code presented in the previous section, this component's code doesn't do anything useful either; it's a framework.

Unlike standalone applications, components must be loaded into parent processes to function and are deployed into the Docbase using DocApps. DocApps are special archive files created with the Documentum Application Builder, and are used to deploy, among other things, components into the Docbase. DocApps, as they relate to deploying components, are discussed later in this chapter. The facts that components reside in the Docbase and must be loaded into parent processes to function make testing and debugging them a little more difficult. This chapter will present two techniques for debugging and testing components.

The component we build in this section is designed to run in the Documentum Desktop by selecting an object in the Windows Explorer and clicking a menu item.

The general procedure to create a component is:

- Create a new ActiveX DLL project in Visual Basic
- Create a form
- Add `IDcComponent_Init()`, `IDcComponent_Run()`, and `IDcComponent_DeInit()` methods to the class module
- Have the `IDcComponent_Run()` method pass the session Id and items collection to the form
- Add all the logic the form needs to operate
- Test and debug the component
- Package and deploy the component in a DocApp

2.2.1 A Word About COM And Documentum Components

Before I discuss setting up a component project and the skeleton code, I thought I should say a few words about COM, Documentum components, and why the project and skeleton code work the way they do. To begin, COM stands for *Component Object Model*, and is an invention of Microsoft. COM is a software architecture that allows applications to be built by *gluing* together binary software components using a standard interface for interoperability. This is accomplished by requiring every component to have a mechanism for dynamically discovering and calling each other's interfaces. This mechanism is called the IUnknown interface, and all COM components are required to implement it.

Documentum takes this concept a step further by requiring components used by the Documentum Desktop to implement the IDcComponent interface, which in turn implements the IUnknown interface in the COM model. Having components implement the IDcComponent interface allows them to be used in both the Documentum Desktop as well as other COM applications. In Documentum components, the IDcComponent interface is implemented with:

```
Implements DCCOMPONENTLib.IDcComponent
```

at the beginning of the code module.

All Documentum components are managed and run by the Documentum Component Dispatcher (DcComponentDispatcher) and the DocApp Runtime (DART), which are integrated into the Microsoft Explorer namespace as part of the Documentum Desktop. These two pieces of code are the heart of the Documentum Desktop. The Documentum Component Dispatcher and DART rely on the Documentum Dynamic Component Delivery system (a COM delivery system based on Microsoft's Internet Component Delivery system) to deliver the right components to the Documentum Desktop when they are needed.

The IDcComponent interface implements three methods that the Documentum Component Dispatcher and DART use to instantiate, run, and destroy Documentum components. These methods are: `IDcComponent_Init()`, `IDcComponent_Run()`, and `IDcComponent_DeInit()`. You will see in the skeleton code that most of the coding is done in these three methods and that you never see any COM code per se; Documentum has graciously shielded you from it.

Though accessible, you should *never* call a Documentum component's `Init()`, `Run()`, or `DeInit()` COM methods directly. Doing so circumvents DART, and operates the component outside of Documentum's component management process. *Always* use the Documentum Component Dispatcher to access components.

2.2.2   Setting Up A Component Project

Following are the steps to set up a new Visual Basic project for developing a Documentum Desktop component.

1. Create a folder on your hard drive with the name of your component to hold the component files. Inside that folder, create another folder named `RefCopy` to hold a reference copy of your DLL.
2. Start Visual Basic.
3. On the **New Project** dialog, choose **ActiveX DLL**, and click **Open**.

4. From the Project menu, choose Properties.
5. The Project Properties dialog box, similar to the one shown in Figure 2.7 should be visible. On the General tab, enter a Project Name. This name becomes the name of your component's type library, not the name of the component. (In this example, MyProjectLib.)

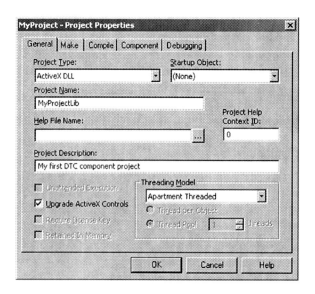

Figure 2.7—Project Properties—General Tab

6. Enter a description of your project in the Project Description field, and ensure the Threading Model is set for Apartment Threaded.
7. Click the Make tab. The Make tab should look similar to Figure 2.8.
8. On the Make tab, select Auto Increment for the Version Number. This is very important since Documentum's Dynamic Component Delivery mechanism won't deliver new components that have the same version as ones already installed on the user's workstation.
9. Enter a title in the Title field. (In this example, MyProjectLib.)
10. You may also want to enter information in the Version Information fields. This information is then available from Microsoft Explorer.
11. Click the Compile tab. The Compile tab should look similar to Figure 2.9.

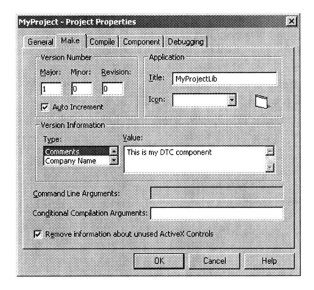

Figure 2.8—Project Properties—Make Tab

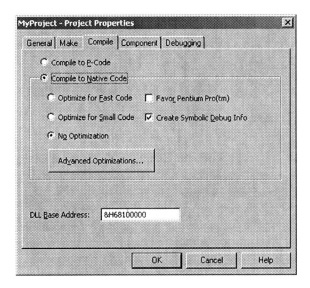

Figure 2.9—Project Properties—Compile Tab

12. Select **Compile to Native Code**, the **No Optimization**, and the **Create Symbolic Debug Information** options.

13. In the **DLL Base Address** field, enter a value between **&H60000000** and **&H68000000** as the base address for your component. You can enter any value you like in this field but it should end with **0000**. Windows will attempt to load your component into this address space. However, if this space is already occupied, Windows must do an expensive and time-consuming memory swap to free the space. By systematically assigning base addresses for your components, you reduce the risk of this happening (a little).
14. Click the **Component** tab. The **Component** tab should look similar to Figure 2.10.

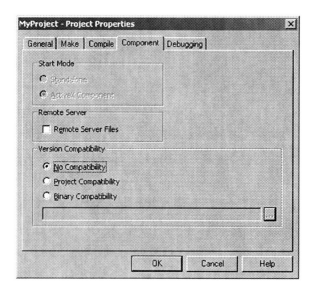

Figure 2.10—Project Properties—Component Tab

15. Select **No Compatibility** in the **Version Compatibility** control group.
16. Click the **Debugging** tab. The **Debugging** tab should look similar to Figure 2.11.
17. Select **Start Program**, and enter `explorer.exe` in the box.
18. Click **OK**.
19. In the **Project Explorer** window of the Visual Basic IDE, select the **Class1** class. In the **Properties** window, give your component a name. (In this example, `MyCompClass`.)
20. Right-click in the **Project Explorer** window, and add a **Form** to your project. Give it a name in the **Properties** window. (For this example, name it `MyCompForm`.) Your project should now look like Figure 2.12.
21. Compile your project by choosing **Make MyProjectLib.dll** from the **File** menu.

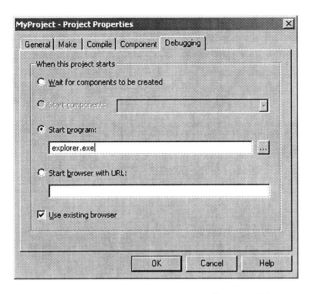

Figure 2.11—Project Properties—Debugging Tab

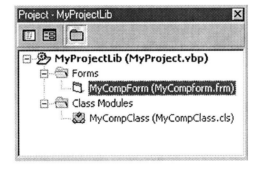

Figure 2.12—Project Explorer Window for MyProject

22. Copy your project's DLL (in this example, MyProjectLib.dll) into the RefCopy subdirectory.
23. In Visual Basic, choose **Properties** from the **Project** menu. The **Properties** dialog box should appear.
24. Click the **Component** tab.
25. Select **Binary Compatibility**, and enter (or navigate to) the DLL in your project's RefCopy subdirectory (see Figure 2.13). Maintaining **Binary Compatibility** will be very important from here on. Usually, when Visual Basic compiles a component it generates a new COM Id, or GUID (Globally Unique Identifier), for the component. This Id distinguishes this version of this

component from all of the COM components in the *world*. By setting **Binary Compatibility**, you are telling Visual Basic to use the same COM Id assigned to the existing component, and not to generate a new one. Documentum uses the COM Id to determine which component to run. If the COM Id of your component and the COM Id in your DocApp are different, your component won't run.

Figure 2.13—Project Properties—Component Tab

26. Click **OK**.
27. Select **References** from the **Project** menu. The **References** dialog box, similar to the one shown in Figure 2.14 should be visible.
28. Add the following references to your project:
    - Documentum Foundation Class Type Library
    - Documentum Item Server Type Library
    - Documentum Login Manager Type Library
    - Documentum Report Manager Type Library
    - Documentum VB Component Development Assistant
    - Documentum Component Dispatcher Type Library
29. Click **OK**.
30. From the **File** menu, choose **Save Project**.

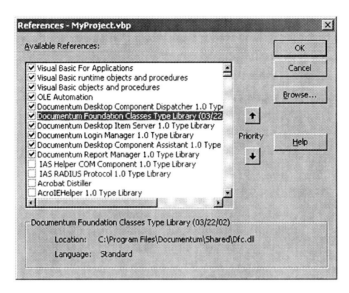

Figure 2.14—References Dialog Box

You are now ready to begin writing your component.

2.2.3 Component Skeleton Code

The following source code implements a skeleton Documentum Desktop component. This code omits most of error checking and other processing that is necessary to implement a robust component. Its intent is to provide the minimum framework necessary for implementing the topics discussed in the remaining chapters of this book. Much of a component's complexity resides not only in what the component does, but also in what it needs for input, and when it is valid and safe to run. If you want to see an example of a more robust component, see the source code for the DcProperties component that is distributed in the Documentum Desktop Component Source archive[*]. The rest of this section assumes you created your project as described above and have one class module named `MyCompClass`, and one form named `MyCompForm`.

The `MyCompClass` module contains only the three methods necessary to instantiate, run, and destroy the component: `IDcComponent_Init()`, `IDcComponent_Run()`, and `IDcComponent_DeInit()`.

- The `IDcComponent_Init() method` receives data passed to the component from the parent process, logs into the Docbase, allocates resources, and—if necessary—processes the input data and saves them to local variables.
- The `IDcComponent_Run()` method is where the component does all of its work. In the skeleton code, the `IDcComponent_Run()` function opens the `MyCompForm` form, and the form actually does all of the work.

---

[*] You can download the Documentum Desktop Component Source archive from the Documentum Download Center (`http://documentum.subscribenet.com`).

- The `IDcComponent_DeInit()` method releases all of the component's resources assigned in `IDcComponent_Init()` and terminates the component.

Source Code A working example of this source code can be found in the "`Chapter2/Component`" directory of the source code archive.

```
' MyCompClass class

Option Explicit

Implements DCCOMPONENTLib.IDcComponent

' private vars
Private cx As DfClientX
Private client As IDfClient
Private session As IDfSession
Private hWndParent As Long
Private myItems As IDcItems
Private myReporter As IDcReport

Private Const GWL_HWNDPARENT As Integer = -8

Private Function IDcComponent_Init(ByVal docbaseName As String, _
                    ByVal userOSName As String, _
                    ByVal domain As String, _
                    ByVal contextID As String, _
                    ByVal items As IDcItems, _
                    ByVal hWndForDialog As Long, _
                    ByVal reporter As IDcReport, _
                    ByVal stringForIID As String, _
                    Optional ByVal itemContainer As _
                    Variant) As Long

    Dim loginMgr As DcLoginManager
    Dim sessionID As String

    ' setup reporter
    Set myReporter = reporter

    On Error GoTo HandleError

    ' do login
    Set loginMgr = New DcLoginManager
```

```
        sessionID = loginMgr.Connect(docbaseName, _
                                     userOSName, _
                                     "", _
                                     domain, _
                                     IS_DOCBASE_CONNECTED)

    ' setup dfc client objects
    Set cx = New DfClientX
    If (sessionID <> "") Then
        Set client = cx.getLocalClient
        Set session = client.findSession(sessionID)
    End If

'   Uncomment this code for debugging
'   cx.setTraceLevel (10)
'   cx.setTraceFileName ("ComponentTrace.txt")

    ' get items and window handles
    Set myItems = items
    myItems.Type = DC_OBJECT_ITEM_IID_STRING
    hWndParent = hWndForDialog

    ' if we got here, success
    IDcComponent_Init = DC_COMP_SUCCESS
    Exit Function

HandleError:

    myReporter.AddEntry Err.Description, True, Err.Source, _
        Err.Number
    IDcComponent_Init = DC_COMP_FAILURE

End Function
```

You will notice that the *IDcComponent_Init()* method requires a lot of input arguments. Fortunately, the Documentum Component Dispatcher provides them so you don't have to. Many of these arguments are saved to local variables for further processing (e.g., reporter, items, and hWndForDialog) by either this method or the *IDcComponent_Run() method*. Most of the other arguments are used by the Login Manager[*] to establish a session with the Docbase.

---

[*] The Login Manager is discussed in Chapter 5, *Proven Solutions to Common Tasks*.

```
Private Function IDcComponent_Run() As Long
    Dim frm As MyCompForm
    Dim item As Variant

    ' assume success
    IDcComponent_Run = DC_COMP_SUCCESS

    On Error GoTo HandleError

    For Each item In myItems

        ' make new form
        Set frm = New MyCompForm

        ' pass vars to form
        frm.objId = item.ID
        frm.sessionID = session.getSessionId

        ' display form
        frm.Show vbModal

        ' unload
        Set frm = Nothing

    Next item

    Exit Function

HandleError:

    myReporter.AddEntry Err.Description, True, Err.Source, _
        Err.Number
    IDcComponent_Run = DC_COMP_FAILURE

End Function
```

As I mentioned earlier, the *IDcComponent_Run()* function is where the component does most of its work. In this component, the *IDcComponent_Run()* function unpacks some of the input arguments, namely the objects selected in the Windows Explorer interface, and ships them off to the MyCompForm, which actually does the work. This is done by iterating over the myItems collection (IDcItems), created by the *IDcComponent_Init()* function, using a For Each loop. Within the loop, I assign the object Id and the session Id to the form's two public variables and show the form. This causes the form to be displayed for each object selected in the Windows Explorer. Note that the form is displayed in *modal* mode. If it wasn't, it would be displayed and instantly destroyed, accomplishing nothing but a blink on your monitor. Also, note that the object Id and session Id are both passed to the form as `String` variables.

The `IDcComponent_DeInit()` method is simple. It destroys the DfClientX, IDfClient, and IDfSession variables instantiated in the `IDcComponent_Init()` function.

```
Private Function IDcComponent_DeInit() As Long

    On Error GoTo HandleError

    Set cx = Nothing
    Set client = Nothing
    Set session = Nothing
    IDcComponent_DeInit = DC_COMP_SUCCESS
    Exit Function

HandleError:

    myReporter.AddEntry Err.Description, True, Err.Source, _
        Err.Number
    IDcComponent_DeInit = DC_COMP_FAILURE

End Function
```

The skeleton code for the component's form is next. It is important to notice that it contains two `Public` variables named `sessionId`, and `objId` that are set by the `IDcComponent_Run()` method when the form is loaded. Also, notice that the form contains its own local instances of the DfClientX, IDfClient, and IDfSession DFC client objects. All forms in your application should follow this model: the session Id and object Ids (if applicable) are passed as `String` variables, and each form contains local DfClientX, IDfClient, and IDfSession DFC client objects.

```
' MyCompForm form

Option Explicit

' public var set from Run
Public sessionId As String
Public objId As String
```

```
' private vars used globally in this form
Private session As IDfSession
Private cx As DfClientX
Private client As IDfClient
Private reporter As New DcReport

Private Sub Form_Load()

    ' setup dfc
    Set cx = New DfClientX
    Set client = cx.getLocalClient
    Set session = client.findSession(sessionId)

    ' your code here . . .

End Sub
```

By declaring the DfClientX, IDfClient, and IDfSession objects global to the form, every subroutine and function on the form can access them—and probably will. It is important to note that instances of the DfClientX, IDfClient, and IDfSession are instantiated in the `Form_Load()` subroutine. Instantiating these variables in the `Form_Load()` subroutine ensures that they are instantiated as soon as the form is loaded and nothing can use them before then.

2.2.4 Debugging And Testing The Component

Run-time debugging and testing of Documentum Desktop components can be difficult, mainly because the components run as in-process servers. This means that you must have a parent process that you can debug and load your component into. I use two different techniques to debug components. The first technique is to setup a test harness program in Visual Basic, and load your component into it. The second technique is to setup a test harness DocApp and let Windows Explorer act as the parent process for your component. I will discuss both methods here, but note that the DocApp approach will utilize techniques not covered until later in this chapter.

2.2.4.1 *Using A Visual Basic Test Harness*

The Visual Basic test harness is a regular .EXE program that references your component's .DLL and loads it into its process. For convenience, you can create a project group that contains both your test harness project and your component project. A project group will make switching between the test harness and the component source code easier. If you examine the code in the Documentum Desktop Component Source archive*, you will find that all of the Documentum components come with project groups and test harnesses.

Below are the steps to create a component test harness:

1. Follow the steps given earlier in this chapter for creating a Standalone application. There is no need to name the module or the form unless you really want to. The procedure below assumes you have *not* given them names.
2. Name your project `testHarness`.
3. Select **Reference** from the **Project** menu and add your component to the project as a reference (see Figure 2.15). In this example, my component is `MyProjectLib`.
4. Save your project.
5. Select **Add Project** from the **File** menu. Click the **Existing** tab, navigate to your component project, and add it. Your **Project Explorer** should now contain both projects: your test harness and your component (see Figure 2.16).
6. Select **Save Project Group** from the **File** menu. (In this example, the project group is named `TestMyComp`).

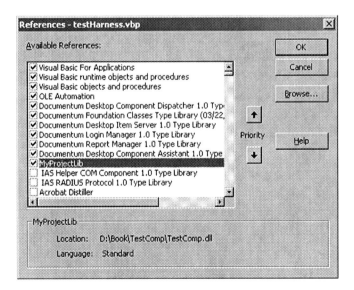

Figure 2.15—TestHarness References Dialog Showing MyProjectLib Component.

---

* You can download the Documentum Desktop Component Source archive from the Documentum Download Center (`http://documentum.subscribenet.com`).

38   A Beginner's Guide to Developing Documentum® Desktop Applications

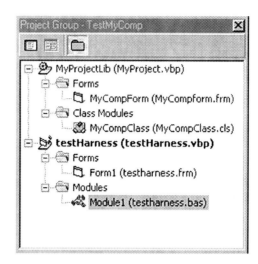

Figure 2.16—Project Explorer Window with both Component Project and Test Harness Project.

Now, both your component and your test harness application are in one group, and can be easily accessed from the **Project Explorer** window. Double-click **Module1** in the **testHarness** project and add the following test harness code.

Source Code A working example of this source code can be found in the "`Chapter2/TestHarness`" directory of the source code archive.

```
Option Explicit

' DCTM globals
Private loginMgr As DCLOGINMGRLib.DcLoginManager
Private sessionId As String

Sub Main()
    Dim frm As Form1

    Set loginMgr = New DCLOGINMGRLib.DcLoginManager

    ' if no session, login
    If (sessionId = "") Then
        sessionId = loginMgr.Connect("", "", "", "", 0)
    End If
```

```
        ' if still no session, error out
    If (sessionId = "") Then
        MsgBox "Could not Log In.", vbCritical, "Could Not" _
            & " Log In"
        Set loginMgr = Nothing
        End
    Else
        ' call form
        Set frm = New Form1
        frm.sessionId = sessionId
        frm.Show vbModal
        Set frm = Nothing
    End If

    loginMgr.disconnect (sessionId)
    Set loginMgr = Nothing

End Sub
```

This code should look familiar. It is essentially the *Main()* subroutine from the standalone application skeleton code discussed earlier in this chapter. This code logs into the Docbase using the Login Manager[*], and then passes the session Id to Form1. Form1 is where the interesting stuff happens.

As illustrated in Figure 2.17, the form for this test harness is very simple, but it doesn't have to be. You can make it as complicated and as interactive as you like. In fact, you can test a whole suite of components from this form if you like. Simply add the projects to the group, add their references to the test harness, and add controls to the form to activate them. For this example, I chose a simple interface: a big button that says **Run Component**. Clicking the button will run the MyProjectLib.MyCompClass component.

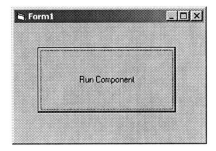

Figure 2.17—testHarness Form1

---

[*] The Login Manager is discussed in Chapter 5, *Proven Solutions to Common Tasks*.

Here is the code behind `Form1`.

```
Option Explicit

Public sessionId As String

Private cx As DfClientX
Private client As IDfClient
Private session As IDfSession
Private reporter As DCREPORTSLib.DcReport

Private Sub Form_Load()

    ' setup dfc client vars
    Set cx = New DfClientX
    Set client = cx.getLocalClient
    Set session = client.findSession(sessionId)

End Sub
```

The `Form_Load()` subroutine runs when the form is loaded and establishes the local DFC variables and a session for the form. When the **Run Component** button is clicked, the `Command1_Click()` subroutine runs—this is where the real work is done.

```
Private Sub Command1_Click()
    Dim itemsCol As New DcItems
    Dim item As New DcObjectItem
    Dim comp As New MyProjectLib.MyCompClass
    Dim dcComp As IDcComponent

    ' cast comp to generic dcComp to get component query
    ' interface
    Set dcComp = comp

    ' hard code a valid object id
    item.ID = "0900218d80053e47"

    ' add item to collection
    itemsCol.Type = DC_OBJECT_ITEM_IID_STRING
    itemsCol.Add item
```

```
    ' init the component using the IDcCompnent interface
    ' you should NEVER do this - except here in a test harness!

    dcComp.Init session.getDocbaseName, _
                session.getUser("").getUserOSName, _
                "", _
                "", _
                itemsCol, _
                Me.hWnd, _
                reporter, _
                DC_OBJECT_ITEM_IID_STRING

    ' run the component
    dcComp.Run

    ' deinit component
    dcComp.DeInit

    Set dcComp = Nothing
    Set comp = Nothing
    Set itemsCol = Nothing
    Set item = Nothing

End Sub
```

The first thing that occurs in this code is a MyProjectLib.MyCompClass object is instantiated and cast to an IDcComponent class. This is necessary because we need to address the object as a COM object. Next, the code sets up the DcItems collection and fills it with one DcObjectItem. Note that the object Id assigned to the DcObjectItem object, `item`, is hard coded, but it doesn't have to be. What your component expects for input determines whether you pass it a DcObjectItem object with a valid object Id, or a DcAbstractItem object with no Id. Components that operate on objects (e.g., DcCheckin, DcCheckout, DcProperties) require DcObjectItem objects with valid object Ids. Components that don't operate on any particular object (e.g., DcFind) require a DcAbstractItem object. Whichever item object type you pass, it must agree with the `items` parameter of the *IDcComponent_Init()* function in your component class file.

Now that the item collection is properly configured, it's time to run the component. After emphasizing that you should always use the Documentum Component Dispatcher to run Documentum components, you can see that the test harness code calls `dcComp`'s *Init()*, *Run()*, and *DeInit()* COM methods directly. I break the rules here with good reason: the component is not yet part of a DocApp. Therefore, neither DART nor the Documentum Component Dispatcher knows anything about it. If you try to use the Documentum Component Dispatcher to run the component, DART will return an error to the effect that it can't find, and doesn't know anything about, your component. In this instance, it really is necessary to circumvent DART.

Set some breakpoints in your component code and run the test harness. Your component will run until it hits your breakpoint and then return you to the Visual Basic debugger where you then have the full facilities of Visual Basic IDE to debug your component (e.g., local window, immediate window, step in).

2.2.4.2 Using A DocApp Test Harness

The test harness DocApp uses Windows Explorer as the parent process for your component. In order to setup the test harness DocApp, you will need to jump ahead and read the next three sections: Section 2.2.5, *Packaging a Component*; Section 2.2.6, *Adding a Component to a DocApp*, and Section 2.3, *Modifying the Documentum Desktop Menu*.

At this point, I assume you have a compiled component (`.DLL`) that has a UI (i.e., a form or message box), followed the steps in the Section 2.2.5, *Packaging a Component*, to create a `.CAB` file, and followed the steps in the Section 2.2.6, *Adding a Component to a DocApp*, to attach it to a DocApp. Depending upon how your component is launched, you may also have edited the Documentum Desktop menu as described in the Section 2.3, *Modifying the Desktop Client Menu*.

Now, open your component's source code in the Visual Basic IDE, set a breakpoint, and run it. Microsoft Explorer should open because you defined it as the debug process in step 17 when you created your component in Section 2.2.2, *Setting up a Component Project*. In Microsoft Explorer, open your Docbase, log in and do whatever is necessary to activate your component (e.g., choose a menu item, or cause an event). Your component will run until it hits your breakpoint and then return you to the Visual Basic debugger where you then have the full facilities of Visual Basic IDE to debug your component (e.g., local window, immediate window, step in).

Both of these testing methods (Visual Basic test harness and DocApp test harness) are equally valid and equally useful. The choice of which to use is solely up to you and your preference. The Visual Basic test harness is quick and simple to build and implement; but doesn't give you a total understanding of how your component will react since it isn't using DART. The DocApp approach is a little more tedious to implement but will give you a thorough understanding of how your component will react when it is installed in the Docbase. However, you might spend more time debugging component delivery than your actual component code. Determine the technique you are most comfortable with and use it.

2.2.5 Packaging A Component

After writing, debugging, and testing your application, you may want to revisit step 12 in Section 2.2.2, *Setting up a Component Project*, to disable debugging, and choose **Optimize for Fast Code**. Once you have recompiled, the easiest way to deploy your application is by using the Package & Deployment Wizard that comes as part of the Microsoft Visual Studio. I am not going to detail the use of the Packaging & Deployment Wizard, but I do want to make two points about the configuration of your deployment file.

First, during the process of creating a deployment file, the wizard will ask you to identify the .DLL files referenced by your application that you would like to bundle in the deployment file. To avoid any licensing or legal issues with redistribution of Documentum binaries, I suggest that you unselect DFC.TLB and any .DLL that starts with Dc, or has Documentum in its path, as shown in Figure 2.18.

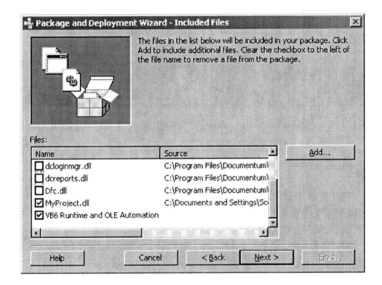

Figure 2.18—Package & Deployment Wizard—Unselect Documentum .DLLs

Second, after deciding which files to include and which files to exclude from the deployment file, the wizard will ask you to identify the source for each of these files. Make sure that you choose **Include in this cab** for each file in the list (see Figure 2.19). The Microsoft files (e.g., VB6 Runtime and OLE Automation) default to **Download from Microsoft Web site**. Depending upon your network's configuration, it could be impossible for users to download these files during installation of the component. It's best to distribute the Microsoft files with your component.

The output of the Package & Deployment Wizard is a .CAB file. This is the file you will use in the next section to include your component in a DocApp.

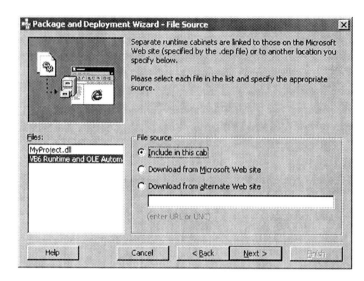

Figure 2.19—Package and Deployment Wizard—Include All Files in this CAB

2.2.6 Adding A Component To A DocApp

Use the Documentum Application Builder to add a component to a DocApp. I am not going to provide a tutorial on the Documentum Application Builder; however, I will briefly discuss attaching components to a DocApp for the purpose of testing them.

In a DocApp, there are two types of components: global components and type-specific components. Global components are not specific to particular object types (e.g., DcFind). Type-specific components implement a functional class on a specific object type (e.g., DcProperties).

The following steps create a DocApp for a global component. It does not contain any custom object types, only an ACX form to hold the component and a global component definition to install it. Remember, the purpose of this DocApp is simply to test the component.

To create a DocApp to test a global component, follow these steps:

1. Start the Documentum Application Builder, and log in.
2. Choose to **New** from the **File** menu.
3. Name your DocApp. (In this example, `MyApp`.)
4. From the **Insert** menu, choose **Forms** and then **ACX Form**.
5. Double-click the new ACX Form to open it for editing.

6. Give the form a name. (In this example, MyComp.)
7. Click the **Add** button.
8. Navigate to the .CAB file for the component you want to add, and select it. The GUID for the component will be automatically inserted in the **Class ID** field (see Figure 2.20).

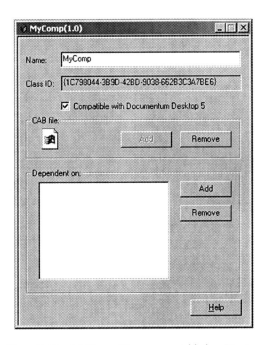

Figure 2.20—MyComp Component Added to DocApp

9. Close the form by clicking the close box in the upper right-hand corner of the form.
10. Select **Checkin Object(s)** from the **DocApp** menu, and click **OK**.
11. Double-click the **Global Components** object to open it for editing.
12. Click the **Add** button.
13. Enter your component's name in the **Class Name** field. (In this example, MyComp.)
14. Click the **Select Component** button.
15. Select the ACX Form you created in step 4, and click **Add** (see Figure 2.21).

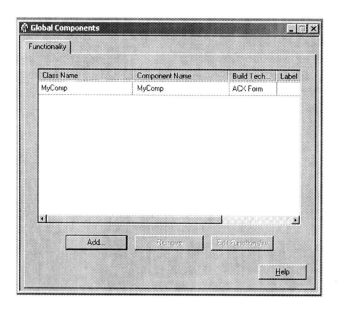

Figure 2.21—MyComp ACX Added to Global Components

16. Click **OK** on the **Functionality Description** form and close the **Global Components** form by clicking the close box in the upper right-hand corner of the form.
17. Select **Checkin Object(s)** from the **DocApp** menu. Click **OK** in the dialog box to checkin the entire DocApp.
18. Select **Checkin DocApp** from the **DocApp** menu. On the **Check In Application** form, click **Version** to activate the drop-down menu and select **Same**. It is crucial that you *always* checkin components and DocApps as the *same version*. Versioned components and DocApps can cause functionality to become disconnected, and cause untold headaches trying to diagnose and repair them.
19. Close Documentum Application Builder.

The process to create a DocApp for testing a type-specific component is essentially the same, except instead of installing the ACX Form as a global component in steps 11—16, you associate it with a functional class of a particular object type in the DocApp.

To create a DocApp for testing a type-specific component, follow these steps.

1. Start the Documentum Application Builder, and log in.
2. Open the DcDesktopClient DocApp, or the DocApp into which you want to insert your type-specific component.
3. From the **Insert** menu, choose **ACX Form**.
4. Double-click the new ACX Form to open it for editing.
5. Give the form a name. (In this example, MyComp.)

6. Click the **Add** button.
7. Navigate to the .CAB file for the component you want to add, and select it. The GUID for the component will be automatically inserted in the **Class ID** field (see Figure 2.20).
8. Close the form by clicking the close box in the upper right-hand corner of the form.
9. Select **Checkin Object(s)** from the **DocApp** menu, and click **OK**.
10. Double-click the object type to which you want to attach your functional class.
11. Click the **Functionality** tab.
12. If you are adding a new function to the object type, click the **Add** button. If you are replacing an existing function with a new one, select the function from the list and click the **Edit Functionality** button (see Figure 2.22).
13. Enter your component's name in the **Class Name** field.
14. Click the **Select Component** button.
15. Select the ACX Form you created in step 4, and click **Add**.
16. Click **OK** on the **Functionality Description** form and close the type description dialog box by clicking the close box in the upper right-hand corner of the form.
17. Select **Checkin Object(s)** from the **DocApp** menu. Click **OK** in the dialog box to checkin the entire DocApp.
18. Select **Checkin DocApp** from the **DocApp** menu. On the **Check In Application** form, click **Version** to activate the drop-down menu and select **Same**. It is crucial that you *always* checkin components and DocApps as the *same version*. Versioned components and DocApps can cause functionality to become disconnected, and cause untold headaches trying to diagnose and repair them.
19. Close Documentum Application Builder.

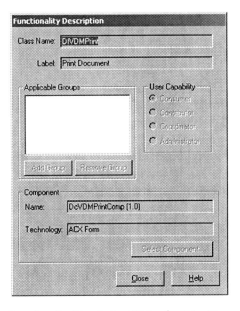

Figure 2.22—Functionality Description Dialog for Print Document Method

You have now successfully installed your component in the Docbase and it is available for use (i.e., testing and debugging). If your component is global, the next step is to provide a mechanism to launch the component. If your component is type-specific, DART will generate the event that invokes the functional class.

2.3 Modifying The Documentum Desktop Menu

One of the easiest ways to launch a component or an application is from the Documentum Desktop menu. Global and type-specific components can easily be added to the menu using the Menu System Designer tool. This section discusses the basics for modifying the Documentum Desktop menu to include new functionality. But first, a few comments about menus.

2.3.1 A Word About Menus

In previous versions of Documentum, the menu existed in the desktop client application (WorkSpace®) and could be modified dynamically by script files when users logged in. This was a blessing and a curse: A good logon script could control the presentation of a lot of menu options, but scripting for WorkSpace was not pretty. In Documentum 4i, the desktop client menu was contained in a file in the Docbase named `MenuSystem.ini`. This was also a blessing and a curse: Documentum provided a nice UI tool to modify menus, but took away the ability to dynamically alter menus with logon scripts. In addition, a quick survey of your Docbase may reveal several `MenuSystem.ini` files. This is a problem. How your Docbase and users are configured, and how you want to allocate access to custom menu options, determines which `MenuSystem.ini` file is used. Documentum 5 is no different from 4i, except the name of the menu file has changed to `MenuSystem5.ini`.

When the Documentum Desktop is initialized, it searches for a `MenuSystem5.ini` file in the following order, *and uses the first one it finds*:

- `/<User's Home Cabinet>/Desktop Client/MenuSystem5.ini`
- `/System/<User's Home Group>/Desktop Client/MenuSystem5.ini`
- `/System/Desktop Client/MenuSystem5.ini`

This means that a user's customizations take precedence over group customizations, and group customizations take precedence over global customizations. This also means that if you add customizations to the global menu (`/System/Desktop Client/MenuSystem5.ini`) they will be lost if a user has a customized menu file in their home cabinet or a group folder. You must choose carefully which `MenuSystem5.ini` file to edit.

2.3.2 Adding A Global Component To The Menu

To add a global component to the Documentum Desktop menu, follow these steps:

1. Login to your Docbase as a Superuser using the Documentum Desktop client.
2. Navigate to the /System/Desktop Client folder. I assume you are updating the global menu file. If this is incorrect, find the appropriate MenuSystem5.ini file instead.
3. Right-click on MenuSystem5.ini and choose **Edit**. This should checkout the MenuSystem5.ini file and launch the Menu System Designer tool.
4. In the left hand pane of the Menu System Designer Tool, scroll down and select the &Applications menu entry.
5. Click the **New** button to create a new Menu Item.
6. On the **Appearance** tab, enter a **Label**, **Description**, **Full Name**, and **ToolTip** for your component (see Figure 2.23).

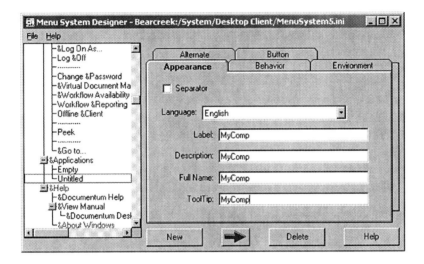

Figure 2.23—Appearance Tab for New Menu Item.

7. Click the **Behavior** tab.
8. Enter the following information on the **Behavior** tab:
   - **Command State Flag:** Choose DC_CSF_ALWAYS so your menu option is always available.
   - **Functional Class:** You must type the name of your functional class in the combo box; it doesn't appear there automatically (In this example, MyComp.). See Figure 2.24.
9. Click the **Environment** tab.

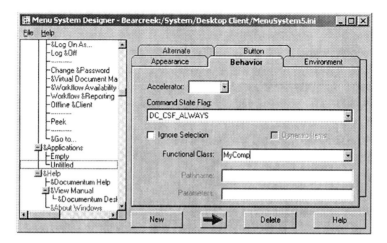

Figure 2.24—Behavior Tab for New Menu Item.

10. Enter the following information on the **Environment** tab:
    - **Global:** Check this box.
    - **Applications:** Type the name of your DocApp in the ComboBox; it doesn't appear automatically (In this example, `MyTestHarness`.). See Figure 2.25.

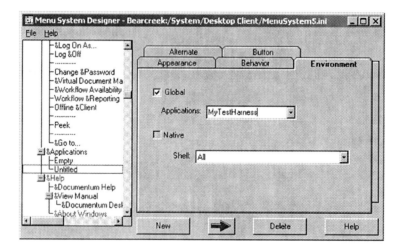

Figure 2.25—Environment Tab for New Menu Item.

11. Close the Menu System Designer Tool and save the menu.
12. Check in the `MenuSystem5.ini` file. You can version this file if you like.
13. Log off and back on to your Docbase to load the new menu file.

If your menu does not reflect the changes you just made, you may need to clear your client-side caches. See Chapter 7, *Tips, Tools and Handy Information,* for details about clearing the client-side caches.

2.3.3 Adding A Type-Specific Component To The Menu

Adding a type-specific component to the menu is very similar to adding a global component.

1. Login to your Docbase as a Superuser using the Documentum Desktop client.
2. Navigate to the `/System/Desktop Client` folder. I assume you are updating the global menu file. If this is incorrect, find the appropriate `MenuSystem5.ini` file instead.
3. Right-click on `MenuSystem5.ini` and choose **Edit**. This should checkout the `MenuSystem5.ini` file and launch the Menu System Designer tool.
4. In the left hand pane of the Menu System Designer Tool, scroll down and select the `&Applications` menu entry.
5. Click the **New** button to create a new Menu Item.
6. On the **Appearance** tab, enter a **Label**, **Description**, **Full Name**, and **ToolTip** for your component.
7. Click the **Behavior** tab.
8. Enter the following information on the **Behavior** tab:
   - **Command State Flag:** Choose the command state flag appropriate for your component. A list of command state flags is supplied in Chapter 7, *Tips, Tools and Handy Information*.
   - **Functional Class:** You must type the name of your functional class in the combo box; it doesn't appear there automatically.
9. Click on the **Environment** tab.
10. Enter the following information on the **Environment** tab:
    - **Global:** Do *not* check this box.
    - **Applications:** Type the name of your DocApp in the ComboBox; it doesn't appear automatically.
11. Close the Menu System Designer Tool and save the menu.
12. Check in the `MenuSystem5.ini` file. You can version this file if you like.
13. Log off and back on to your Docbase to load the new menu file.

If your menu does not reflect the changes you just made, you may need to clear your client-side caches. See Chapter 7, *Tips, Tools and Handy Information,* for details about clearing the client-side caches.

2.3.4 Adding An Executable Application To The Menu

Sometimes you want a menu item to run an executable file on your hard disk, instead of a component in a DocApp. This is also easy to accomplish with the Menu System Designer Tool.

1. Login to your Docbase as a Superuser using the Documentum Desktop.
2. Navigate to the /System/Desktop Client folder. I assume you are updating the global menu file. If this is incorrect, find the appropriate MenuSystem5.ini file instead.
3. Right-click on MenuSystem5.ini and choose **Edit**. This should checkout the MenuSystem5.ini file and launch the Menu System Designer tool.
4. In the left hand pane of the Menu System Designer Tool, scroll down and select the &Applications menu entry.
5. Click the **New** button to create a new Menu Item.
6. On the **Appearance** tab, enter a **Label**, **Description**, **Full Name**, and **ToolTip** for this menu item.
7. Click the **Behavior** tab.
8. Enter the following information on the **Behavior** tab:
   - **Command State Flag:** Choose the command state flag appropriate for your component. A list of command state flags is supplied in Chapter 7, *Tips, Tools and Handy Information*.
   - **Functional Class:** Choose DcOpenFile. This will activate the **Pathname** and **Parameter** fields.
   - **Pathname:** Enter the fully qualified path name to the application you want to run (e.g., c:\winnt\notepad.exe)
   - **Parameters:** Enter a parameter to pass to the application you named in **Pathname** above. Unfortunately, I haven't found this to be too useful. You can't pass "%1" like you can in DOS to indicate a filename; you can't pass an r_object_id; and you can't pass the result of an API call like *getcontent()*. The only thing you can pass is a literal string, like "test.txt." For example, choosing this menu option would launch NotePad and open a file named "test.txt " *every* time the menu option is selected.
9. Close the Menu System Designer Tool and save the menu.
10. Check in the MenuSystem5.ini file. You can version this file if you like.
11. Log off and back on to your Docbase to load the new menu file.

If your menu does not reflect the changes you just made, you may need to clear your client-side caches. See Chapter 7, *Tips, Tools and Handy Information,* for details about clearing the client-side caches.

2.4 Modifying Documentum Desktop Components

Documentum has made it easy to modify several of their stock Desktop components. First, they provide the source code[*] for the most common components. Second, each component has three subroutines that were designed for you to implement, and are called automatically by the component's logic. Table 2.1 summarizes these subroutines.

---

[*] You can download the Documentum Desktop Component Source archive from the Documentum Download Center (http://documentum.subscribenet.com).

The following procedure is applicable to customizations using both the `DcCustomOnXXXCode()` subroutines and purely custom code. Certainly, implementing the `DcCustomOnXXXCode()` subroutines is easier than customizing other parts of the code, however, often what you need is not achievable with the `DcCustomOnXXXCode()` subroutines. Regardless of where you implement your customizations, remember that if you ever upgrade your Documentum Desktop, you will need to re-implement your customizations, so make them easy to identify in your source code.

Table 2.1—Customizable Subroutines in Documentum Desktop Components

Subroutine Name	Description
`DcCustomOnLoadingCode()`	This subroutine is automatically called at the end of the `Form_Load()` subroutine. You can use it to implement custom initialization you want the component to have before it is displayed.
`DcCustomOnSavingCode()`	This subroutine is automatically called whenever form data is saved. You can use it to implement specialized save routines.
`DcCustomOnUnloadingCode()`	This subroutine is automatically called by the `Form_Unload()` event handler before the form is unloaded. You can use it to implement any post-processing necessitated by your customizations.

The procedure for modifying existing Documentum Desktop components is generally the same as for creating a new component. However, instead of starting with a new Visual Basic project, we will copy an existing one.

1. Copy the component's folder containing all of its Visual Basic files to a new location.
2. Double-click the component's project file (.vbp) to start Visual Basic.
3. Choose **Save Project As** from the **File** menu to save the project with a new name.
4. Choose **Properties** from the **Project** menu.
5. On the **General** tab, change the name of the project.
6. On the **Application** tab, change the title of the application.
7. On the **Component** tab, select the **No Compatibility** radio button. Selecting **No Compatibility** will break this component's binary compatibility with its former project and force Visual Basic to generate a new COM Id. Breaking binary compatibility ensures that this component will not overwrite the original. In addition, breaking binary compatibility and generating a new COM Id ensures that this component will only apply to the object types to which you attach it.
8. Click **OK** to save the project properties.

9. Choose **Replace** from the **Edit** menu. Enter the old project name in the **Find What** field and the new project name in the **Replace With** field. Also, select **Current Project** in the **Search** frame. Click **OK** and replace all occurrences of the old project name with your new project name.
10. Choose **Save** from the **File** menu.
11. If you broke binary compatibility in step 7, you should now compile your component, and then reset its binary compatibility. See steps 21—28 in Section 2.2.2, *Setting up a Component Project*, earlier in this chapter.

You are now ready to modify the component. Whether you choose to totally customize the inner workings of the component or stick to using the `DcCustomOnXXXCode()` subroutines, it doesn't matter. From here on, it's all the same: code, compile, test, and deploy.

2.5 Troubleshooting Component Delivery

Debugging and troubleshooting failed component delivery can be very frustrating. Improvements to the Documentum Desktop and Microsoft Windows have alleviated many of the earlier problems associated with the delivery of COM objects to clients. If you are encountering a problem with component delivery, here are a few things to try.

1. Reboot your workstation. This often knocks things loose.
2. Reboot the Content Server®. This, too, often knocks things loose.
3. Remove the component from the `%Windows%\Downloaded Program Files` directory on your workstation. To do this, locate the component in Windows Explorer, right-click on the component and choose **Remove**.
4. Review your Package & Deployment Wizard script and ensure that the **File Source** for all files is marked as **Include in this cab** and *not* **Download from Microsoft Web site** or **Download from alternate Web site**. Some files default to **Download from Microsoft Web site** which, depending upon your networking environment, can be unreachable. I have found that components fail without indication when this occurs.
5. See Documentum's publication, *Frequently Asked Questions for Deploying, Downloading and Creating Documentum Desktop Client Components*.
6. See Documentum Tech Support Note #14740. This support note is the consolidation of four support notes regarding deployment of Desktop components.
7. See Microsoft Knowledgebase article #Q252937. This article discusses why code download fails and offers some suggestions and tools to trace the download process.

2.6 Chapter Summary

This chapter provided an overview of the process for creating Documentum applications, both standalone and components. The two types of applications are similar, though implemented differently. For example, they both use a similar routine to launch themselves; however, standalone applications are easier to debug than components.

In addition to the basic structure of standalone and component applications, this chapter also discussed techniques for testing them using test harnesses. There are two types of test harnesses: Visual Basic test harnesses which involve creating a project group and direct instantiation of the component; and the DocApp approach which leverages DART to instantiate the component. Both methods have advantages and disadvantages, which method you use is up to you.

This chapter also discussed making modifications to the Documentum Desktop menu system using the Menu System Designer Tool. It discussed how to add three types of applications to the menu system: global, type-specific, and executable.

The chapter concluded with a brief overview of the process for modifying Documentum's stock Desktop components. Although you are free to completely rewrite any Desktop component, Documentum has provided hooks in their source code to accommodate quick and easy modifications.

This chapter provided a foundation and framework on which the rest of the techniques in this book can be implemented. In the remaining chapters of this book, I discuss specific techniques and approaches for solving problems, and will no longer discuss the infrastructure of the application. The following chapters' code snippets will be short (relatively), and context-less, meaning that certain variables will be assumed (e.g., IDfSession, DfClient, and IDfClientX), and no further mention of the application or component framework will be made.

3

Working With Queries And Collections

Now that you have an understanding of the application and component framework, this chapter will begin your exploration of what happens inside the application. This chapter covers four related topics:

- Techniques for querying the Docbase
- Different types of queries
- Methods for processing collections
- Common, useful queries

Queries ask questions of the Docbase, which responds with a collection of answers. Queries and collections are one of the basic constructs in a Documentum application, and you don't have one without the other.

You will learn that there are several techniques to query the Docbase and several different types of queries. Each query technique and query type serves a different purpose and each has a time for use. You will also learn several techniques for processing collections and common pitfalls to avoid. The last part of this chapter presents an assortment of common, useful queries for your use.

3.1 How To Query The Docbase

I will present three ways to programmatically query the Docbase in this section:

- Using the Run Query (IDcRunQuery) interface of the DcFindTarget class
- Using the Query Manager (IDfQueryMgr) class
- Using the query (IDfQuery) class

Each of these techniques has advantages and disadvantages. The Run Query is extremely simple to implement and leverages the Documentum Desktop to process the query and display the results. However, it is restricted to only running SELECT queries.

The Query Manager is a high-level DFC class that lets you build queries by setting properties of the class. The Query Manager is a powerful class that can, among other things, query multiple Docbases simultaneously and aggregate the results. However, the Query Manager doesn't handle complex queries well and provides no functionality for processing the results of the query.

Using the IDfQuery class is the most common approach to querying. With it, you can meet all your querying needs. However, it also requires the most work to implement.

Each of these techniques is examined in detail in the following sections.

3.1.1 Using Run Query

A simple way to programmatically query the Docbase is to use the Run Query interface (IDcRunQuery) of the DcFindTarget class. This is essentially the same interface used by the Query screen of the Documentum Desktop. As the following code snippet demonstrates, all that is required to execute a query is to instantiate an IDcRunQuery object and call the *RunQuery()* method while passing it a Docbase name and query string. Your project must reference the Documentum Find Target Server 1.0 Type Library to use this code.

Source Code A working example of this source code can be found in the "`Chapter3/Run Query`" directory of the source code archive.

```
Dim findTargetObj As New DcFindTargetObj
Dim runQueryObj As IDcRunQuery

Set runQueryObj = findTargetObj
runQueryObj.RunQuery "Docbase", "select * from dm_document " _
          & "where folder('/Temp')"
```

The DcFindTarget class takes care of logging into the Docbase, parsing the query string, running the query, and displaying the results. The results are displayed in a Documentum Desktop window, and can be manipulated (see Figure 3.1). That's a lot of functionality for four lines of code. However, this technique takes a lot for granted and probably doesn't meet your needs as an application developer. It is also restricted to only executing simple SELECT queries; you cannot issue a query that results in a change to the Docbase (e.g., you cannot use ALTER or UPDATE DQL commands).

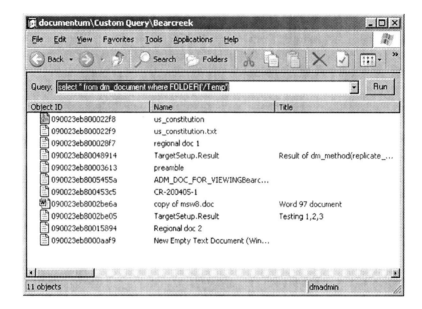

Figure 3.1—Run Query Results

3.1.2 Using The Query Manager

The Query Manager (IDfQueryMgr) is a high-level DFC class that provides better control for the construction and execution of queries than IDcRunQuery. This class is well suited for building queries from data entered on forms since each element of the query is added to the class before it is executed. It also has the ability to save queries as SmartLists and to query multiple Docbases simultaneously and aggregate the results.

The following code snippet demonstrates a simple use of the Query Manger. Query Manager queries are built one property at a time. First, the SELECT variables are added to the class and given order and display characteristics. Next, the object types are added. Finally, the WHERE clause is built with all of its variables and conditions. The query is then executed in an asynchronous fashion.

> **Source Code** A working example of this source code can be found in the "`Chapter3/Query Manager`" directory of the source code archive.

```
Dim qMgr As IDfQueryMgr
Dim a1 As IDfAttrLine
Dim l1 As IDfQueryLocation
Dim r1 As IDfQueryResultItem
Dim strTmp As String
Dim i As Integer
Dim j As Integer
Dim sobj As IDfSysObject
Dim tObj As IDfTypedObject

' DQL: select object_name, r_object_id from dm_document where
'           owner_name = 'dmadmin' and folder('/Temp') order by
'           object_name

' init
Set qMgr = cx.getQueryMgr
qMgr.Initialize session

' set up SELECT
qMgr.insertDisplayAttr -1, "object_name", 20
qMgr.insertDisplayAttr -1, "r_object_id", 20

' set up FROM
qMgr.setObjectType ("dm_document")

' setup WHERE
Set a1 = qMgr.insertAttrLine(0, -1, 0)
a1.SetAttr ("owner_name")
a1.setValue ("dmadmin")
a1.setRelationalOp (1)
a1.setLogicOp ("AND")

Set l1 = qMgr.insertLocation(-1)
l1.setPath "/Temp"
l1.setDescend False

' setup ORDER BY
qMgr.insertSortAttr -1, "object_name", True
```

```
' execute
qMgr.startSearch

While (Not qMgr.isSearchFinished)
    sleep (1)
Wend

' get results
strTmp = "DQL: " & qMgr.getDQL & vbCrLf & vbCrLf
strTmp = strTmp & qMgr.getResultItemCount & " " _
    & qMgr.getObjectType & "(s) found." & vbCrLf & vbCrLf

' get columns
For i = 0 To qMgr.getDisplayAttrCount - 1
    strTmp = strTmp & qMgr.getDisplayAttr(i) & vbTab
Next i
strTmp = strTmp & vbCrLf & vbCrLf

' process results
For i = 0 To qMgr.getResultItemCount - 1
    Set r1 = qMgr.getResultItem(i)
    Set tObj = r1.getTypedObject

    For j = 0 To qMgr.getDisplayAttrCount - 1
        strTmp = strTmp & tObj.getString(qMgr.getDisplayAttr(j)) _
                    & vbTab
    Next j
    strTmp = strTmp & vbCrLf
Next i

' show results
MsgBox strTmp, vbInformation, "Results"
```

As you can see, querying using the IDfQueryMgr is simply a matter of assigning values to the IDfQueryMgr's property fields. This is why it works well behind a form. In this example the full query was:

```
select object_name, r_object_id from dm_document where
    owner_name = 'dmadmin' and folder('/Temp') order by
    object_name
```

The code first initializes the Query Manager object with a valid session and then adds the two attributes to search on, `object_name` and `r_object_id`, using the *insertDisplayAttr()* method. This method requires three arguments: the placement of the attribute (-1 is the beginning of the list); the name of the attribute; and the width of the display column. The width of the display column attribute only comes into play when you save the query as a Smart List, since the Query Manager class has no display capabilities. The object type is set using *setObjectType()* and then the WHERE clause is built by adding IDfAttrLine objects. IDfAttrLine objects encapsulate WHERE clause variables and describe the conditions they must meet, as well as their relation to each other. Lastly, a search path is added to the Query Manager object using an IDfQueryLocation object, and a sort order is added using the *insertSortAttr()* method.

Of particular interest is the use of the While loop and the *sleep()* function*. The *IDfQueryMgr.execute()* method runs the query asynchronously and returns immediately. Therefore, you must continually poll the Query Manager to determine if the query has completed. The reason the Query Manager operates in this manner is so it can execute multi-Docbase queries. Naturally, some of these queries will take longer to complete than others. Therefore, instead of blocking the application thread waiting for a remote query to complete, the queries are executed asynchronously and application control is returned immediately.

This code snippet also includes some code to process the results returned by the Query Manger. The logic is similar to processing a two-dimensional array where i enumerates the rows and j enumerates the columns (see Figure 3.2). I included this code primarily to highlight the difference between accessing the Query Manager's results, and accessing an IDfCollection, which will be examined later in this chapter.

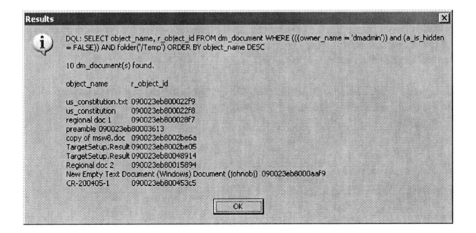

Figure 3.2—Query Manager Results

---

* The *sleep()* function is discussed in Chapter 5, *Proven Solutions for Common Tasks*.

One of the stated benefits to using the Query Manager class is that it can save its query as a Smart List (`dm_smart_list`). In a sense, this is really the class' display and results processing mechanism, since a Smart List can be opened and its query results viewed in the Documentum Desktop. Saving the query as a Smart List is accomplished with a simple call to the `save()` method of the Query Manager object. Interestingly, the `save()` method saves the Smart List on your *hard drive*, not in the Docbase as you would expect. I don't often have a reason to save a query to a user's hard drive, so when I need to save a query, I save it as a Query object (`dm_query`) in the Docbase. Like a Smart List, doubling-clicking the Query object in the Documentum Desktop executes the query and displays the results in a Documentum Desktop window. Unlike a Smart List, a Query object cannot be opened or edited with the Documentum Desktop Find component.

The code snippet on the following pages illustrates the use of the `save()` method as well as how to save the query in the Docbase as a `dm_query` object. I duplicated the previous snippet here to provide context, and highlighted the added lines with bold typeface.

> **Source Code** A working example of this source code can be found in the "`Chapter3/Query Manager`" directory of the source code archive.

```
Dim qMgr As IDfQueryMgr
Dim al As IDfAttrLine
Dim ll As IDfQueryLocation
Dim rl As IDfQueryResultItem
Dim strTmp As String
Dim i As Integer
Dim j As Integer
Dim sobj As IDfSysObject
Dim tObj As IDfTypedObject

' DQL: select object_name, r_object_id from dm_document where
'            owner_name = 'dmadmin' and folder('/Temp') order by
'            object_name

' init
Set qMgr = cx.getQueryMgr
qMgr.Initialize session

' set up SELECT
qMgr.insertDisplayAttr -1, "object_name", 20
qMgr.insertDisplayAttr -1, "r_object_id", 20
```

```
' set up FROM
qMgr.setObjectType ("dm_document")

' setup WHERE
Set a1 = qMgr.insertAttrLine(0, -1, 0)
a1.SetAttr ("owner_name")
a1.setValue ("dmadmin")
a1.setRelationalOp (1)
a1.setLogicOp ("AND")

Set l1 = qMgr.insertLocation(-1)
l1.setPath "/Temp"
l1.setDescend False

' setup ORDER BY
qMgr.insertSortAttr -1, "object_name", True

' execute
qMgr.startSearch

While (Not qMgr.isSearchFinished)
    sleep (1)
Wend

' save as smartlist
If (Not qMgr.save("C:\Temp\qMgr.smartlist")) Then
    MsgBox "Error Saving SmartList.", vbCritical, "Error"
End If

'save as query
Set sObj = session.newObject("dm_query")
sObj.setContentType ("crtext")
sObj.setContent cx.StringToByteArrayOutputStream (qMgr.getDQL)
sObj.setObjectName "Test Query"
sObj.link "/Temp"
sObj.save

Set qMgr = Nothing
```

After running this code, you should find a file named `qMgr.smartlist` in the `C:\Temp` directory on your hard drive, and an object named `Test Query` in the /Temp cabinet in the Docbase. The `dm_query` object can be checked out and edited, or double-clicked and executed in the Documentum Desktop.

Again, the Query Manager is a good choice for constructing a query from a user interface (UI) since it is relatively easy to map UI field values into the properties of the Query Manager object. UI-controlled queries are less likely to use "SELECT *", wild cards, and joins, which the Query Manager doesn't handle well. The Query Manager is also well suited for enterprise-level, multi-Docbase searches.

A few disadvantages of using the Query Manager are: it doesn't handle complex queries well (e.g., "SELECT *", joins, or sub-queries), it doesn't provide any result processing capabilities, and there is a resource cost for using it. The resource cost is, of course, only temporary while the object is instantiated and running, but it can be high and should be considered if performance is an issue.

For more information regarding the use of the Query Manager or any of its properties or methods, see the *Documentum Foundation Classes API Specification*.

3.1.3 Using The IDfQuery Class

As useful as the Query Manager is, its overhead and shortcomings do not make it the best class for general-purpose queries. For the best control and most flexibility when querying, use the IDfQuery class. The IDfQuery class is the basic query class in the DFC, and is the most common class used for querying. It is well designed and simple, but does require more work on your part, as the following code snippet illustrates.

> **Source Code** A working example of this source code can be found in the "`Chapter3/Query Class`" directory of the source code archive.

```
Dim query As IDfQuery
Dim col As IDfCollection

Set query = cx.getQuery
query.setDQL ("select r_object_id, object_name, r_object_type" _
    & " from dm_document where FOLDER('/Temp')")
Set col = query.execute(session, DF_READ_QUERY)

' process the results returned in the collection object here

col.Close
```

The IDfQuery object is instantiated using the object factory in the DfClientX object (represented here by the `cx` variable). The `setDQL()` method is used to pass the DQL query string to the object. The object does not validate the DQL, you must ensure the DQL is valid. The `execute()` method is called to run the query. There are three important things to note about the `execute()` method:

- It returns an IDfCollection object (processing of collection objects is discussed later in this chapter).
- The first parameter is an IDfSession object.
- The second parameter is a constant indicating the type of query to perform. The constant values and their affects are listed in Table 3.1.

As this example illustrates, the IDfQuery object is simple to use. The query runs synchronously within the application thread and the results are returned in an IDfCollection object for processing. The down side to this technique is that it requires more coding on your part: you have to write code to validate and assign the DQL string; you have to write code to process and display the results; and you have to write code to trap errors. As you will see later in this chapter, these things are simple to implement, and this process is probably closer to what you expect as a developer.

Table 3.1—Query Type Constants

Constant Name	Value	Affect
DF_READ_QUERY	0	A read query does not allow changes to be made to the Docbase by the DQL statement (e.g., you cannot use ALTER or UPDATE). Think of it as a read-only query.
DF_QUERY	1	This is a general-purpose query. This type must be used if the DQL statement makes a change to the Docbase (e.g., you use ALTER or UPDATE).
DF_CACHE_QUERY	2	A cached query stores its results in the client's local cache for later reuse. Cached queries can improve performance, but also have the potential for returning stale data. Cached queries are discussed later in this chapter.
DF_EXEC_QUERY	3	The execute query is the same as the DF_QUERY constant except it is used for queries whose syntax exceeds 256 characters.
DF_EXECREAD_QUERY	4	The execute read query is the same as the DF_READ_QUERY constant except it is used for queries whose syntax exceeds 256 characters.
DF_APPLY	5	The apply query is a special type of query that invokes system administration functions or runs external procedures. See the *Documentum Content Server Administrator's Guide* for more information.

3.2 Types Of Queries

This section discusses and gives examples of three types of queries that are other than the basic DQL-variety. These types are: SQL pass-through queries, cached queries, and full-text queries. SQL pass-through queries are queries that affect the underlying RDBMS and are not concerned with Documentum objects. Cached queries are queries whose results are stored locally, and can be quickly retrieved without having to access the Documentum Server. These queries are very useful for populating user controls on a UI. Full-text queries are queries that utilize the full-text index to retrieve objects that contain certain words, or whose content matches certain linguistic constructs.

3.2.1 SQL Pass-Through Queries

A SQL pass-through query is a query targeted at the underlying RDBMS, and not Documentum. To execute a SQL pass-through query, use the DQL EXECUTE statement with the `exec_sql` method. EXECUTE is the DQL equivalent of the Documentum API *apply()* method. The format of an EXECUTE query is:

```
EXECUTE exec_sql WITH query = 'sql_query'
```

where `sql_query` is the actual pass-through SQL query string.

A common use for SQL pass-through queries is to programmatically CREATE, DROP, UPDATE, and INSERT tables in the RDBMS schema. Usually, creating, dropping, and manipulating RDBMS tables in this manner is achieved via a script or other RDBMS interface, and not an application. The following example drops, and then creates a table named USSTATES with two columns: STATE_NAME and STATE_ABBR, and inserts a row for the state of Virginia.

```
execute exec_sql with query = 'drop table usstates'
go
execute exec_sql with query = 'create table usstates
    (state_name varchar2(25), state_abbr varchar2(2))'
go
execute exec_sql with query = 'insert into usstates
    (state_name, state_abbr) values (''Virginia'',''VA'')'
go

execute exec_sql with query = 'commit'
go
```

This example can be run from `idql32.exe`, Documentum's interactive DQL editor*.

Here is the same process in Visual Basic using the DFC.

Source Code A working example of this source code can be found in the "Chapter3/SQL PassThrough" directory of the source code archive.

```
Dim q As IDfQuery
Dim col As IDfCollection
Dim msg As String

Set q = cx.getQuery

' drop table if it already exists
q.setDQL ("execute exec_sql with query = 'drop table usstates'")
Set col = q.execute(session, DF_QUERY)
msg = session.getMessage(3)
If (msg <> "") Then
    MsgBox "Drop: " & msg
End If
col.Close

' (re) create table
q.setDQL ("execute exec_sql with query = 'create table " _
        & "usstates (state_name varchar2(25), state_abbr " _
        & "varchar2(2))'")
Set col = q.execute(session, DF_QUERY)
msg = session.getMessage(3)
If (msg <> "") Then
    MsgBox "Create: " & msg
End If
col.Close

' insert row
q.setDQL ("execute exec_sql with query = 'insert into usstates" _
        & " (state_name, state_abbr) values " _
        & (''Virginia'',''VA'')'")
Set col = q.execute(session, DF_QUERY)
msg = session.getMessage(3)
```

---

* See Chapter 7, *Tips, Tools and Handy Information*, for more information regarding the `idql32.exe` utility

```
If (msg <> "") Then
    MsgBox "Insert: " & msg
End If
col.Close
```

The length of this code snippet compared to the script example illustrates one of the advantages of doing this type of query in a script environment. Another advantage to the script environment is the built-in error handling of `idql32.exe`. The `EXECUTE` statement returns a collection with only one column, `result`, that holds an integer indicating the result of executing the statement, not the result of the query. This is not very useful for error trapping. A better technique is to access the `getMessage()` method of the IDfSession object and check its length. If its length is greater than zero, an error occurred and can be trapped. This code snippet simply displays the error message in a message box.

There are many other uses for the `EXECUTE` statement. See the *Documentum Content Server DQL Reference Manual* for more information.

3.2.2 Cached Queries

Cached queries are the same as other queries in form and structure, but different in execution. When the query engine receives a request for a cached query, it first looks in the local query cache to determine if the same query has previously been saved. If it has, and it's still valid[*], the query results are returned from the local query cache and the actual query is never executed on the server. This results in a much faster response for the user. If the query does not exist in the local query cache (or it is deemed to be invalid), the query engine executes the query on the Documentum Server and saves the results in the local query cache for the next time they are needed.

Cached queries are most useful with data that is fairly static in nature. Since the queries stored in the local query cache are not continually updated, the risk of them growing stale and out of synch with the Docbase is real. For this reason, cached queries should only be used for queries whose results do not change frequently. For example, a good candidate for a cached query would be one that retrieves the names and postal abbreviations for the 50 United States from a registered table. It is not likely that this query will grow stale over the course of a day or even weeks.

You will frequently see cached queries used for populating UI controls. The queries might be executed when the user logs into the application, and cached for the duration of the user's session. Using cached

---

[*] The period of time a cached query remains valid and the criteria used to make that determination can be adjusted by changing the `effective_date` attribute on the Docbase config object. The validity of the query cache is determined when the user logs in.

queries to populate fairly static data in UI controls can increase performance dramatically, especially if you have a complex UI with many query-driven controls.

To execute a cached query, simply use the DF_CACHE_QUERY type constant with the *IDfQuery.execute()* method:

    Set collection = query.execute(session, DF_CACHE_QUERY)

The local query cache is usually:

    c:\documentum\dmcl\qrycache\<server name>\<docbase id>\<user name>\

The query cache map (`cache.map`) and result files are plain text files and can be examined with a text editor. You should not manipulate query cache result files directly. Always use the *IDfQuery.execute()* method with the DF_CACHE_QUERY type constant to manipulate cached queries and their result files.

You can flush the query cache programmatically using the *IDfSession.flushCache()* method. You may want your application to do this when it starts to ensure all of its cached queries are current.

3.2.2.1 Cached Query Configuration

To use cached queries you must make two configuration changes to your environment, one on your client, and one on the server.

- On the client computer, add the line:

    cache_queries = T

    to the [DMAPI_CONFIGURATION] section of your `dmcl.ini` file. The `dmcl.ini` file is usually found in your `C:\Windows` directory. For example, your `dmcl.ini` file might look like this:

```
[DOCBROKER_PRIMARY]
host = 192.168.0.1

[DMAPI_CONFIGURATION]
cache_queries = T
```

- On the server, you will need to set the `effective_date` attribute of the Docbase config object to a valid date. By default, this attribute is set to `NULLDATE`, which disables query caching. The server uses the value of the `effective_date` attribute to determine if the client query cache is valid or needs to be flushed. If the date of the query cache files and the value of the `effective_date` attribute are the same, or the value of the `effective_date` is greater than the current system time, the cache is deemed valid. Otherwise, the cache is deemed invalid and flushed. Use the Documentum Administrator to update the `effective_date` attribute of the Docbase config object.

If you make changes to data you know is cached by clients (e.g., values used by a UI control), you can change the `effective_date` attribute and invalidate everyone's cache. Doing so will cause the clients to reload the data from the Documentum Server.

3.2.2.2 Cached Query Example

The following code snippet illustrates the use of a cached query and the performance improvement it provides. It uses the Win32 API method *GetTickCount ()* to compare the execution times of two queries.

Source Code A working example of this source code can be found in the "`Chapter3/Cached Query`" directory of the source code archive.

```
' Win32 API declaration
Private Declare Function GetTickCount Lib "kernel32" () As Long

Dim q As IDfQuery
Dim col As IDfCollection
Dim startTime As Long

' flush the cache to make sure this query isn't there
session.flush "querycache"

' first query is not found in cache
Set q = cx.getQuery
q.setDQL ("select * from dm_user")
startTime = GetTickCount
Set col = q.execute(session, DF_CACHE_QUERY)
MsgBox "Elapsed time = " & GetTickCount() - startTime, _
    vbInformation, "Initial Query"
col.Close
Set col = Nothing
```

```
' second query is in cache
q.setDQL ("select * from dm_user")
startTime = GetTickCount
Set col = q.execute(session, DF_CACHE_QUERY)
MsgBox "Elapsed time = " & GetTickCount() - startTime, _
    vbInformation, "Cached Query"
col.Close
```

This snippet queries for all of the user objects in the Docbase. This is a good cached query since it is unlikely that the number of user objects in the Docbase will change during the lifetime of your session. When I run this snippet, the first message box reports a duration of 42 milliseconds[*] for the execution of the first query. The second message box reports 3 milliseconds to retrieve the query results from the cache—a 93% improvement in performance.

This example makes the utility of cached queries obvious. However, be aware of the data being cached, and the risk should it fall out of synch with the Docbase.

3.2.3   Full-Text Queries

Up to this point, I have discussed queries that retrieve objects from the Docbase based upon the values of discrete attributes (e.g., object_name), or some relationship among these attributes. Full-text queries allow you to search for words, phrases, values, and word relationships in the content of objects. A full-text search is akin to using an Internet search engine to locate a word or phrase on the Internet. In Documentum, this capability is provided by an embedded Verity®, Inc. full-text search engine. The Verity engine is distributed and fully integrated with the Documentum Server. This integration allows you to execute very effective full-text searches on your Docbase without leaving the Documentum environment. In fact, for queries involving large numbers of objects and massive table scans, full-text searching is often more efficient than DQL. However, sheer volume alone doesn't always make full-text searches more attractive. The use of some DQL predicate functions (e.g., *LOWER ()*), or wildcard characters in search strings (e.g., %book%), will disable RDBMS indexes and force Documentum to execute slow table scans. Both of these situations can be overcome by using full-text searching.

Documentum full-text queries come in two flavors: document searches, and TOPIC® searches. Document searches follow a more traditional DQL format in which the clause SEARCH DOCUMENT CONTAINS is appended to or replaces the WHERE clause in the query. For example:

---

[*] Your execution times will probably be different from mine; however, the point should hold: cached queries are much faster.

```
select * from dm_document search document contains 'Union'
    where any author = 'Madison';
```

TOPIC searches utilize the advanced features of the Verity search engine and the Verity Query Language (VQL) and have a syntax or their own. They are implemented with the `SEARCH TOPIC` clause, which can also be appended to or replace the WHERE clause. For example:

```
select * from dm_document search topic '<word> Union'
    where any author = 'Madison';
```

VQL provides modifiers and operators for creating full-text queries that can handle non-discrete data, fielded data, and word relationships. In addition, the Verity search engine installs and uses KeyView® format filters so it can read and index the most common file formats. A list of these formats can be found in Chapter 7, *Tips, Tools and Handy Information*.

As useful as full-text searches are, they do have some drawbacks. One is objects in the Docbase that do not have any content (e.g., folders), are not full-text indexed. Therefore, to find content-less objects, you must use traditional DQL. Another problem is not all of the DQL predicate functions have equivalents in VQL (e.g., `FOLDER()`). Therefore, to search a folder structure, you must append a DQL WHERE clause to your full-text search. Finally, there is a lag between when an object's content enters the Docbase and when it is available in the full-text index. This lag is governed by the frequency with which the `dm_FulltextMgr` job runs. Therefore, documents are not always immediately available in the full-text index.

3.2.3.1 Full-Text Configuration

Before full-text searching will work, you must create full-text indexes on the Documentum Server, and then indicate which objects to include in the index. To create full-text indexes, and keep them up-to-date, schedule and run the `dm_FulltextMgr` job using the Documentum Administrator. This job also automatically updates the full-text index as objects are add, deleted, and updated in the Docbase. The more frequently this job runs, the more quickly content is available in the full-text index. However, too frequent of execution of this job can impair performance.

To indicate that an object should be included in the full-text index, set its `a_full_text` attribute to true. You can accomplish this in many ways: at checkin when using the Documentum Desktop, by writing a custom checkin procedure that sets it, or by running a DQL query[*].

---

[*] This query and several others relating to full-text searching are discussed in the Section 3.3, *Useful Queries*.

3.2.3.2 Document Searches

Document searches are simple, almost brute-force style full-text searches. A document search uses the SEARCH DOCUMENT CONTAINS clause instead of or in addition to the standard WHERE clause in its DQL. The general format of a document search DQL statement follows:

    select * from dm_document search document contains
        'search_word'

where search_word is the word you are searching for. Notice that this is a search *word*, and not a phrase. White spaces are not supported. You can search for several words as long as you relate them with a Boolean operator, as in:

    select * from dm_document search document contains
        'search_word' AND 'another_search_word'

Document searches do not support wildcards, phrases, or any sort of linguistic relationship between words (e.g., words *near* each other). You cannot search for a particular attribute/value pair using a document search alone. However, you can combine SEARCH DOCUMENT CONTAINS clauses and WHERE clauses to achieve this type of search. For example:

    select * from dm_document search document contains
        'search_word' AND 'another_search_word' where
        attribute_name = 'value'

If you want to perform full-text searches that can implement wildcards, phrases, and linguistic relationships, you need to use TOPIC searches.

3.2.3.3 TOPIC Searches

TOPIC searches utilize VQL to create robust and comprehensive full-text searches. TOPIC searches append or replace the DQL WHERE clause with a SEARCH TOPIC clause. The general format is:

    select * from dm_document search topic 'Vertiy syntax here'
        where atribute_name = 'value'

Notice the Verity syntax is enclosed in single quotes (' '). In the examples that follow, you will also notice that operators and modifiers are enclosed in angle brackets (< >).

The Verity syntax used in DQL is comprised of a combination of operators and modifiers. These operators and modifiers are used to construct DQL predicates that define the qualifications that objects must meet for retrieval. There are four categories of operators:

- Evidence operators
- Relational operators
- Concept operators
- Proximity operators

Each of these categories and their operators are discussed next.

3.2.3.3.1 Evidence Operators

Evidence operators expand your search criteria by adding fuzziness to your search terms. Fuzziness is generated by automatically including related or similar words to the search, thereby expanding the possible result set. Table 3.2 summarizes the Verity evidence operators.

Table 3.2—Verity Evidence Operators

Operator	Description
SOUNDEX	Expands the search to include words that sound like or have a similar letter pattern as your search term. This expansion is done using the Soundex algorithm. *Example*: `select * from dm_document search topic '<soundex> white'` Returns objects containing "wait", "weed", "wheat", or "wood". These words all have the same Soundex value, W300.
STEM	Expands the search to include words that have the same linguistic stem as the search term. *Example*: `select * from dm_document search topic '<stem> train'` Returns objects containing "train", "trains", "trained", or "training".
THESAURUS	Expands the search to include synonyms for the search term as defined in the Verity thesaurus. *Example*: `select * from dm_document search topic '<thesaurus> staff'` Returns objects also containing "stick", "cane", or "rod".

Operator	Description
TYPO/N	Expands the search to include words that have *N* letters different from the search term, thus emulating a typo. *Example*: `select * from dm_document search topic '<typo/1> cat` Returns objects containing "hat", "rat", "sat", or "cot".
WILDCARD	Allows the use of wildcard characters in the search term. *Example*: `select * from dm_document search topic '<wildcard> comp*'` Returns objects containing "compare", "compose", or "computer".
WORD	Performs an exact match (case insensitive) full-text word search. This is the basic full-text search operator and is analogous to the Documentum SEARCH DOCUMENT CONTAINS-style full-text search. *Example*: `select * from dm_document search topic '<word> Documentum'` Returns objects containing the word "Documentum".

3.2.3.3.2 Relational Operators

Relational operators allow you to search the values of fielded RDBMS data (i.e., object attributes) that have been included in the full-text index. Since Documentum 4.2, all string attributes of `dm_sysobjects` (and subtypes) are automatically included in the full-text index for all objects with content. Table 3.3 summarizes the Verity relational operators.

Table 3.3—Verity Relational Operators

Operator	Description
CONTAINS	Performs a search using the attribute and the indicated value. *Example*: `select * from dm_document search topic 'title <contains> Documentum'` Returns objects whose title attribute contain the word "Documentum".

Operator	Description
ENDS	Performs similarly to the CONTAINS operator but only matches on the ending of the value. *Example*: `select * from dm_document search topic 'authors <ends> son'` Returns objects whose author attribute contains values ending with "son", such as: "Gibson", "Morrison", and "Stevenson".
MATCHES	Performs an exact search using the attribute and the indicated value. *Example*: `select * from dm_document search topic 'title <matches> Documentum Content Server Administrators Guide'` Returns objects whose title attribute exactly match "Documentum Content Server Administrators Guide".
STARTS	Performs similarly to the ENDS operator but matches on the beginning of the values. *Example*: `select * from dm_document search topic 'title <starts> Documentum'` Returns objects whose title attribute start with "Documentum".
SUBSTRING	Performs a substring search using the attribute and the indicated value. *Example*: `select * from dm_document search topic 'title <substring> guide` Returns objects whose title attribute contain the string "guide".
=, >, >=, <, <=	These operators select objects whose attributes contain values that are equal to (=), greater than (>), greater than or equal to (>=), less than (<), less than or equal to (<=) the indicated values. *Example*: `select * from dm_document search topic 'r_creation_date >= 1/1/2002'` Returns objects whose r_creation_date values are greater than or equal to "1/1/2002". Note that these operators are not enclosed in angle brackets.

3.2.3.3.3 Concept Operators

Concept operators allow you to apply Boolean operators to search terms or other operators. The Verity concept operators are summarized in Table 3.4.

Table 3.4—Verity Concept Operators

Operator	Description
AND	Selects objects that contain all of the search terms. *Example*: `select * from dm_document search topic 'Documentum <and> Administrator'` Returns objects that contain the words "Documentum" and "Administrator".
ACCRUE	Functions similarly to the AND operation but ranks objects who have more occurrences of the search terms higher in the relevancy ranking. *Example*: `select * from dm_document search topic 'Documentum <accrue> Administrator'` Returns objects that contain the words "Documentum" and "Administrator" but ranks those that contain both words higher.
OR	Selects objects that contain at least one of the search terms. *Example*: `select * from dm_document search topic 'Docbase Server <or> Content Server'` Returns objects that contain either the word "Docbase Server", "Content Server", or both.

3.2.3.3.4 Proximity Operators

Verity's proximity operators allow you to write queries that describe how words relate to each other in a grammatical construct, for example, a paragraph. The Verity proximity operators are summarized in Table 3.5.

Table 3.5—Verity Proximity Operators

Operator	Description
IN	Searches document zones[*] for the search terms. *Example*: `select * from dm_document search topic 'Documentum <in> summary'` Returns objects that have the word "Documentum" in their summary zone.
WHEN	Allows you to put conditions on a zone search. *Example*: `select * from dm_document search topic 'Documentum <in> A <when> (href <contains> www.documentum.com)'` Returns objects that have the word "Documentum" in a zone named "A" which also contains the string "www.documentum.com" in an "href" attribute. For example: `<a href="http://www.documentum.com">Documentum</a>`.
NEAR/N	Selects objects that contain the search terms within N words of each other. *Example*: `select * from dm_document search topic 'Documentum <near/3> server'` Returns objects that contain the phrases: "Documentum Content Server", and "…Documentum. The server …"
PARAGRAPH	Selects objects that contain the search terms in the same paragraph. *Example*: `select * from dm_document search topic 'ship <paragraph> wreck'` Returns objects that have the words "ship" and "wreck" in the same paragraph.

---

[*] Document zones are defined in custom Verity style files, and added to Documentum using SETSTYLE_FTINDEX (an *apply()* method). For more information about custom style files, see *The Documentum Content Server Administrator's Guide*.

Operator	Description
PHRASE	Selects objects that contain the specified string. *Example*: `select * from dm_document search topic '<phrase> (Documentum Content Server Administrators Guide)'` Returns objects that contain the phrases: "Documentum Content Server Administrators Guide".
SENTENCE	Functions similarly to the PARAGRAPH operator but selects objects that contain the search terms in the same sentence. *Example*: `select * from dm_document search topic 'ship <sentence> wreck'` Returns objects with sentences that contain "ship" and "wreck".

3.2.3.3.5 Modifiers

Modifiers change how the operators work, or how the query results are returned. The Verity modifiers are summarized in Table 3.6.

Table 3.6—Verity Modifiers

Operator	Description
CASE	Forces a case *sensitive* search. By default, searches are performed in case *insensitive* mode. *Example*: `select * from dm_document search topic '<case> IT'` Returns only objects containing "IT" and not "it" or "It".

Operator	Description
MANY	This modifier considers the density of the search terms in the text when calculating the relevancy score. Typically, shorter documents have greater density and produce higher relevancy scores than long documents with the same number of occurrences of the search terms. *Example*: `select * from dm_document search topic '<many> documentum'` Ranks objects with a higher occurrence of "Documentum", higher in the relevancy score.
NOT	Eliminates words from consideration when performing a selection. *Example*: `select * from dm_document search topic 'computer <and> Mac <and><not> IBM'` Returns objects containing "Macintosh computer" but not "IBM computer".
ORDER	Stipulates the order in which search terms must occur in the text to constitute a match. *Example*: `select * from dm_document search topic '<order> <paragraph> (little, red, corvette)'` Returns only objects containing paragraphs with "little", "red", and "corvette" in that order.

3.2.3.3.6 Other Verity Features

The Verity search engine has a number of other features worth mentioning. Some of these are:

- **Thesaurus**—The Verity search engine utilizes a thesaurus file on the Documentum Server. This file allows users to search for word synonyms. The thesaurus is located in `%DM_HOME%\verity\common\English\vdk20.syd`.
- **Stop Word File**—Verity also utilizes a stop word file on the Documentum Server when it generates its indexes. (Stop words are words like "a" and "the" that are excluded from the index.) The stop word file is located in `%DM_HOME%\verity\common\English\dm_default.stp`.
- **Term Hit Highlighting**—If Verity finds a search word in a document that contains a PDF and PDFTEXT rendition, it will highlight the word in the document when you view the rendition.

- **Topics**—Verity can utilize topic trees when conducting searches to return a broader range of results. A topic tree is a hierarchical ontology of a subject area, for example, the zoological phyla of animals. Topics differ from synonyms in that topics are related and may have an implied hierarchical relationship (e.g., microprocessors to computers), whereas synonyms simply mean the same thing (e.g., sickness and illness). By default, no topic trees exist on the Documentum Server. You can create them using Verity's `mktopic` utility.

For details regarding these features, consult the Documentum and Verity documentation.

The Verity full-text search engine adds additional power and ease to searching in Documentum. Not only does it allow you to easily implement single-field searches for attributes, but with the VQL extensions to DQL, you can also search for text using very sophisticated and precise linguistic constructs.

3.2.3.4 Documentum Full-Text Search Keywords

Regardless of the flavor of full-text search you conduct (document search or TOPIC search), there is a set of special DQL keywords you can use to return additional information about your query results. These keywords are used as `SELECT` variables and can be processed as such after the query. Four of the most common keywords are described in Table 3.7. See the *Documentum Content Server DQL Reference Manual* for more details and an explanation of the other keywords.

Table 3.7—Full-Text Search Keywords

Keyword	Description

HITS	Returns an integer representing the total number of times the search word or phrase matched in the document.
	
	Example: `select object_name, r_object_id, HITS`
	`        from dm_document search document contains`
	`             'Virginia'`

SCORE	Returns a number representing the relevance ranking for each object. See Verity's documentation for a discussion of scoring. *Example*: `select object_name, r_object_id, SCORE` `        from dm_document search topic 'Virginia'`

SUMMARY	Returns a summary of each document matched by the query. The summary consists of four sentences selected by the Verity full-text search engine based upon its analysis of the document. Note that the summary may be truncated depending upon the total length of the sentences chosen, and the maximum length of string variables defined by the RDBMS.
	
	Example: `select object_name, r_object_id, SUMMARY`
	`        from dm_document search document contains`
	`             'Virginia'`

Keyword	Description
TEXT	Returns the actual words matched by a non-specific full-text search criteria such as STEM or SOUNDEX. *Example*: `select object_name, r_object_id, TEXT from dm_document search topic '<stem> train'`

3.3 How To Process Collections

This section deals with processing collection objects. A collection object, IDfCollection, contains the results of a query. It is often helpful to think of a collection as a table with rows and columns. The columns represent the SELECT variables requested in the DQL query, and the rows represent objects, which met the query criteria. Processing a collection refers to retrieving the data from a collection and doing something with it. This is one of the most basic and common tasks you will implement as a Documentum developer. It is a simple task, yet it does require care to avoid some pitfalls that can crash your application or affect its performance. The following sections discuss some best practices for processing collections.

3.3.1 Basic Collection Processing

The basic technique for processing a collection is simple, as the following code snippet illustrates.

Source Code A working example of this source code can be found in the "`Chapter3/Collection`" directory of the source code archive.

```
Dim q As IDfQuery
Dim col As IDfCollection

Set q = cx.getQuery

' do query
q.setDQL("select r_object_id, object_name, r_object_type from" _
    & " dm_document where owner_name = user")

Set col = q.execute(session, DF_READ_QUERY)

' process collection
While (col.Next = true)
```

```
    ' print each column for each row of collection . . .
    Debug.Print col.getString("r_object_id")
    Debug.Print col.getString("object_name")
    Debug.Print col.getString("r_object_type")
Wend
col.Close
```

An IDfCollection object is returned by the query and processed in a `While` loop. The process is propelled forward by the `IDfCollection.Next()` method that advances the collection pointer to the next row. Inside the loop, you use the `getXXX()` methods of the IDfCollection object to access individual values.

Always issue the `IDfCollection.Close()` method call as soon as you are finished processing the collection—even in an error state (See Chapter 5, *Proven Solutions for Common Tasks*). This seems like a simple thing—and it is—yet it is often overlooked. Documentum allows only ten (10) simultaneous, open collections per-session[*]. Ten seems like a lot, but depending upon what you are doing, you can quickly exceed the need for ten simultaneous, open collections. When this occurs, Documentum will refuse to open an eleventh and raise an exception in your application. See Section 3.3.2, *Tracing for Open Collections*, below for a technique to find open collections in your source code.

There are two pitfalls you should avoid when processing collections like this. The first is using the `IDfCollection.getTypedObject()` method. This method returns an entire row of the collection as an IDfTypedObject object. Unless you specifically need the functionality an IDfTypedObject object provides (e.g., persistence of the row after the collection has advanced), you are just wasting time and resources. Instead, access each individual column of the row using the `IDfCollection.getXXX()` methods.

The second pitfall to avoid is fetching an object from inside the collection-processing loop. This can be detrimental to your application's performance and should be avoided, if possible, even though it seems like a logical thing to do. Instead, change the query to return the attributes you need and access them using the `IDfCollection.getXXX()` methods.

These two pitfalls are illustrated below:

```
    Dim q As IDfQuery
    Dim col As IDfCollection
```

---

[*] Actually, this number is configurable in the `dmcl.ini` file. However, the default is 10. See Chapter 7, *Tips, Tools and Handy Information,* regarding the `dmcl.ini` file.

```
Dim tObj As IDfTypedObject
Dim pObj As IDfPersistentObject
Dim idObj As IDfId

Set q = cx.getQuery

' do query
q.setDQL("select * from dm_document where owner_name = user")

Set col = q.execute(session, DF_READ_QUERY)

' process collection
While (col.Next = true)

    ' !!! AVOID THIS UNLESS ABSOLUTELY NECESSARY!!!
    Set tObj = col.getTypedObject
    Debug.Print tObj.getString("r_object_id")

    ' get the object Id
    Set idObj = cx.getId(col.getString("r_object_id"))

    ' !!! AVOID THIS UNLESS ABSOLUTELY NECESSARY!!!
    Set pObj = session.GetObject(idObj)
    Debug.Print pObj.getObjectName

Wend
col.Close
```

The *IDfSession.GetObject()* method fetches the entire object from the server to your workstation and is thus very expensive. If your only reason for fetching the object is to retrieve its attributes, rewrite the query and the code inside the processing loop to specifically get the attributes you want using methods of the IDfCollection object. For example:

```
Dim q As IDfQuery
Dim col As IDfCollection
Dim idObj As IDfId

Set q = cx.getQuery

' do query
q.setDQL("select r_object_id,object_name from dm_document" _
    & " where owner_name = user")
```

```
    Set col = q.execute(session, DF_READ_QUERY)

    ' process collection
    While (col.Next = true)

        ' get attrs
        Debug.Print col.getString("r_object_id")
        Debug.Print col.getString("object_name")

    Wend
    col.Close
```

Getting individual attributes from the Docbase is much less expensive than fetching the entire object. However, sometimes it is unavoidable (and necessary) to fetch objects from within a collection-processing loop. For example, if you want to check them out for editing. In that case, a fetch is required. The rule of thumb is: if you are only retrieving attributes, use one of the *IDfCollection.getXXX()* methods. If you are manipulating the object, you need to fetch it.

3.3.2 Tracing For Open Collections

So, you have an application with several dozen queries. After testing it for a while you receive an error saying there are no more collections available. Somewhere you didn't close a collection after processing it. But where?

One way to find the offending collection is to turn on client-side tracing and make the application crash again. Chapter 5, *Proven Solutions for Common Tasks,* discusses turning on client-side tracing in detail. Set the trace level to 11 when trying to find open collections. Be aware that trace level 11 produces *a lot* of output.

After the application crashes, review the trace log. The DFC will enter a statement similar to the one below for each collection left open.

```
DFC DIAGNOSTIC - YOUR PROGRAM DID NOT CLOSE THIS DfCollection.
(QueryId=q0; DQL=select r_object_id, object_name, r_object_type from
dm_document where owner_name = user)
```

This statement gives you two clues to find the offending query:

- the query Id, which is equivalent to the collection Id, and
- the offending query string.

By knowing the query Id and the query string, you should be able to track down the offending query in your code and correct it.

3.3.3 Calculating The Size Of Collections

It is common practice to display the size of the result set (i.e., the number of rows returned, or "hits") to a user after executing a query. Unfortunately, the IDfCollection object does not contain an attribute or method to provide this information. Here are two techniques to calculate the size of the result set. The first is to simply increment a counter variable every time a row in the collection is processed. The advantage to this technique is that you only have to execute the query once. The drawback is that you don't know the size of the result set until *after* it has been processed. The following code snippet demonstrates this idea.

> **Source Code** A working example of this source code can be found in the "`Chapter3/Collection Size`" directory of the source code archive.

```
Dim q As IDfQuery
Dim col As IDfCollection
Dim count As Integer
Dim dql As String

' query
Set q = cx.getQuery
q.setDQL("select r_object_id, object_name, r_object_type from " _
    & "dm_document where owner_name = user")
Set col = q.execute(session, DF_READ_QUERY)

' process collection
While (col.Next = true)

    ' process the collection . . .

    ' increment the counter
    count = count + 1

Wend
col.Close
Debug.Print "Results = " & count
```

The second technique requires executing the query twice. To implement this approach, first strip the SELECT clause out of the DQL statement, replace it with COUNT(*), and execute the query. Obtain the value of COUNT(*) from the collection, and then run the original query. The advantage to this technique is that you know the size of the result set before you process it. The drawbacks are you have to execute the query twice, and the COUNT(*) command can be expensive resource-wise. The following code snippet demonstrates this technique.

Source Code A working example of this source code can be found in the "Chapter3/Collection Size" directory of the source code archive.

```
Dim q As IDfQuery
Dim col As IDfCollection
Dim count As Integer
Dim dql As String
Dim i As Integer
Dim countDQL As String

Set q = cx.getQuery
dql = "select r_object_id, object_name, r_object_type from " _
    & "dm_document where owner_name = user"

'find the end of the select statement
i = InStr(1, LCase(dql), "from", vbTextCompare)

' build the countDQL query string
countDQL = "select count(*) " & Right(dql, Len(dql)-i + 1)

' do query to get count
q.setDQL (countDQL)
Set col = q.execute(session, DF_READ_QUERY)

' this collection only has one row so there is no need for a loop
col.Next
    count = col.getInt("count(*)") ' get the count
col.Close
Debug.Print "Results = " & count

' do query to get results
q.setDQL (dql)
Set col = q.execute(session, DF_READ_QUERY)

' this collection will hold the actual results of the query so
' a loop IS necessary
While (col.Next = True)
```

```
    ' process the collection…

Wend
col.Close
```

Both of these techniques work well. Which one you use depends upon your application and your needs. I tend to favor the second approach, because knowing the size of the result set ahead of time gives you the ability to cancel the query if the result set is too large. You will see an example of this in the sample application in Chapter 8, *Putting It All Together In A Sample Application*.

3.3.4 Recursive Processing Of Collections

Occasionally, it is necessary to do recursive or nested collection processing. For example, when you need to traverse a folder structure or gather workflow statistics. Both of these processes require using the results of one query to drive a nested query. Processing the resulting collections can be very tricky and require great attention to collection management. This section presents a technique to recursively process collections without breaking the ten collections-per-session limit.

The following example illustrates one way to traverse a folder structure to determine the size of its contents. There are other, more efficient ways to accomplish this task (e.g., clever DQL as you will find in Section 3.4.8, *Content, Cabinet and Folder Queries*); however, traversing a folder structure is an easy-to-understand example of recursion. The function begins by taking the `r_object_id` of the specified folder and getting the object Id, content size, and object type for all the `dm_sysobject` objects it contains. It then simply iterates over the collection summing the content size and recursively calling itself when it encounters a `dm_folder` object. On the surface, this seems like a simple recursion example. In reality, it's a good example of how *not* to do recursion with collection objects.

```
Function doRecursiveQuery(ByVal fold_id As String) As Long
    Dim q As IDfQuery
    Dim col As IDfCollection
    Dim totalSize As Long

    Set q = cx.getQuery
    q.setDQL ("select r_object_id,r_content_size, " _
        & "r_object_type from dm_sysobject where " _
        & "folder(id('" & fold_id & "'))")
    Set col = q.execute(session, DF_READ_QUERY)

    While (col.Next = True)
```

```
        If (col.getString("r_object_type") = "dm_folder") Then

            ' !!! THIS RECURSIVE CALL SHOULD BE AVOIDED!!!
            totalSize = totalSize +
                    doRecursiveQuery(
                        col.getString("r_object_id"))
        Else
            totalSize = totalSize +
                    col.getInt("r_content_size")
        End If
    Wend
    col.Close

    doRecursiveQuery = totalSize

End Function
```

The problem with this example is that the recursive call is made from inside the loop processing the collection. When the recursive call is made, the current collection is left open and a new one is created by the recursive call. The current collection won't be closed until the recursive call returns. In all likelihood, the recursive call will make a recursive call, and so on…. Eventually you will run out of collection objects.

The following code snippet illustrates a technique to avoid running out of collection objects when doing this type of recursion. Instead of processing the collection as it iterates over it, this code saves the information in each collection row to a Visual Basic array as a delimited string. It then closes the collection, and processes the array. The recursive call is made from within the array-processing loop, so there is only ever one collection open at a time.

Source Code A working example of this source code can be found in the "`Chapter3/Recursive Collection`" directory of the source code archive.

```
Function doRecursiveQuery(ByVal fold_id As String)
    Dim q As IDfQuery
    Dim col As IDfCollection
    Dim totalSize As Long
    Dim arrObj() As String
    Dim row As Variant
    Dim emptyDir As Boolean
    Dim colRow() As String
```

```
q.setDQL ("select r_object_id,r_content_size, " _
    & "r_object_type from dm_sysobject where " _
    & "folder(id('" & fold_id & "'))")
Set col = q.execute(session, DF_READ_QUERY)

While (col.Next = True)

    ' if array uninitailized, init to 1
    If (emptyDir = True) Then
        ReDim arrObj(1)
        emptyDir = False
    ' extend array by one
    Else
        ReDim Preserve arrObj(UBound(arrObj) + 1)
    End If

    ' save collection to array as delimited string
    ' for example:   0000000000000000::1234::dm_document

    arrObj(UBound(arrObj)) = col.getString("r_object_id") _
        & "::" _
        & col.getString("r_content_size") _
        & "::" _
        & col.getString("r_object_type")

Wend
col.Close

' process array of delimited strings
If (Not emptyDir) Then
    For Each row In arrObj
        If (row = "") Then
            ' noop
        Else
            ' split on delimter
            colRow = Split(row, "::")

            ' if it's not a folder, add the objects size
            If (colRow(2) <> "dm_folder") Then
                totalSize = totalSize + colRow(1)
            Else
                ' if it is a folder, recurse into it
```

```
                        totalSize = totalSize + _
                                    doRecursiveQuery(colRow(0))
                End If
            End If
        Next row
    End If
    doRecursiveQuery = totalSize

End Function
```

This code snippet illustrates a very simple implementation of recursive processing. You can easily imagine examples that are more complicated. The drawbacks to this technique are it's slow, and resource expensive. Both of these faults are primarily due to how Visual Basic handles dynamic arrays, of which this examples utilizes two (`arrObj` and `colRow`). If you really need to calculate the size of a folder's content, use one of the DQL queries discussed later in this chapter instead of a recursive, Visual Basic function.

3.3.5   Processing Collections With Unknown Content

You will discover that in the quest to write generic and multi-use application code, you will often need to process collections that have unknown content. These collections may contain the results of a user-generated query, or contain the results of any of numerous application-generated queries that are centrally processed. For example, you might have a custom search screen that allows the user to input DQL to be executed. You have no idea what attributes or objects they might search on, so how can you process the results? In these cases, you don't know the attribute names or types contained in the collection and; therefore, you cannot process it by simply issuing `IDfCollection.getXXX()` method calls. The solution is to interrogate the IDfCollection object regarding its contents *before* you process it. The following code snippet demonstrates how to process the contents of any collection.

The first step is to get a row from the IDfCollection object before you issue the `IDfCollection.Next()` method call to advance the collection pointer. This allows you to work with the collection object itself before you process its rows. Once you have the collection, get the number and names of the attributes to process.

> **Source Code** A working example of this source code can be found in the "`Chapter3/Unknown Collection`" directory of the source code archive.

```
Dim attr As IDfAttr
Dim q As IDfQuery
Dim col As IDfCollection
Dim numCols As Integer
Dim colName As String
Dim colValue As String
Dim i As Integer

Set q = cx.getQuery
q.setDQL ("select * from dm_document where owner_name = user")
Set col = q.execute(session, DF_READ_QUERY)

' get number of attrs in collection
numCols = col.getAttrCount

' get column names from attrs in collection
For i = 1 To numCols
    colName = col.GetAttr(i - 1).getName

    ' process colName
    Debug.Print "col " & i & " = " & colName
Next i
```

The next step is to iterate over the collection. You do this as you would any collection, with one catch. The catch is that you must specifically process the value in each column by assigning it to an IDfAttr object and testing the IDfAttr object's content type to determine how to retrieve its value.

```
' iterate over collection and process each row
While (col.Next = True)

    ' process each column in a row
    For i = 1 To numCols
        Set attr = col.GetAttr(i - 1)

        ' get value in column
        Select Case attr.getDataType
            Case DF_BOOLEAN
```

```
                colValue = col.getBoolean(attr.getName)
            Case DF_DOUBLE
                colValue = col.getDouble(attr.getName)
            Case DF_ID
                colValue = col.getId(attr.getName).toString
            Case DF_INTEGER
                colValue = col.getInt(attr.getName)
            Case DF_STRING
                colValue = col.getString(attr.getName)
            Case DF_TIME
                colValue = col.getTime(attr.getName).toString
        End Select

        ' process colValue
        Debug.Print "col " & i & " val = " & colValue
    Next i
Wend
col.Close
```

This is the recommended technique for processing collections with unknown content. The important thing to remember is you can interrogate the IDfCollection object for information about itself and use that information to process its contents accordingly.

3.4 Useful Queries

This section presents an assortment of useful queries I have developed or collected over the years. I have not put a lot of effort into explaining each query other than providing a brief description of what each one does and why you would use it. In that regard, this section is much more how-oriented than why-oriented. The queries are grouped in the following broad categories:

- Full-Text Queries
- Full-Text Index Queries
- Registered Table Queries
- Virtual Document Queries
- Workflow Queries
- Object Queries
- Content, Cabinet and Folder Queries

All of the queries are written in DQL, as opposed to Visual Basic.

3.4.1 Full-Text Queries

This collection of queries provides several examples of full-text queries. Some queries are written as both `SEARCH DOCUMENT CONTAINS` queries and `SEARCH TOPIC` queries to illustrate the nuance of each syntax. Several of these queries use special DQL full-text search keywords to demonstrate their use also. These queries assume an object containing the text of the U. S. Constitution is in the Docbase.

3.4.1.1 Basic Single-Word Search

These queries illustrate a basic, single-word search of the full-text index. Notice the use of `HITS`, `SCORE`, and `SUMMARY` keywords to return specific information about each object and not just it's object Id and name. I have also included a `WHERE` clause for further illustration. These queries return the objects with the highest score first.

```
select object_name, r_object_id, hits, score, summary from
    dm_document search document contains 'constitution' where
    any author = 'Madison' order by score desc;
```

Or, using the `TOPIC SEARCH` form:

```
select object_name, r_object_id, hits, score, summary from
    dm_document search topic 'constitution' where any author =
    'Madison' order by score desc;
```

Another option when doing a single-word search is to use the Verity evidence operator `<word>`.

```
select object_name, r_object_id, hits, score, summary from
    dm_document search topic '<word> constitution' where any
    author = 'Madison' order by score desc;
```

This query will return similar results as the previous two queries; however, you will notice the `<word>` operator affects the score and ranking of the results.

3.4.1.2 Basic Multi-Word Search

This set of queries illustrates searching for multiple words in a document with no qualification on their relationship (i.e., They can be next to each other, in different paragraphs, or one in the text of the object and one in the metadata.).

```
select object_name, r_object_id, hits, score, summary from
    dm_document search document contains 'constitution' and
    'people' order by score desc;
```

Or, using the SEARCH TOPIC form:

```
select object_name, r_object_id, hits, score, summary from
    dm_document search topic 'constitution <and> people' order
    by score desc;
```

3.4.1.3 Search For A Phrase

Search for the phrase "more perfect union."

```
select * from dm_document search topic '<phrase> (more perfect
    union)';
```

Beware of using stop words when searching for phrases. Searching for "a more perfect union" will not produce any results because the word "a" is not in the index. Also, note the parentheses are necessary to denote the phrase.

3.4.1.4 Search For Words Near Each Other

This query demonstrates how to search for words that are near each other, in this case, within four words of each other.

```
select * from dm_document search topic 'people <near/4>
    state';
```

3.4.1.5 Search For Words In The Same Paragraph

This query finds objects whose content contains the words "people" and "state" in the same paragraph.

```
select * from dm_document search topic 'people <paragraph>
    state';
```

3.4.1.6 Find A Particular Object In The Full-Text Index

This query will return all of the attributes for the object with `r_object_id` of `0900218d80034d35`.

```
select * from dm_sysobject search topic '0900218d80034d35';
```

3.4.1.7 Find An Attribute Value

This query finds objects that have a particular attribute value. In this case, the `object_name` contains the word "Constitution".

```
select * from dm_sysobject search topic 'object_name
    <contains> constitution';
```

3.4.2 Full-Text Index Queries

This collection of queries concerns the full-text index itself. These are not full-text queries, rather queries about the full-text index.

3.4.2.1 Find All Objects In The Full-Text Index

This query finds all the objects in the Docbase that have been full-text indexed.

```
select * from dm_sysobject search topic '';
```

3.4.2.2 Counting The Number Of Objects In The Full-Text Index

This query counts the number of objects in the Docbase that have been full-text indexed.

```
select count(*) from dm_sysobject (all) search topic '';
```

3.4.2.3 Determine If An Object Type Can Be Full-Text Indexed

This query returns a list of format types that can be full-text indexed.

```
select * from dm_format where can_index = true;
```

3.4.2.4 Mark An Object For Full-Text Indexing

This query marks the object with `r_object_id` of `0900218d80034d35` for full-text indexing by setting it's `a_full_text` attribute to `true`. The `dm_FulltextMgr` job will put this object in the index the next time it runs.

```
update dm_sysobject object
    set a_full_text = true
    where r_object_id = '0900218d80034d35';
```

3.4.2.5 Find Objects That Passed Indexing

This query returns the objects that were successfully full-text indexed.

```
select * from dm_sysobject where a_full_text = 1 and
    r_object_id in
        (select parent_id from dmr_content where any
            update_count = 0 and any index_set_times <=
            date(now));
```

3.4.2.6 Find Objects That Failed Indexing

This query returns all the objects that failed full-text indexing.

```
select * from dm_sysobject where a_full_text = 1 and r_object_id in
    (select parent_id from dmr_content where any
        update_count < 0 and any index_set_times <=
        date(now));
```

3.4.2.7 Find Objects Pending Indexing

This query returns all the objects in the Docbase that are awaiting full-text indexing.

```
select * from dm_sysobject where a_full_text = 1 and r_object_id in
    (select parent_id from dmr_content where any
        index_operations != 2 and any index_set_times >=
        date(now));
```

3.4.3 Registered Table Queries

This section discusses registered table queries. Registered tables are RDBMS tables that you add to the database to work in conjunction with Documentum. Registered tables serve many purposes from holding lookup values, to gluing together disparate applications. Registering RDBMS tables in Documentum allows you to query and/or update these tables using DQL. The following queries all assume the underlying RDBMS is Oracle®. These queries may need to be altered slightly for Microsoft SQL Server™ or other RDBMS.

3.4.3.1 Register A Table

To register a table, you must know the table's schema (structure) and be logged into Documentum as the Docbase Owner (dm_dbo). For example, assume you have created an RDBMS table named USSTATES that contains the names and postal abbreviations of the 50 United States, in two columns:

- `state_name varchar2(25)`
- `state_abbr varchar2(2)`

To register the USSTATES table in Documentum, use the following DQL statement.

```
register table usstates (state_name string(25), state_abbr
    string(2));
```

The result of this query is the `r_object_id` of a newly created `dm_registered` object. This object contains the table's column descriptions in its attributes. You can query this newly created registered table like this:

```
select * from dm_dbo.usstates;
```

Note you must preface the table name with `dm_dbo` since the table lives in the Docbase Owner's table space.

An interesting shortcut exists for the `register table` command: you don't have to explicitly describe the table's schema to register the table. You can (and Documentum does!) get away with just listing a dummy column description and still have access to the entire table structure. Therefore, to simplify registering tables, you can use syntax like this:

```
register table usstates (dummy string(10));
```

and still be able to perform queries like this:

```
select state_name, state_abbr from dm_dbo.usstates;
```

3.4.3.2 Unregister A Table

Unregistering a table makes it inaccessible from Documentum. It does not drop the table from the RDBMS. It only destroys the `dm_registered` object that points to it. The syntax is very simple:

```
unregister table usstates;
```

You can re-register the table without affecting the actual RDBMS table itself.

3.4.3.3 Registered Table Permissions

By default, registered tables are given the following access controls:

```
world_permit  = 3*
group_permit  = 5
owner_permit  = 7
```

These permissions govern what can be done to the `dm_registered` object. You must have at least Browse (2) permission to query a registered table.

The underlying RDBMS table receives these access controls:

```
world_table_permit  = 1
group_table_permit  = 1
owner_table_permit  = 1
```

These permissions govern what can be done to the RDBMS table. Other than the Browse permission required to see the `dm_registered` object, these permission sets have nothing to do with one another. To give users the ability to update, insert, or delete from the RDBMS table, you must change the values of the table permits listed above. The following DQL illustrates updating the RDBMS permissions for the USSTATES registered table to allow the world and group to insert rows, and the owner full control.

```
update dm_registered objects
    set world_table_permit = 4,
    set group_table_permit = 4,
    set owner_table_permit = 15
    where object_name = 'usstates';
```

3.4.3.4 Insert Into A Registered Table

Inserting rows into a registered table is no different from inserting rows into any RDBMS table, with the exception that the registered table name should be prefaced with the Docbase Owner's alias, `dm_dbo`. For example:

```
insert into dm_dbo.usstates (state_name,state_abbr) values
    ('Texas','TX')
```

Make sure your table permits allow you to make insertions (see Section 3.4.3.3, *Registered Table Permissions*).

---

* See Chapter 7, *Tips, Tools and Handy Information*, for a list of object permissions.

3.4.4 Virtual Document Queries

These queries deal with virtual documents. Virtual documents are a Documentum construct that allows multiple files to be bound and managed as a single entity. For example, each chapter of a book can be an individual file, and a book virtual document will allow you to manage them all as a single entity—a book. Virtual documents are best dealt with through the DFC or the API, but sometimes you need to access them from DQL too. So, here are a few useful queries

3.4.4.1 Find Virtual Documents

This query finds all the virtual documents in the Docbase.

```
select * from dm_sysobject where r_is_virtual_doc = true;
```

3.4.4.2 Find The Number Of Components In A Virtual Document

For a virtual document with an object Id of `0900218d8000ad97`, this query will return its number of components (child documents, or nodes).

```
select r_link_cnt from dm_sysobject where r_object_id =
    '0900218d8000ad97';
```

Remember, this count includes the object itself, so the actual number of children is really one less than the value returned.

3.4.4.3 Find Components Of A Virtual Document

For a virtual document with object Id of `0900218d8000ad97`, this query will return its children and descendants.

```
select * from dm_sysobject in document id('0900218d8000ad97')
    descend;
```

3.4.4.4 Find An Object's Virtual Document Parent

For a document with an `i_chronicle_id` of `0900218d8008d71`, this query will return the document's virtual document parent.

```
select parent_id from dmr_containment where component_id =
    '0900218d80008d71';
```

3.4.5 Workflow Queries

To put these queries into context, let me begin with a brief overview of workflow objects and their relationships. Workflows are created using the Workflow Editor, a graphical tool included with the Documentum Application Builder. The product of the Workflow Editor is a workflow template represented by a `dm_process` object. Each activity definition in the template is represented by a `dm_activity` object. One workflow template will contain many activity objects.

When a workflow template is instantiated (when a user starts a workflow), it is instantiated as a `dm_workflow` object. As each of the activities in the workflow are activated, the `dm_activity` objects that represent them create two other objects: `dmi_workitems` and `dmi_package`. The `dmi_workitem` object represents the task that each performer must complete, and the `dmi_package` contains the content on which the activities are to occur. By querying this hierarchy of objects, we can elicit information and statistics about nearly every aspect of a workflow.

The following queries were designed to work together to provide an in-depth look at workflows. Each of these queries uses the results from queries that precede it as input. The queries use the DQL keyword `as` to identify values that are needed in the succeeding queries. Those values are then referenced as `<value name>` in the queries. Each occurrence of this convention is in bold typeface to help you readily identify it.

3.4.5.1 Get Workflow For Specific Object

This query finds the workflow in which the object with object Id of `0900218d8008d71` is a participant.

```
select distinct r_workflow_id from dmi_package where any
    r_component_id = '0900218d8008d71';
```

`r_workflow_id` is the `r_object_id` of the workflow object.

3.4.5.2 Get All Active Workflows

This query will return all of the workflow objects that are dormant, running, or finished.

```
select distinct r_object_id as wfid from dm_workflow where
    r_runtime_state < 3;
```

Returns: `wfid`, the `r_object_id` of the workflow object

3.4.5.3 Get Workflow Information

This query uses the `wfid` value from the previous query to retrieve statistical data about the workflow.

```
select r_start_date, r_runtime_state, w.r_object_id,
    p.object_name, supervisor_name, w.object_name from
    dm_workflow w, dm_process p where w.r_object_id = '<wfid>'
    and w.process_id = p.r_object_id order by r_start_date;
```

3.4.5.4 Get Activities Information

This query uses the `wfid` value from a previous query to retrieve information about the workflow's activities.

```
select distinct r_object_id, r_act_def_id, a.object_name,
    message, due_date, priority, task_name, r_act_seqno as
    seqno, r_workflow_id from dmi_workitem w, dmi_queue_item
    q, dm_activity a where w.r_workflow_id = '<wfid>' and
    w.r_act_def_id = a.r_object_id and w.r_queue_item_id =
    q.r_object_id;
```

Returns: `seqno`, the `r_act_seqno` for each of the workflow's activities.

3.4.5.5 Get Packages Information

This query gets all of the packages referenced by a particular activity. It uses the `seqno` of the activity, and `wfid` of the workflow from previous queries.

```
select r_object_id as pkgid, r_package_name, r_package_label
    from dmi_package where r_act_seqno = <seqno> and
    r_workflow_id = '<wfid>';
```

Returns: `pkgid`, the `r_object_id` of each package.

3.4.5.6 Get Components

This query uses `pkgid` from the previous query to select the package's components. These components are the actual content objects, which the workflow passes among its participants for processing.

```
select r_component_id as compid, r_note_id, r_note_flag,
    r_note_writer from dmi_package where r_object_id =
    '<pkgid>';
```

Returns: `compid`, the `r_object_id` of each component.

3.4.5.7 Get Components Information

This query retrieves basic information from the `dm_sysobject` that is the component of the package. It uses the `compid` from the previous query.

```
select r_object_id, object_name, owner_name, r_version_label
    from dm_sysobject where r_object_id = '<compid>';
```

3.4.5.8 Get Activity Performers

This query returns information about an activity's performers. It uses the `wfid` of the workflow and the `seqno` of the activity from previous queries.

```
select i.r_object_id, name, due_date, priority, task_state,
    r_workflow_id, exec_type from dmi_workitem i,
    dmi_queue_item q, dm_activity a where i.r_workflow_id =
    '<wfid>' and i.r_act_seqno = <seqno> and a.exec_type = 0
    and i.r_act_def_id = a.r_object_id and i.r_queue_item_id =
    q.r_object_id);
```

3.4.5.9 Determine Who Has An Object

Occasionally, you need to know in whose Inbox an object's workflow task resides. You may find this important if you are debugging a workflow, or generating a report on workflow activity. For an object Id of 0900218d8008d71, this query will return the names of the users that have an Inbox item associated with this object.

```
select distinct name from dmi_queue_item where router_id in
    (select r_object_id from dm_workflow where r_object_id in
        (select r_workflow_id from dmi_package where any
            r_component_id = '0900218d8008d71')
    ) and delete_flag = false;
```

3.4.5.10 Get The Id Of An Object In A Workflow Package

The last workflow-related query I will share with you is particularly useful when it is used in an automated workflow activity. Automated workflow activity methods have workflow-related arguments passed to them by the workflow engine. Two of these arguments are the workflow Id (named `router_id`) and the current activity's sequence number (named `task_number`). Using these two arguments you can determine the object Id of the objects in the package.

```
select r_component_id from dmi_package where r_workflow_id =
    '<router_id>' and r_act_seqno = '<task_number>';
```

Once you have obtained the Ids of the objects in the package, you can manipulate the objects as part of the automated workflow activity's processing.

3.4.6 Inbox Queries

Closely related to the operation of workflows is the Inbox. The queries in this section perform some common tasks on the Inbox.

3.4.6.1 Check For Inbox Notifications

This query determines if there are any new, unread notifications in your Inbox.

```
select count(*) from dmi_queue_item where name = user and
    delete_flag = false;
```

Note this query uses the DQL `user` keyword to indicate the user running the query.

3.4.6.2 Get Inbox Notifications

This query retrieves any new or unread notifications in your inbox.

```
select task_name, sent_by, message, date_sent, due_date,
    priority from dmi_queue_item where name = user and
    delete_flag = false;
```

3.4.6.3 Delete Inbox Notifications

Occasionally, you need to delete a bunch of Inbox notifications en masse. For example, suppose a job failed overnight and sent dmadmin a notification every minute. There could be thousands of notifications in dmadmin's Inbox before you know it. Deleting these notifications using the Documentum Desktop UI is cumbersome; it would be easier just to delete them with a query. This query deletes notifications in your Inbox that are associated with a particular event.

```
update dmi_queue_item objects
    set delete_flag = true
    where event = '<event name>' and name = user;
```

where <event name> is the name of a particular event, for example, Job_Failure. This query doesn't really delete the notifications, it just flags them for deletion. The dm_QueueMgt job actually deletes them.

3.4.7 Object Queries

This section contains a miscellaneous collection of queries that deal with objects in the Docbase.

3.4.7.1 Find All Objects With The Same Root Object

By default, the Documentum Server only returns the *current* version of objects. The DQL keyword (all) forces the server to return all versions of objects. This query assumes you have an object with an r_object_id of 0900218d800492a2.

```
select * from dm_sysobject (all) where i_chronicle_id in
    (select i_chronicle_id from dm_sysobject where
    r_object_id = '0900218d800492a2');
```

Without the use of (all) in the above query, your result set would only contain one object: 0900218d800492a2.

3.4.7.2 Find Your Locked Objects

This query returns all objects in the Docbase locked by you.

```
select * from dm_sysobject where r_lock_owner = user;
```

You can change the value tested in the predicate to any valid Docbase user's login Id (user_os_name) and return the objects locked by them also.

3.4.7.3 Unlock A Locked Object

This query assumes an object with an object Id of 0900218d8000ad97 is checked out. It releases the lock on the object, which effectively cancels the checkout.

```
update dm_sysobject object
    set r_lock_owner = '',
    set r_lock_machine = '',
    set r_lock_date = date('nulldate')
    where r_object_id = '0900218d8000ad97';
```

You must have Superuser privileges in the Docbase to perform this query.

3.4.7.4 Unlock All Locked Objects

This query will unlock all the objects in the Docbase that are currently locked (checked out). Be careful, this query could cause you a lot of trouble.

```
update dm_sysobject object
    set r_lock_owner = '',
    set r_lock_machine = '',
    set r_lock_date = date('nulldate')
    where r_object_id in
    (select r_object_id from dm_sysobject where
        r_lock_owner is not nullstring);
```

You must have Superuser privileges in the Docbase to perform this query.

3.4.8 Content, Cabinet, and Folder Queries

The queries in this section deal with object content, cabinets, and folders.

3.4.8.1 Determine The Content Size Of A Cabinet (Method I)

This query summarizes the size of all of the content in the /Temp cabinet and its sub-folders. You can replace /Temp with any cabinet you like.

```
select sum(r_content_size) from dm_document (all) where
    cabinet('/Temp',descend);
```

Using the *folder()* predicate function instead of *cabinet()* will also work. For example:

```
select sum(r_content_size) from dm_document (all) where folder
    ('/System/Applications',descend);
```

3.4.8.2 Determine The Content Size Of A Cabinet (Method II)

This query is a variation on the previous one. Given a cabinet, /System in this example, it summarizes and displays the size of the content in each individual sub-folder.

```
select f.object_name, sum(d.r_content_size) from dm_folder
    (all) f, dm_document (all) d where any d.i_folder_id =
    f.r_object_id and cabinet('/System', descend) group by
    f.object_name;
```

This query is much more impressive if you see the output. Take a look.

```
object_name                           sum(d.r_content_size)
-------------                         ---------------------
Actions                                               18421
Applications                                              0
DataDictionary                                            0
DcDesktopClient                                       22106
Default XML Application                                4590
Desktop Client                                       182865
Distributed References                                    0
FileSystem                                                0
Jobs                                                      0
Methods                                              152999
Procedures                                             4821
Reports                                              805154
Startup Items                                        159470
Views                                                  3238
Workspace Customizations                                  0
```

Again, using the *folder()* predicate function instead of *cabinet()* will also work. For example:

```
select f.object_name, sum(d.r_content_size) from dm_folder
    (all) f, dm_document (all) d where any d.i_folder_id =
    f.r_object_id and folder('/System/Applications',descend)
    group by f.object_name;
```

Be aware, this query can take a *long* time to run.

3.4.8.3 Find Deleted Content

When you delete an object in Documentum, the content is not deleted immediately. Instead, a delete simply disconnects the record in the RDBMS from the content on the file system. The dm_DMClean and dm_DMFileScan jobs then search for these disconnected fragments and permanently delete them.

This query finds all of the content objects that have been disconnected from their dm_sysobject objects, but have not yet been deleted by the dm_DMClean job.

```
select * from dmr_content where any parent_id is NULL and
    content_size > 0 order by set_time;
```

It is possible to recover this content by retrieving its file system path using the `apply()` API method with the `GET_PATH` function, and assigning it to a new `dm_sysobject`.

3.4.8.4 Find Folder Paths From An Object Id

Given an object Id of `0900218d80034d35`, this query will return the object's folder paths in the Docbase. This concept is addressed again in Chapter 5, *Proven Solutions for Common Tasks*.

```
select r_folder_path from dm_folder where r_object_id in
    (select i_folder_id from dm_sysobject where r_object_id =
    '0900218d80034d35');
```

3.4.9 Setting Up Indexes

If you know your application will make numerous queries on a particular attribute, or set of attributes, it may be advantages to set up indexes on these attributes. Indexes are RDBMS constructs that improve query performance on particular table columns (i.e., attributes) by setting up special search and retrieval mechanisms on them. Once these indexes are set up, they are automatically updated with each change to the table, and are automatically used by Documentum when querying.

To create indexes, use the EXECUTE DQL command with the `MAKE_INDEX` function, or the `apply()` API method. The basic format for the DQL statement is:

```
execute make_index with type_name='<object name>',
    attribute='<attribute name>', attribute='<attribute
    name>'...
```

For example:

```
execute make_index with type_name='regional_doc',
    attribute='region', attribute='usstate';
```

This query creates an index for `reginal_doc` object type on the `region` attribute and the `usstate` attribute.

3.5 Chapter Summary

This chapter discussed three ways to create and execute queries: `IDcRunQuery.RunQuery()`, the Query Manager (IDfQueryMgr), and the IDfQuery class. Each of these techniques has its role and purpose. Generally, the IDfQuery class gives you the greatest flexibility, but also requires the most programming. Conversely, `RunQuery()` requires little programming, but you have no control over the processing or display of the results. The Query Manager falls somewhere in between. It provides an easy way to construct queries from UIs, while still allowing you to manipulate the results. It is also the preferred method for searching multiple Docbases simultaneously.

Hand-in-hand with generating queries, this chapter discussed handling and processing their results, IDfCollection objects. Several techniques for processing collections were discussed to include: calculating its size, recursive processing, and processing collections of unknown content.

This chapter also discussed three types of queries: SQL pass-through queries, cached queries, and full-text queries. SQL pass-through queries target RDBMS tables, are rare, and require the use of the EXECUTE DQL command. Cached queries can be very beneficial if used in the right circumstance and having been properly configured. Full-text searches were examined in-depth to expose their power. For searching document content and attributes not involved in complex joins, you should use a full-text search for speed and accuracy.

Finally, this chapter presented a collection of useful queries regarding full-text indexes, registered tables, virtual documents, workflows, and other Docbase objects.

Implementing Core Document Management Functions

This chapter discusses implementing core document management functions. These functions are often called *library services* because they control the movement of objects into and out of the Docbase. The core document management functions[*] I will discuss are:

- Create
- Delete
- Copy
- Checkout
- View
- Cancel checkout
- Checkin

These seven actions represent the basic functions of any document management system and its clients. That being true, you can expect to encounter the need to implement them frequently. In this chapter, I will demonstrate how to implement each of these functions in two different ways: first, with custom code using only the DFC, queries, and custom logic. These implementations will explore the logic behind these

---

[*] Technically, Import and Export are also considered library services, but they are not discussed here.

functions. Second, the same operations will be implemented using Documentum's IDfOperation classes. IDfOperation classes encapsulate all of the process logic for these functions and allow you to implement them with little programming. The IDfOperation classes provide a simple and consistent implementation of these core functions, and are your best choice for implementation.

4.1 Implementing Library Functions With The DFC

This section demonstrates implementing the core document management functions using only basic DFC classes and queries. Several of the core functions in this section have interesting and important variations that are explored. For example, objects can be created with or without content, or from a template. Deleting objects can be done individually, as a group, or as a hierarchical folder structure.

4.1.1 Creating Objects

Creating new objects in the Docbase is a simple task, as the following example illustrates. However, as you expect your code to do more than just create an object, this process becomes more involved. This example creates an object with the name, "regional doc 1," and saves it to the user's default (Home) cabinet. This is the minimum implementation for object creation.

```
Dim sobj As IDfSysObject

Set sobj = session.newObject("dm_document")
sobj.setObjectName ("regional doc 1")
sobj.save
```

4.1.1.1 Creating Objects With Content And Location

What if you want your new object to contain content and reside in a specific folder? A slight augmentation to the code can accomplish this. The following code snippet adds content to a newly created object by using the *IDfSysObject.setFile()* method. Before you can save an object with content, you must specify the format of the content using *IDfSysObject.setContentType()*[*]. After the content and the format are set, the object is placed in the /Temp cabinet by using the *IDfSysObject.link()* method. When the object is saved, the file is automatically transferred from your workstation, to the Content Server.

---

[*] Valid values for content type can be found in Chapter 7, *Tips, Tools and Handy Information*.

> **Source Code** A working example of this source code can be found in the "`Chapter4/From Scratch/Create`" directory of the source code archive.

```
Dim sobj As IDfSysObject

Set sobj = session.newObject("dm_document")
sobj.setContentType ("crtext")
sobj.setFile ("c:\reports\regions\ne\q1.txt")
sobj.setObjectName ("regional doc 1")
sobj.link ("/Temp")
sobj.save
```

4.1.1.2 Creating Object Content From A Variable

What if you want to use the content of a Visual Basic variable and not a file on the file system as the content for an object? This might be the case if you are dynamically creating content, for example, as the result of a DQL query or XML operation. To set the content of an object from a variable, you need to convert the variable to a ByteArrayOutputStream, and use the *IDfSysObject.setContent()* method. Of course, ByteArrayOutputStream variable types don't exist in Visual Basic. Fortunately, the IDfClientX class will manufacture one for you using the *StringToByteArrayOutputStream()* method if you give it a String.

The following code snippet illustrates using the *setContent()* and *StringToByteArrayOutputStream()* methods to set an object's content from a variable. In this example, the Preamble to the U. S. Constitution is stored in a string variable and used as the content for a new dm_document object.

> **Source Code** A working example of this source code can be found in the "`Chapter4/From Scratch/SetContent`" directory of the source code archive.

```
Dim sobj As IDfSysObject
Dim content As String

content = "We the People of the United States, in Order to " _
    & "form a more perfect Union, establish Justice, insure " _
    & "domestic Tranquility, provide for the common defence, " _
    & "promote the general Welfare, and secure the Blessings " _
    & "of Liberty to ourselves and our Posterity, do ordain " _
    & "and establish this Constitution for the United States " _
    & "of America."
```

```
Set sobj = session.newObject("dm_document")
sobj.setContentType ("crtext")

' convert string to BAOS
sobj.setContent cx.StringToByteArrayOutputStream(content)

sobj.setObjectName ("Preamble")
sobj.link ("/Temp")
sobj.save
```

4.1.1.3 Creating An Object From A Template

This last snippet of code dealing with object creation demonstrates how to create a new object from a template in the Docbase. This is something you might do if you have a standard format for documents of a specific type (e.g., an inter-office memo). Documentum allows you to store a blank document as a template and then create new documents from it. As you will see, this is the most complicated way to create a new object in the Docbase.

To begin, this code retrieves the template. To simplify this example, I hard coded the template's object Id. In a real application, you could use *IDfSession.getObjectByQualification()* to retrieve the template. Once I have the template, I save it as a new object using the *IDfSysObject.saveAsNew()* method. The *IDfSysObject.saveAsNew()* method saves the object as a new instance in the Docbase, and generates a new object Id.

Source Code A working example of this source code can be found in the "`Chapter4/From Scratch/Template`" directory of the source code archive.

```
Dim templateSObj As IDfSysObject
Dim copySObj As IDfSysObject
Dim foldObj As IDfFolder
Dim id As IDfId

' get MS Word 8 template
Set templateSObj =
    session.GetObject(cx.getId("0900218d80079051"))

' make a copy
Set id = templateSObj.saveAsNew(False)
Set copySObj = session.GetObject(id)
```

The *IDfSysObject.saveAsNew()* method saves the new object in the same folder as the original. This is, of course, not what you want. To move the new object, it first must be unlinked from its current location, and then linked to the new one. Both the *IDfSysObject.link()* and *IDfSysObject.unlink()* methods accept strings as input arguments that contain either a folder path or a folder Id. The last step is to rename the object and save it.

```
' move copy
Set foldObj = session.GetObject(copySObj.getFolderId(0))
copySObj.unlink (foldObj.getFolderPath(0))
copySObj.link ("/Temp")

' rename copy
copySObj.setObjectName ("copy of " & copySObj.getObjectName)

'save copy
copySObj.save
```

4.1.2 Deleting Objects

Deleting a single object from the Docbase is a simple task: call *IDfSysObject.destroy()*, or if you want to remove all of an object's versions, *IDfSysObject.destroyAllVersions()*. The following example illustrates deleting an object with an object Id of 0900218d8003d538.

```
Dim sObj As IDfSysObject

' get the object
Set sObj = session.GetObject(cx.getId("0900218d8003d538"))

' destroy current object
sObj.destroy

' or, destroy them all
sObj.destroyAllVersions
```

You can also delete objects using DQL. The following examples are analogous to the Visual Basic code above. The first example deletes a single object, even if it isn't the current version. The second example deletes all versions of an object.

```
delete dm_document objects where r_object_id =
    '0900218d8003d538'
```

```
delete dm_document (all) objects where i_chronicle_id =
    '0900218d8003d538'
```

In general, it is more efficient to delete objects with DQL than with the DFC. The DFC method fetches the object to your workstation only to delete it. This wastes time and bandwidth. With the DQL method, there is no fetch, so the delete is much more efficient.

4.1.2.1 Deleting Collections Of Objects

Deleting a collection of objects is also straight forward as long as the objects are all content-type objects (e.g., `dm_document`), and are not hierarchical folders or cabinets. The problem with deleting cabinets and folders is that they must be empty before they can be deleted. This problem and its solution are examined later in this section.

Using the DFC, deleting a collection of objects can be accomplished like this:

Source Code A working example of this source code can be found in the "`Chapter4/From Scratch/Delete1`" directory of the source code archive.

```
Dim sObj As IDfSysObject
Dim q As IDfQuery
Dim col As IDfCollection
Dim cnt As Integer

' get a collection of objects
Set q = cx.getQuery
q.setDQL ("select r_object_id from dm_document where folder " _
    & "('/News/2002',descend)")
Set col = q.execute(session, DF_QUERY)
cnt = 0

' loop to destroy them
While (col.Next = True)

    ' fetching the object just to delete it is inefficient
    ' and expensive
    Set sObj = session.GetObject(cx.getId( _
        col.getString("r_object_id")))
    sObj.destroyAllVersions
    cnt = cnt + 1
Wend

MsgBox "Deleted " & cnt & " objects"
col.Close
```

The same task can be accomplished more efficiently using DQL, as follows.

Source Code A working example of this source code can be found in the "Chapter4/From Scratch/Delete2" directory of the source code archive.

```
Dim q As IDfQuery
Dim col As IDfCollection

' delete objects using dql
Set q = cx.getQuery
q.setDQL ("delete dm_document (all) objects where folder" _
    & " ('/News/2002',descend))")

' get results
Set col = q.execute(session, DF_QUERY)
While (col.Next = True)

    ' display number of deleted objects
    MsgBox "Deleted " & col.getString(col.GetAttr(0).getName) _
        & " objects "
Wend
col.Close
```

Using the DQL technique is a better choice for implementation in this case. In the first code snippet, each object is fetched from the Docbase and instantiated on the client workstation, only to be deleted. This consumes a lot of unnecessary overhead. In the second code snippet, DQL does all of the deleting, very efficiently. The key to the success of the DQL is the DQL *folder()* function. It collects the r_object_ids of the objects in the folder structure indicated so the DELETE statement can delete them en masse. The collection processing loop in this code snippet is only necessary to retrieve the number of objects deleted.

4.1.2.2 Deep Delete

Deletes get tricky when you want to delete a collection of objects *and* a folder hierarchy (i.e., prune a folder structure). This is often referred to as a *deep delete*. To avoid any problems you must delete a folder's contents first and then the folder. This is accomplished bottom up, so that no folder you delete contains any content or other folders.

The code snippet below accomplishes this using a recursive algorithm. For input, the `DeepDelete()` subroutine expects an IDfPersistentObject that represents a folder, and performs a query to gather the object Ids of all of the `dm_sysobject` objects contained in it. The query results are then analyzed, and if one of the returned objects is a folder, the `DeepDelete()` subroutine calls itself, passing the folder object as the input argument.

Source Code A working example of this source code can be found in the "`Chapter4/From Scratch/Deep Delete`" directory of the source code archive.

```
Sub DeepDelete(fold As IDfPersistentObject)
    Dim q As IDfQuery
    Dim col As IDfCollection
    Dim rows() As String
    Dim pObj As IDfPersistentObject
    Dim i As Integer
    Dim emptyDir As Boolean

    emptyDir = True
    Set q = cx.getQuery

    ' get all sys_objects in this folder
    q.setDQL ("select r_object_id from dm_sysobject (all) " _
        & "where folder(id('" & fold.getObjectId.toString _
        & "'))")

    Set col = q.execute(session, DF_READ_QUERY)
```

The collection processing here is the same as in the recursive example in Chapter 3, *Working with Queries and Collections*. Instead of manipulating the objects inside the collection-processing loop, they are stored in a dynamic array and the collection is closed. *This is extremely important.* These object Ids must be persisted during recursive calls, but the IDfCollection object cannot stay open.

```
' process collection
While (col.Next = True)

    ' if array uninitialized, init to 1
    If (emptyDir = True) Then
        ReDim rows(1)
        emptyDir = False
    ' extend array by one
    Else
        ReDim Preserve rows(UBound(rows) + 1)
    End If

    ' put obj id in array
    rows(UBound(rows)) = col.getString("r_object_id")

Wend
col.Close      ' IMPORTANT! close collection
```

Each object Id in the `rows()` array is tested to determine whether its object is a `dm_folder` object. This is accomplished by doing a quick string compare on the Id. If it starts with "0b" it's a folder. This technique has the added benefit of catching custom subtypes of `dm_folder` also. If the object is a folder (or subtype), a recursive call is made to *DeepDelete()* and the object is passed as the argument. The processing of the current iteration of the subroutine is put on hold until the recursive call returns. When the recursive call returns, processing of the current iteration continues. The object is ultimately deleted by the *IDfPersistentObject.destroy()* method. Thus, each object is deleted while iterating over the array, not while processing the collection.

```
        ' process array if it was initialized
    If (emptyDir = False) Then
        For i = 1 To UBound(rows)

            ' get the object
            Set pObj = session.GetObject(cx.getId(rows(i)))

            ' if it's a folder, recurse into it
            If ((InStr(1, rows(i), "0b", vbTextCompare) _
                = 1)) Then
                Call DeepDelete(pObj)
            End If

            ' delete object
            pObj.destroy
        Next i
    End If

End Sub
```

To call the *DeepDelete()* function, use code like this:

```
    ' get a folder
    Set pObj = session.GetObject(cx.getId("0b0023eb800001db"))
    Call DeepDelete(pObj)
```

An improvement to this subroutine would be to delete all of the content in the folder hierarchy first. DQL similar to that found in the second example of Section 4.1.2.1, *Deleting Collections of Objects*, would do it. Then the recursive part of the function would only have to delete folders.

That code might look like this:

```
    ' delete objects using dql
    Set q = cx.getQuery
    q.setDQL ("delete dm_document (all) objects where folder" _
        & " (id(""0b0023eb800001db"",descend))")

    Set col = q.execute(session, DF_QUERY)
    While (col.Next = True)
```

```
        cnt = col.getString(col.GetAttr(0).getName)
Wend
col.Close

Set pObj = session.GetObject(cx.getId("0b0023eb800001db"))
Call DeepDelete(pObj)
```

4.1.3 Copying Objects

You have already seen the code that copies objects in the Docbase, it was used in Section 4.1.1.3, *Creating an Object from a Template*. It is present here in a more concise form. The key to this piece of code is the `sObj.saveAsNew()` method, which actually makes the copy in the Docbase. Unlike the previous version of this code, this example does not move the copy to a new location. It continues to reside in the folder with the original. Again, assume the object Id of the object to copy is 0900218d80079051.

```
Dim sObj As IDfSysObject
Dim copySObj As IDfSysObject
Dim id As IDfId

' get object to copy
Set sObj = session.GetObject(cx.getId("0900218d80079051"))

' make a copy
Set id = sObj.saveAsNew(False)
Set copySObj = session.GetObject(id)

' rename copy
copySObj.setObjectName ("copy of " & copySObj.getObjectName)

'save copy
copySObj.save
```

4.1.3.1 Deep Copy

In a deep copy, you copy a folder and all of its contents—including other folders with content—to a new location. Where a deep delete pruned of a tree structure, a deep copy is analogous to a graft. This is similar to the old DOS xcopy function or the UNIX `cp -r` function. As with the deep delete code discussed previously, deep copy offers some interesting challenges and recursion.

The following code snippet demonstrates how to copy one folder hierarchy into another. As input, it requires two IDfFolder objects that represent the *from folder* and the *to folder*, respectively. The code loops through the from folder and copies the objects it finds there to the to folder. If it happens to find a folder in the from folder, it recurses into it.

The first thing you will notice about this code snippet is that it uses many variables. The number of variables could be reduced, but I wanted to be explicit concerning each variable's purpose to make the code easier to read. Also, note this subroutine is broken into two distinct parts. The first part runs the query within each folder to obtain a list of objects to copy, and the second part actually does the copy and the recursive call.

Source Code A working example of this source code can be found in the "`Chapter4/From Scratch/Deep Copy`" directory of the source code archive.

```
Sub DeepCopy(FromFold As IDfFolder, ToFold As IDfFolder)
    Dim q As IDfQuery
    Dim col As IDfCollection
    Dim rows() As String
    Dim i As Integer

    Dim sobj As IDfSysObject
    Dim copyIdObj As IDfId
    Dim copySObj As IDfSysObject
    Dim foldObj As IDfFolder
    Dim newFolderId As String
    Dim newFoldObj As IDfFolder
    Dim thisFold As IDfFolder
    Dim emptyDir As Boolean
```

The structure of the query and `while` loop used to gather the object Ids of the objects to copy is similar to those used in the `DeepDelete()` function in Section 4.1.2.2, *Deep Delete*. The object Id in each row of the collection is saved to a row in the dynamic array, `rows()`, to be processed later.

```
        emptyDir = True
        Set q = cx.getQuery
        q.setDQL ("select r_object_id from dm_sysobject where " _
            & "folder(id('" & FromFold.getObjectId.toString _
            & "'))")
        Set col = q.execute(session, DF_READ_QUERY)

        While (col.Next = True)

            ' if array uninitialized, init to 1
            If (emptyDir = True) Then
                ReDim rows(1)
                emptyDir = False
            ' extend array by one
            Else
                ReDim Preserve rows(UBound(rows) + 1)
            End If

            ' put obj id in array
            rows(UBound(rows)) = col.getString("r_object_id")
        Wend
        col.Close
```

The second section of this subroutine processes the objects selected by the query. First, each object is fetched from the Docbase. This is an expensive process, but because we have to fetch each object to copy it anyway, it's tolerable. After each object is fetched, it is tested to determine if it is a folder (dm_folder) or not. If it is, a folder is created in the target location. Then the DeepCopy() subroutine is called recursively with the current folder and this newly created folder as arguments. If it is not, the object is copied to the target location.

To create new folders I call a subroutine named dmMkDir() and pass the path of the folder to create as an argument. dmMkDir() is a subroutine discussed in Chapter 5, *Proven Solutions for Common Tasks*. For now, just know that it creates a folder hierarchy to match the path passed into it, and returns the r_object_id of the leaf folder it creates.

```
    ' process array if it was initialized
If (emptyDir = False) Then
     For i = 1 To UBound(rows)

          ' get the object
          Set sobj = session.GetObject(cx.getId(rows(i)))

          ' if it's a folder...
          If (sobj.getType.getName = "dm_folder") Then

               ' cast it to a folder
               Set thisFold = sobj

               ' create it,
               newFolderId = dmMkDir(session,
                              ToFold.getFolderPath(0) _
                              & "/" & sobj.getObjectName)
               Set newFoldObj =
                    session.GetObject(cx.getId(newFolderId))

               ' and recurse into it
               Call DeepCopy(thisFold, newFoldObj)
```

If the object being processed is not a folder, it is copied to the `toFold` location. The code to copy the object is similar to that discussed in Section 4.1.3, *Copying Objects*, and utilizes the *IDfSysObject.saveAsNew()* method to do the copy.

```
            Else

                ' make a copy of object
                Set copyIdObj = sobj.saveAsNew(False)
                Set copySObj = session.GetObject(copyIdObj)

                ' move it
                Set foldObj =
                    session.GetObject(copySObj.getFolderId(0))
                copySObj.unlink (foldObj.getFolderPath(0))
                Set foldObj =
                    session.GetObject(ToFold.getObjectId)
                copySObj.link (foldObj.getFolderPath(0))

                'save
                copySObj.save
            End If
        Next i
    End If
End Sub
```

To initiate the *DeepCopy()* subroutine, use code like this:

```
    Dim from_folder As IDfFolder
    Dim to_folder As IDfFolder

    Set from_folder =
        session.GetObject(cx.getId("0b00218d8007e3a5"))
    Set to_folder =
        session.GetObject(cx.getId("0b00218d8007e294"))

    Call DeepCopy(from_folder, to_folder)
```

Assuming `0b00218d8007e3a5` and `0b00218d8007e294` are the object Ids of two folders in your Docbase.

4.1.4 Checking Out And Editing Objects

A necessity of any Documentum Desktop application is the ability to check documents out of the Docbase for editing. The checkout function, as you know it from using the Documentum Desktop, is actually a combination of actions that result in the document being locked in the Docbase, its content transferred to your workstation, and the appropriate editing application invoked. The following code snippet demonstrates this process in its most basic form.

This snippet relies on the Windows API to determine and execute the default application for editing the file you checked out. To make this happen, the code appends a DOS extension to the filename when it is transferred from the Docbase to the workstation. It gets the default DOS extension from the object's associated IDfFormat object, and appends it to the filename during the execution of the *IDfSysObject.getFile()* method. The file is copied to your checkout directory, as defined in your Documentum registry key. This snippet assumes an object with object Id of 0900218d80034d35 exists in the Docbase.

Source Code A working example of this source code can be found in the "`Chapter4/From Scratch/Edit`" directory of the source code archive.

```
' Win32 API declares
Public Declare Function GetDesktopWindow Lib "user32" () As Long
Public Declare Function ShellExecute Lib "shell32.dll" Alias _
    "ShellExecuteA" (ByVal hwnd As Long, ByVal lpOperation As _
    String, ByVal lpFile As String, ByVal lpParameters As _
    String, ByVal lpDirectory As String, ByVal nShowCmd As _
    Long) As Long

Dim sObj As IDfSysObject
Dim Path As String
Dim fmtObj As IDfFormat
Dim regObj As IDfClientRegistry

' fetch the object
Set sObj = session.GetObject(cx.getId("0900218d80034d35"))

' if its not already checked out, check it out
If (Not sObj.isCheckedOut) Then

   sObj.checkout

   ' if it has content, get it
   If (sObj.getContentSize > 0) Then
```

```
        ' make sure the DOS extension is part of filename
        Set fmtObj = sObj.GetFormat

        ' get local checkout path
        Set regObj = cx.getClientRegistry
        Path = regObj.getCheckoutDirectory

        ' put content in the check out dir
        Path = sObj.getFile(Path & "\" & sObj.getObjectName _
            & "." & fmtObj.getDOSExtension)

        ' open in the default application
        ShellExecute GetDesktopWindow(), "open", Path, "", "", 1

    End If
End If
```

This example is a very basic implementation, but gives you a sense of what is required to check out and edit an object in the Docbase.

This implementation is hampered because it doesn't register the checked out files in the Windows registry. Therefore, it won't interface correctly with the Documentum Desktop or other applications that expect checked out files to be registered in the Windows registry.

4.1.5 Viewing Objects

Viewing an object in the Docbase uses the same logic as checking one out. The exception is you don't have to check if the object is already checked out, or call the *IDfSysObject.checkout()* method. Other than that, the code is the same. The same limitations exist for this viewing process as for the checkout process.

Source Code A working example of this source code can be found in the "Chapter4/From Scratch/View" directory of the source code archive.

```
Dim sObj As IDfSysObject
Dim Path As String
Dim fmtObj As IDfFormat
Dim regObj As IDfClientRegistry
```

```
' fetch the object
Set sObj = session.GetObject(cx.getId("0900218d80034d35"))

' if it has content, get it
If (sObj.getContentSize > 0) Then

    ' get format
    Set fmtObj = sObj.GetFormat

    ' get local checkout path
    Set regObj = cx.getClientRegistry
    Path = regObj.getCheckoutDirectory

    ' get content to the check out dir
    Path = sObj.getFile(Path & "\" & sObj.getObjectName _
        & "." & fmtObj.getDOSExtension)

    ' open in the default application
    ShellExecute GetDesktopWindow(), "open", Path, "", "", 1

End If
```

4.1.6 Canceling A Checkout

Canceling the checkout of an object reverses any changes you have made to it locally. The cancel is achieved by calling `IDfSysObject.cancelCheckout()` to release the object's lock in the Docbase. The code snippet below demonstrates canceling the checkout of an object and removing the local copy of the file from your hard drive. It assumes that the checkout directory is the user's default checkout directory as defined by the Documentum key in the Windows registry, and that the object's file name is the `object_name` plus the DOS extension. The object I use in this example has an object Id of `0900218d80034d35`.

Source Code A working example of this source code can be found in the "`Chapter4/From Scratch/Cancel Checkout`" directory of the source code archive.

```
Dim sObj As IDfSysObject
Dim fmtObj As IDfFormat
Dim Path As String
Dim regObj As IDfClientRegistry
```

```
Set sObj = session.GetObject(cx.getId("0900218d80034d35"))

' cancel checkout
sObj.cancelCheckout

' get local checkout path
Set regObj = cx.getClientRegistry
Path = regObj.getCheckoutDirectory

' get obj format
Set fmtObj = sObj.GetFormat

' remove local file
Kill Path & "\" & sObj.getObjectName & "." _
    & fmtObj.getDOSExtension
```

4.1.7 Checking In Objects

Programmatically checking objects back into the Docbase is, as you would expect, just the opposite of checking them out. This code snippet assumes that the checked out object has an Id of 0900218d80034d35, and is located in your default Documentum checkout directory on your hard drive.

Source Code A working example of this source code can be found in the "Chapter4/From Scratch/Checkin" directory of the source code archive.

```
Dim sObj As IDfSysObject
Dim fmtObj As IDfFormat
Dim Path As String
Dim regObj As IDfClientRegistry

Set sObj = session.GetObject(cx.getId("0900218d80034d35"))

' get format object
Set fmtObj = sObj.GetFormat

' get local checkout path
Set regObj = cx.getClientRegistry
```

```
Path = regObj.getCheckoutDirectory

' set content type from format object
sObj.setContentType fmtObj.getName

' setfile and checkin
sObj.setFile (Path & "\" & sObj.getObjectName & "." _
    & fmtObj.getDOSExtension)
sObj.checkin False, ""
```

To save changes to the content as well as the object's attributes, you must connect the updated file on your hard drive to the object in the Docbase. You do this by calling `IDfSysObject.setFile()`. Notice that before I call the `setFile()` method, I set the content type of the object with the `IDfSysObject.setContentType()` method. This is only necessary if the IDfSysObject has never had content until now, or if you are changing the type of its content (e.g., MS Word to WordPerfect, JPG to GIF).

The `IDfSysObject.checkin()` method performs the following actions:

- Automatically creates a new version of the object in the Docbase,
- Increments the minor version number of the object,
- Transfers the file to the Content Server,
- Saves the new object, and
- Removes the object's lock in the Docbase.

If you want to checkin an object *without* versioning, use the `IDfSysObject.save()` method instead of the `IDfSysObject.checkin()` method.

4.2 *Implementing Library Functions With DFC Operation Classes*

Now that you have seen some of the logic required to implement the core library functions, we turn to the Documentum Operation classes, which implement this logic for you. Documentum has generalized the core library functions into the IDfOperation classes to allow developers to concentrate on solving business problems instead of the details of implementing these functions. If you browse the source code for any of the Documentum Desktop components[*] and you will see that when it comes to implementing any of these functions, Documentum uses the IDfOperation classes.

---

[*] You can download the Documentum Desktop Component Source archive from the Documentum Download Center (http://documentum.subscribenet.com).

I took the time to discuss and demonstrate how to implement the core library functions in the previous section without the IDfOperation classes for several reasons:

- It provided a good introduction to Documentum programming.
- It provided an understanding of how these functions really work and the effort involved to implement them.
- It will help you appreciate the Operation classes.

One of the problems with the code in the previous section is if Documentum changes any of its objects, methods, or the way the Docbase operates, these subroutines may break and need to be rewritten. Documentum alleviated this problem by creating the IDfOperation classes; that way, if and when changes occur in how the Docbase operates or the DFC works, only these classes need to be updated.

There are numerous other advantages to using Documentum's Operation classes instead of creating your own. A few are:

- Take advantage of the years of thought and testing Documentum invested in these classes.
- You can do more with less code.
- Since these classes are used internally by Documentum, they will be continually updated (and fixed!) to account for new capability at no cost or expense to you.
- They allow you to easily work within Documentum's application framework.
- They provide hooks into other functionality that is otherwise cumbersome to create (e.g., abort, undo, progress monitors, error handlers).
- They are all XML-aware, meaning that they can be used to process XML documents.

By using the IDfOperation classes, you ensure your library functions will always work—regardless of how complex your content becomes. In addition, you gain the assurance that you are working within the Documentum application framework, which will insulate you from future changes in implementation of the Docbase and the DFC. The Table 4.1 summarizes the Documentum IDfOperation classes.

Table 4.1—IDfOperation Classes

Operation	Class	Remark
Delete	IDfDeleteOperation	The delete operation deletes objects from the Docbase, including deep folder structures and virtual documents, and updates the Windows registry.
Copy	IDfCopyOperation	The copy operation copies objects in the Docbase from one location to another, including deep folder structures and virtual documents.
Checkout	IDfCheckoutOperation	The checkout operation locks objects in the Docbase, exports content to the client for manipulation, and updates the Windows registry.
Checkin	IDfCheckinOperation	The checkin operation releases the Docbase lock, imports updated content and attribute data, and updates Windows registry entries.
CancelCheckout	IDfCancelCheckoutOperation	The cancel checkout operation releases the Docbase lock, deletes the local content file, and updates Windows registry entries.
Import	IDfImportOperation	The import operation imports new content into the Docbase.
Export	IDfExportOperation	The export operation exports content from the Docbase to the local file system.
Move	IDfMoveOperation	The move operation moves objects in the Docbase from one location to another.
Transform	IDfXMLTransformOperation	The transform operation performs XSL transformations on XML documents.
Validate	IDfValidationOperation	The validate operation performs XML validations on XML documents.

To provide contrast, this section will discuss the same core library functions as the previous section. Additionally, I will discuss how to use the progress bar and how to process an aborted operation—things not easily achieved without these classes.

4.2.1 Overview Of Using Operations

Each Operation class contains methods and attributes specific to a particular operation (e.g., checkin, checkout). Although each class performs a different operation, they all work in generally the same way. The basic process for using an operation class is:

- Instantiate object—instantiate an interface class for the particular operation you want to implement, usually through the DfClientX factory class.
- Populate object—populate the object with the necessary data and set execution options.
- Execute—run the operation.
- Check errors—check for execution errors.
- Process results—process the results of the operation for additional error checking, undo requests, or abort requests.

In code, this generic process might look like this (note the use of XXX where specific operation names should be used):

```
Dim opObj As IDfXXXOperation
Dim sObj As IDfSysObject
Dim retVal As Boolean
Dim i As Integer

' get operation obj
Set opObj = cx.getXXXOperation

' get sysobj
Set sObj = session.GetObject(cx.getId("0900218d8003d538"))

' add object to operation
opObj.Add sObj

' do operation
retVal = opObj.execute

' check for errors
For i = 0 To (opObj.getErrors.getCount - 1)
    MsgBox opObj.getErrors.getString(i), vbCritical, _
```

```
        "Operation Error"
Next I
```

The following sections look at the specific implementation of this process for each Operation class.

4.2.2   Creating And Viewing Objects

As you may have noticed in Table 4.1, there are no IDfOperation classes for creating or viewing objects in the Docbase. These functions remain in the realm of custom code as demonstrated previously in Sections 4.1.1, *Creating Objects*, and 4.1.5, *Viewing Objects*, respectively.

4.2.3   Deleting Objects

The following code snippet implements the same deep delete functionality as demonstrated in Section 4.1.2.2, *Deep Delete*. You will notice it is a lot less complicated to implement using the IDfDeleteOperation class.

First, the delete operation is instantiated. Next, the object to delete is fetched from the Docbase (in this case a `dm_folder` object with Id of 0b00218d8007e237) and added as a node to the delete operation object. Notice the *object* is added to the operation class, not just its Id. Finally, the operation is executed and queried for errors.

Source Code A working example of this source code can be found in the "`Chapter4/Operations/Delete`" directory of the source code archive.

```
Dim opObj As IDfDeleteOperation
Dim sObj As IDfSysObject
Dim retVal As Boolean
Dim i As Integer

' get op obj
Set opObj = cx.getDeleteOperation

' get obj to delete
Set sObj = session.GetObject(cx.getId("0b00218d8007e237"))

' add object to operation
opObj.Add sObj

' do operation
retVal = opObj.execute
```

```
' check for errors
For i = 0 To (opObj.getErrors.getCount - 1)
    MsgBox opObj.getErrors.getString(i), vbCritical, "Delete " _
        & "Error"
Next i
```

By default, the delete operation class implements a deep delete. I think you will agree, this code is significantly less complex than the `DeepDelete()` function discussed in Section 4.1.2.2, *Deep Delete*. In addition, this deep delete automatically handles XML and virtual documents, something the previous code did not.

4.2.4 Copying Objects

This code snippet implements the copy operation using the IDfCopyOperation class. The structure and function of the code is nearly identical to the IDfDeleteOperation class discussed in Section 4.2.3, *Deleting Objects*, except for one detail: the IDfCopyOperation class requires the destination folder to be identified and added to the operation. The copy operation class implements a deep copy by default. In addition, it can also handle XML and virtual documents. In this example, I copy an object with Id of `0900218d8003d538` to a folder with Id of `0b0023eb80002f17`.

Source Code A working example of this source code can be found in the "`Chapter4/Operations/Copy`" directory of the source code archive.

```
Dim opObj As IDfCopyOperation
Dim sObj As IDfsysObject
Dim retVal As Boolean
Dim i As Integer

' get op obj
Set opObj = cx.getCopyOperation

' get obj to copy
Set sObj = session.GetObject(cx.getId("0900218d8003d538"))

' setup operation
opObj.Add sObj
opObj.setDestinationFolderId cx.getId("0b0023eb80002f17")
```

```
' do operation
retVal = opObj.execute

' check for errors
For i = 0 To (opObj.getErrors.getCount - 1)
    MsgBox opObj.getErrors.getString(i), vbCritical, "Copy Error"
Next i
```

4.2.5 Checking Out And Editing Objects

The following code snippet implements the same checkout functionality as demonstrated in the Section 4.1.4, *Checking Out and Editing Objects*, but uses the IDfCheckoutOperation class. However, to edit the checked out object, it relies on the same Win32 API code.

> **Source Code** A working example of this source code can be found in the "`Chapter4/Operations/Edit`" directory of the source code archive.

```
' Win32 API declares
Public Declare Function GetDesktopWindow Lib "user32" () As Long
Public Declare Function ShellExecute Lib "shell32.dll" Alias _
    "ShellExecuteA" (ByVal hwnd As Long, ByVal lpOperation As _
    String, ByVal lpFile As String, ByVal lpParameters As _
    String, ByVal lpDirectory As String, ByVal nShowCmd As _
    Long) As Long

Dim opObj As IDfCheckoutOperation
Dim sObj As IDfSysObject
Dim retVal As Boolean
Dim i As Integer

' get op obj
Set opObj = cx.getCheckoutOperation

' get obj to checkout
Set sObj = session.GetObject(cx.getId("0900218d80034d35"))
```

```
' setup operation
opObj.Add sObj

' get local checkout path
Set regObj = cx.getClientRegistry
opObj.setDestinationDirectory regObj.getCheckoutDirectory

' do operation
retVal = opObj.execute

' check for errors
For i = 0 To (opObj.getErrors.getCount - 1)
    MsgBox opObj.getErrors.getString(i), vbCritical, "Checkout" _
        & " Error"
Next i

' open files in editor
For i = 0 To (opObj.getRootNodes.getCount - 1)
    ShellExecute GetDesktopWindow(), "open", _
            opObj.getRootNodes.get(i).getFilePath, "", "", 1
Next i
```

Again, this code follows the same general implementation pattern as the IDfOperation classes discussed previously. The notable exception is the use of the *setDestinationDirectory()* method to identify where the checkout object should reside on the client computer. In this case, I use the default Documentum checkout directory as defined in the Windows registry.

The IDfCheckoutOperation object in this example does all of the following actions for you:

- Obtains the Docbase lock on the object (If the object is a virtual document or an XML document, it obtains locks for all of the object's parts).
- Avoids file system collisions by constructing a unique file name.
- Transfers the object's content to the your workstation.
- Updates the Windows registry to include the object's Id, filename, and checkout directory.

The only thing the checkout operation does not do is launch the file's native editor. You still have to launch the appropriate application yourself; thus, the use of the Win32 API method, *ShellExecute()* and *GetDesktopWindow()*.

4.2.6 Canceling Checkout Of Objects

The cancel checkout operation does more than just release the Docbase lock on the checked out object. It reverses the entire checkout process by releasing the lock, updating the Windows registry, and removing the local file. It is implemented similarly to the checkout operation, as the code snippet below illustrates. This example assumes an object with an Id of `0900218d80034d35` was previously checked out.

> **Source Code** A working example of this source code can be found in the "`Chapter4/Operations/Cancel Checkout`" directory of the source code archive.

```
Dim opObj As IDfCancelCheckoutOperation
Dim sObj As IDfSysObject
Dim retVal As Boolean
Dim i As Integer

' get op obj
Set opObj = cx.getCancelCheckoutOperation

' get obj to cancel checkout
Set sObj = session.GetObject(cx.getId("0900218d80034d35"))

' setup operation
opObj.Add sObj
opObj.setKeepLocalFile False

' do operation
retVal = opObj.execute

' check for errors
For i = 0 To opObj.getErrors.getCount - 1
    MsgBox opObj.getErrors.getString(i), vbCritical, "Cancel " _
        & "Checkout Error"
Next i
```

Simple and clean, the IDfCancelCheckoutOperation class provides a lot of power for very little code. One nice feature of the cancel checkout operation, is it can remove the local copy of the file from the user's computer simply by passing `False` to the `setKeepLocalFile()` method. The IDfCancelCheckoutOperation class can do this by scanning the Windows registry for the key written there by the IDfCheckoutOperation class. Once it finds the key, it can determine where the file resides on the hard drive and delete it. This small feature points to one large drawback to the "from scratch" functions implemented in the first half of this chapter: they did not use the Windows registry to communicate among operations.

4.2.7 Checking In Objects

Checking in objects using the IDfCheckinOperation class is just as easy as checking them out. This code snippet checks in the object as the next minor version, and removes the local copy of the file. This example assumes an object with an Id of `0900218d80034d35` was previously checked out.

> **Source Code** A working example of this source code can be found in the "`Chapter4/Operations/Checkin`" directory of the source code archive.

```
Dim opObj As IDfCheckinOperation
Dim sObj As IDfSysObject
Dim retVal As Boolean
Dim i As Integer

' get op obj and cast it
Set opObj = cx.getCheckinOperation

' get obj to checkin and cast it
Set sObj = session.GetObject(cx.getId("0900218d80034d35"))

' setup operation
opObj.Add sObj
checkinOp.setKeepLocalFile False
checkinOp.setCheckinVersion 1      ' NEXT MINOR VERSION

' do operation
retVal = opObj.execute

' check for errors
For i = 0 To (opObj.getErrors.getCount - 1)
    MsgBox opObj.getErrors.getString(i), vbCritical, "Checkin " _
        & "Error"
Next i
```

The checkin operation creates a new version of the object in the Docbase, transfers the content file (If the object was a virtual document or an XML document, it transfers all of the object's parts.), updates the Windows registry, and releases the Docbase lock. Again, because of the operation's use of the Windows registry, it is not necessary to indicate which file on the hard drive to transfer back to the Documentum Server, it already knows.

4.2.8 Implementing An Operation Monitor

One exciting feature of the IDfOperation classes is their ability to integrate with the operation monitor class, IDfOperationMonitor. The operation monitor is a Documentum Desktop UI class. It provides user feedback and the ability to abort an operation during its execution. When an operation monitor object is used with an IDfOperation, the operation monitor automatically shows and updates itself during the execution of the operation. The UI and functionality of the operation monitor is predefined, but somewhat configurable. Figure 4.1 shows a typical operation monitor in action.

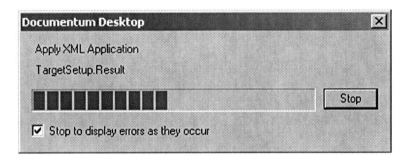

Figure 4.1—Example of IDfOperationMonitor

The following code snippet demonstrates how to add an operation monitor to the checkout operation previously discussed in Section 4.2.5, *Checking Out and Editing Objects*. That code is repeated here for context with the operation monitor code shown in bold typeface. Note that you need to add a reference in your project for the Documentum Progress Monitor Component 1.0 Type Library to use this code.

Source Code A working example of this source code can be found in the "`Chapter4/Operations/Operation Monitor`" directory of the source code archive.

```
' Win32 API declares
Public Declare Function GetDesktopWindow Lib "user32" () As Long
Public Declare Function ShellExecute Lib "shell32.dll" Alias _
    "ShellExecuteA" (ByVal hwnd As Long, ByVal lpOperation As _
    String, ByVal lpFile As String, ByVal lpParameters As _
```

```
        String, ByVal lpDirectory As String, ByVal nShowCmd As _
        Long) As Long

Dim opObj As IDfCheckoutOperation
Dim progressMonitor As New DcProgressMonitor
Dim opMonitor As IDfOperationMonitor
Dim sObj As IDfSysObject
Dim retVal As Boolean
Dim i As Integer
Dim regObj As IDfClientRegistry

' get op obj
Set opObj = cx.getCheckoutOperation

' get obj to checkout
Set sObj = session.GetObject(cx.getId("0900218d800c2fde"))

' setup operation
opObj.Add sObj

' get local checkout path
Set regObj = cx.getClientRegistry
opObj.setDestinationDirectory regObj.getCheckoutDirectory
```

After instantiating the progress monitor, cast it to an operation monitor and install it in your operation. Then *start()* the monitor before you *execute()* the operation, and *stop()* it afterward. The operation object and the operation monitor object take care of the necessary synchronization.

```
' setup the progress monitor
progressMonitor.Delay = 0
progressMonitor.StopEnabled = True

' cast and install the progress monitor
Set opMonitor = progressMonitor
Call opObj.setOperationMonitor(opMonitor)

' start monitor
Call progressMonitor.start(GetDesktopWindow)
```

```
' do operation
retVal = opObj.execute

' stop monitor
Call progressMonitor.Stop

' check for errors
For i = 0 To opObj.getErrors.getCount - 1
    MsgBox opObj.getErrors.getString(i), vbCritical, "Checkout" _
        & " Error"
Next i

' open files in editor
For i = 0 To (opObj.getRootNodes.getCount - 1)
    ShellExecute GetDesktopWindow(), "open", _
            opObj.getRootNodes.get(i).getFilePath, "", "", 1
Next i
```

In addition to providing a nice feedback mechanism, the operation monitor also provides the ability to abort an operation, as discussed next.

4.2.9 Processing An Operation Abort

Another advantage of using an operation monitor with an IDfOperation class is it allows users to abort and undo operations. For example, in Figure 4.1, if the user clicks the **Stop** button on the operation monitor UI, an abort request is registered with the underlying Operation object, and the Operation object halts the execution of the operation. With the addition of a few lines of code, you can undo the operation and return the Docbase and/or the content objects to their previous state. The only additional code necessary to implement this feature is that which processes the abort request. The following code snippet demonstrates how to add this code to the code snippet discussed in Section 4.2.8, *Implementing An Operation Monitor*. That code is repeated here for context with the abort code shown in bold typeface.

> **Source Code** A working example of this source code can be found in the "Chapter4/Operations/Operation Monitor" directory of the source code archive.

```
' Win32 API declares
Public Declare Function GetDesktopWindow Lib "user32" () As Long
Public Declare Function ShellExecute Lib "shell32.dll" Alias _
    "ShellExecuteA" (ByVal hwnd As Long, ByVal lpOperation As _
    String, ByVal lpFile As String, ByVal lpParameters As _
```

```vb
        String, ByVal lpDirectory As String, ByVal nShowCmd As _
        Long) As Long

Dim opObj As IDfCheckoutOperation
Dim progressMonitor As New DcProgressMonitor
Dim opMonitor As IDfOperationMonitor
Dim sObj As IDfSysObject
Dim opProperties As IDfProperties
Dim retVal As Boolean
Dim i As Integer
Dim regObj As IDfClientRegistry

' get op obj
Set opObj = cx.getCheckoutOperation

' get obj to checkout
Set sObj = session.GetObject(cx.getId("0900218d800c2fde"))

' setup operation
opObj.Add sObj

' get local checkout path
Set regObj = cx.getClientRegistry
opObj.setDestinationDirectory regObj.getCheckoutDirectory

' setup the progress monitor
progressMonitor.Delay = 0
progressMonitor.StopEnabled = True

' cast and install the progress monitor
Set opMonitor = progressMonitor
Call opObj.setOperationMonitor(opMonitor)

' start monitor
Call progressMonitor.start(GetDesktopWindow)

' do operation
retVal = opObj.execute

' stop monitor
Call progressMonitor.Stop
```

The code to check for the abort request is placed after the `IDfOperation.execute()` method call. When the user aborts the operation, the `IDfOperation.execute()` method returns and the code continues running from that point. The fact that an abort request occurred is only captured in the operation's property object, so you must query that object for the presence of an `IDfOperation.AbortRequested` property. If it exists, a call to the `IDfOperation.abort()` method takes care of reversing the operation and all of the clean up.

```
' get operation properties
Set opProperties = opObj.getProperties()

' process abort event
If (opProperties.containsProperty("AbortRequested")) Then
    Call opObj.abort
End If

' check for errors
For i = 0 To opObj.getErrors.getCount - 1
    MsgBox opObj.getErrors.getString(i), vbCritical, "Checkout" _
        & " Error"
Next i

' open files in editor
For i = 0 To (opObj.getRootNodes.getCount - 1)
    ShellExecute GetDesktopWindow(), "open", _
            opObj.getRootNodes.get(i).getFilePath, "", "", 1
Next i
```

The addition of the operation monitor to your application will give it a polished and professional look. In addition, the ability to process abort requests and undo operations will further add to your application's usability.

4.3 Chapter Summary

This chapter introduced you to seven core library functions: create, delete, copy, checkout, view, cancel checkout, and checkin. These functions are essential to any document management system and its clients, so you can expect to implement them frequently. The first part of the chapter examined implementing these functions "from scratch", meaning each step of the processing logic had to be thought out and implemented using basic DFC classes and queries.

The second half of the chapter demonstrated how to implement the same functions using the IDfOperation classes. These classes allow developers to concentrate on solving business problems instead of the details of implementing these functions. Using the IDfOperation classes to implement the core library functions give you many benefits, not the least of which is the ability to use the operation monitor. The operation monitor is a UI class, which integrates with the IDfOperation classes to provide user feedback during an operation as well as the opportunity for the user to cancel the operation. Other benefits of the IDfOperation classes include better integration with other Documentum-aware products by recording actions in the Windows registry, insulation from future changes in Documentum architecture, and the ability to handle XML and virtual documents.

Proven Solutions For Common Tasks

This chapter presents a variety of proven solutions for common tasks. These solutions are implemented frequently, because no matter the purpose of the application, solutions to these common tasks are required. I think of these solutions as *staples of the trade*, and this chapter contains more than a dozen of them I have collected over the years.

Unlike previous chapters that focused on single topics with sections of related information, this chapter is composed of many unrelated topics. For example, previous chapters were devoted to queries and collections, and core library functions. This chapter discusses topics ranging from logging in and auditing, to creating paths in the Docbase and Dump and Load. These solutions provide real, value-added functionality to applications and are techniques you need to be familiar with.

The techniques presented in this chapter fall into four broad categories:

- DFC programming techniques and best practices,
- Debugging and auditing techniques,
- Interfacing with resources outside of Documentum, and
- Automating things inside the Docbase.

5.1 Login Using The DFC

The first task any Documentum application or component must accomplish is logging in. The following code snippet illustrates this process in its most basic form..

First, an IDfLoginInfo object is obtained from the IDfClientX object, and populated with a username and password. These values can be hard coded, as in this example, or obtained from the user. The IDfLoginInfo object is then passed to the *IDfClient.newSession()* method, along with the Docbase name, to login and establish a session. If an error occurs, the *IDfClient.newSession()* method raises an exception and Visual Basic displays an error message. There is no need to specifically code an error message for a failed login using this technique.

> **Source Code** A working example of this source code can be found in the "`Chapter5/DFC Login`" directory of the source code archive.

```
Dim cx As DfClientX
Dim client As IDfClient
Dim session As IDfSession
Dim li As IDfLoginInfo

Set cx = New DfClientX
Set client = cx.getLocalClient
Set li = cx.getLoginInfo

li.setUser ("username")
li.setPassword ("password")

Set session = client.newSession("docbase", li)

If (session Is Nothing) Then
    End
End If
```

This is a very simple login technique and is particularly useful in applications that do not prompt the user to login, for example, server methods.

5.2 Login Using The Login Manager

Using the IDfLoginInfo class, as explained above, is fine for applications that don't require direct user input to login. However, if your application requires users to provide a username and password, use the Login Manager to manage the login process. Using the Login Manager makes obtaining and managing sessions easier than with custom code. The Login Manager provides a standard and consistent UI (see Figure 5.1) for logging in, as well as a comprehensive set of rules and methods for obtaining and managing sessions, including "silent logins" or Windows trusted Logins. The Login Manager is the preferred technique for interactive logins.

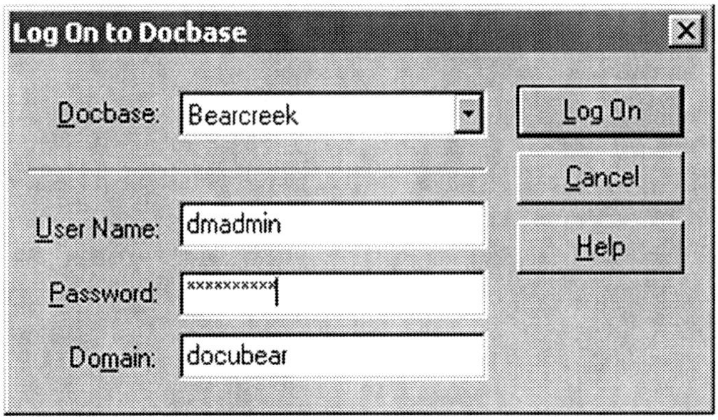

Figure 5.1—Login Manager UI

Using the Login Manager is simple: instantiate one and call the Connect() method. For Example:

```
Dim sessionId As String
Dim loginMgr As New DcLoginManager

sessionId = loginMgr.Connect("docbase", "username", _
                    "password", "domain", ConnectFlag)
```

The combination of variables passed to the Connect() method affect how the login is performed and what options are available in the UI. These variable combinations work as follows:

Docbase and User Name Provided:

1. The Login Manager determines if a session already exists for the given docbase and username (the domain is assumed). If a session exists, its Id is returned, otherwise, the process continues.

2. The Login Manager tries to match the `username` and the `domain` with a profile in the Authentication Manager. The Authentication Manager is a part of the Documentum Desktop that runs silently in the background and coordinates the authentication of users with the OS. If a match is made, the Authentication Manager returns an encrypted password to the Login Manager, which logs in and returns a session Id. If no match is found, the process continues.
3. The Login Manager determines if a session for `docbase` exists under a different user's name. If it does, the Login Manager prompts the user that he will be disconnected from all Docbases by making this connection. If the user chooses to proceed, Login Manager returns a session Id, otherwise, the process continues.
4. The login UI is displayed and the user must provide a `docbase`, `username`, `password`, and `domain` (optional).

Only Docbase Name Provided:

1. The Login Manager determines if a session already exists for the `Docbase`, the `username` is not important. If a session exists, its Id is returned, otherwise, the process continues.
2. The Login Manager attempts to retrieve the current user's profile from the Authentication Manager, login silently, and return the session Id. If no profile exists, the process continues.
3. The login UI is displayed and the user must login by providing `username`, `password`, and `domain` (optional).

Only Home Docbase Name Provided:

1. The Login Manager retrieves the Home Docbase name from the Authentication Manager. If the Home Docbase name passed into the Login Manager matches the Home Docbase name retrieved from the Authentication Manager:
    a. If a `username` is provided, use the same process as **Docbase and User Name Provided**, beginning at step 1.
    b. If no `username` is provided, use the same process as **Docbase and User Name Provided**, beginning at step 2.
2. If the Home Docbase name passed into the Login Manager is blank or does not match the Home Docbase name retrieved from the Authentication Manager, then the process continues.
3. The login UI is displayed and the user must login by providing `docbase`, `username`, `password`, and `domain` (optional).

No Parameters Provided:

1. The login UI is displayed and the user must login by providing `docbase`, `username`, `password`, and `domain` (optional).

The last argument in the `DcLoginManager.Connect()` method signature is the `ConnectFlag`. This argument is an integer value (usually defined as a constant) that adds additional constraints to how the session is established. Table 5.1 describes these values.

Table 5.1—Login Manager ConnectFlag Values

Constant Name	Value	Purpose
DOCBASE_IS_READ_ONLY	1	Forces the **Docbase** combo box on the Login Manager UI to be disabled.
HOME_DOCBASE_TITLE	2	Forces the user to login to their Home Docbase.
IS_DOCBASE_CONNECTED	4	If a session has been previously established, this flag instructs the Login Manager to return the session Id of that session.
USER_IS_READ_ONLY	8	Forces the **User** field on the Login Manager UI to be disabled.
DO_UNIFIED_LOGIN	16	Instructs the Login Manager to perform a Windows Trusted Login, which will attempt to login to the Docbase using the user's current Windows credentials.
DOCBASE_CHOOSER	32	Forces the Login Manager into Docbase chooser mode, allowing only the selection of a Docbase. All other flags are ignored.
	0	Forces the Login Manager into its default behavior. The default behavior is: • look for an existing session (`IS_DOCBASE_CONNECTED`), • attempt a silent login (`DO_UNIFIED_LOGIN`), • finally, display the Login Manager UI.

The following code snippet demonstrates using the Login Manager to connect to a Docbase, obtain a session, and disconnect from the Docbase. Your project must reference the Documentum Login Manager Type Library to use this code.

> **Source Code** A working example of this source code can be found in the "`Chapter5/LoginMgr`" directory of the source code archive.

```
Dim loginMgr As New DcLoginManager
Dim cx As DfClientX
Dim client As IDfClient
Dim session As IDfSession
Dim sessionId As String

' if no session, login
If (sessionId = "") Then
    sessionId = loginMgr.Connect("", "", "", "", 0)   ' force GUI
End If

' if still no session, error out
If (sessionId = "") Then
    MsgBox "Could not Login.", vbCritical, "Could Not Login"
    Set loginMgr = Nothing
    End
Else
    ' set up dfc
    Set cx = New DfClientX
    Set client = cx.getLocalClient
    Set session = client.findSession(sessionId)
End If

' program code here. . .

' disconnect with login mgr
loginMgr.disconnect(sessionId)
Set loginMgr = Nothing
```

Notice passing the `DcLoginManager.Connect()` method empty strings and a `ConnectFlag` of zero will always force the Login Manager to display the login UI. If you would prefer to pre-populate some of the arguments and use a different `ConnectFlag`, you can use any number of techniques to obtain these values from the operating system.

To make the best use of the Login Manager, declare it and the `sessionId` variable global to the main module in your application. This ensures that both exist throughout the life of the application, and makes it easier to manage the session. The DfClientX, IDfClient, and IDfSession variables should be defined locally on each form where they are required.

When you connect to a Docbase using the Login Manager, it returns a session Id string for a shared DFC session. A shared session can be used by any component in the same process as the Login Manager. Thus, you can pass it to forms and other objects. The caveat is that each process must lock and unlock the session when used to prevent collisions. Passing session Ids to forms and session locking are both discussed later in this chapter.

It's important to remember that if you connect to the Docbase using the Login Manager, you *must* disconnect from the Docbase using the Login Manager. Directly disconnecting a session established with the Login Manager can cause instability in your application.

As wonderful as the Login Manager is, it still leaves you with a session that you must manage throughout the life of your application. This management entails passing the session to forms and functions, as well as explicitly locking it during Docbase operations. These tasks are not difficult to implement, and will be discussed later in this chapter.

5.3 Passing A Session To A Form

Most applications consist of more than one form, and most of those forms interact with the Docbase. Therefore, each form must have access to the session. The best way to give a form access to the session is by passing it the session Id (not the session *object*) and requiring each form to instantiate its own DfClientX, IDfClient, and IDfSession objects.

This may not seem like an obvious best practice so let's take a closer look. More than likely, each form will require access to the session or access to the DFC client objects (DfClientX and IDfClient). Since passing objects among forms runs counter to Microsoft best practice, the only options left are: declare the objects global to the application, or instantiate them locally on each form. Declaring the objects global to the application and having each form reach back to the main module to access them is not good programming style and ruins many of the modular and reuse aspects of your code. Therefore, the only option left is to instantiate the objects locally on each form. Though instantiation of these objects does consume overhead, it's not too bad, and the localization of the objects helps to scope and modularize your code.

You saw a preview of this technique in Chapter 2, *Getting Started with Applications and Components*. The following code snippets illustrate this idea in more detail. These code snippets assume you have a form in your application named `aForm` that has a public string variable named `sessionId`. It also assumes the session identifier (returned by the Login Manager) is named `sessionId`.

The calling code looks like this:

Source Code A working example of this source code can be found in the "`Chapter5/Passing Session Id`" directory of the source code archive.

```
Dim theForm As New aForm

' pass session Id to form
theForm.sessionId = sessionId

' show form
theForm.Show vbModal
```

The form code looks like this:

```
' FORM

' passed in
Public sessionId As String

' global to form
Private cx As DfClientX
Private client As IDfClient
Private session As IDfSession

Sub Form_Load()

' this code is usually in the Form_Load method
' to insure it runs first

    ' set up dfc client vars
    Set cx = New DfClientX
    Set client = cx.getLocalClient
    Set session = client.findSession(sessionId)

    ' other code

End Sub
```

It is best to define the DfClientX, IDfClient, and IDfSession objects globally for the form since nearly all of the form's methods will require access to them. To ensure the DfClientX, IDfClient, and IDfSession objects are instantiated first, put their initialization code in the `Form_Load()` subroutine.

As mentioned previously, passing session Ids to forms as strings and instantiating the DFC client objects locally, as demonstrated here, is a Documentum best practice. Passing the session to a form as an IDfSession object is not recommended.

5.4 Session Locking

Shared sessions are great. Using them avoids every process in your application having to establish its own session with the server and consuming memory and resources. They also facilitate data sharing since each process uses the same DMCL cache. However, because they are shared, they require careful management to avoid processes from colliding while accessing the Docbase. To keep processes from clashing over session access, have each process exclusively lock the session before reading data from, or writing data to, the Docbase, and unlock it as soon as the operation is completed.

The easiest way to achieve session locking is to use the DcSessionLock class in your application. Unlike other DFC classes, this one is not packaged as a `.DLL` that must be referenced in your Visual Basic project. Instead, DcSessionLock is a Visual Basic class file that must be added to the project as part of the source code. The `DcSessionLock.cls` file is found in the Documentum Desktop Component Source archive[*]. This class makes session locking easy: simply instantiate a DcSessionLock object, and call its two methods, `GetLock()` and `ReleaseLock()` as appropriate. Your Visual Basic project must reference the Documentum Desktop Client Utilities Manager Type Library because the DcSessionLock class uses it. The following code snippet demonstrates the use of the DcSessionLock class.

> **Source Code** A working example of this source code can be found in the "`Chapter5/Session Lock`" directory of the source code archive.

```
Dim sessionLock As DcSessionLock
Dim sObj As IDfSysObject

Set sessionLock = New DcSessionLock

sessionLock.GetLock session, True, "Lock 1"
```

---

[*] You can download the Documentum Desktop Component Source archive from the Documentum Download Center (`http://documentum.subscribenet.com`).

```
Set sObj = session.GetObject(cx.getId("0900218d8000d145"))
sObj.setTitle ("Testing 1,2,3")
sObj.save

sessionLock.ReleaseLock
```

The `GetLock()` method requires three arguments:

- The session as an IDfSession object,
- `True` or `False`, indicating if tracing should be used, and
- The context string to write to the trace file.

DcSessionLock objects should be defined as needed and not globally. I recommend *not* creating a global DcSessionLock object, but rather instantiating one whenever a session lock is needed. There is no advantage to instantiating one global object and reusing it throughout your application. By instantiating a new one each time it is needed, you can pass a new `context` string and more easily manage the locks, the lock objects, and debug problems. As long as the same IDfSession object is passed to the DcSessionLock object, the same session will be locked.

The DcSessionLock class is useful; however, if a session cannot be locked, the `GetLock()` method just returns `False` instead of retrying. To remedy this problem, I wrote the `lockSession()` function below that wraps the `GetLock()` method.

Source Code A working example of this source code can be found in the "`Chapter5/Lock Session`" directory of the source code archive.

```
Function lockSession(session As IDfSession, context As String) As
        DcSessionLock

    Dim sessLock As New DcSessionLock
    Dim locked As Boolean

    locked = False

    ' Lock the session.  Keep trying until successful
    While (locked = False)
        locked = sessLock.GetLock(session, True, context)
```

```
            If (locked = False) Then
                Debug.Print "Sleeping. . ."
                sleep (1)
            End If
        Wend

        Set lockSession = sessLock
        Set sessLock = Nothing

End Function
```

The `lockSession()` function requires two arguments:

- The session as an IDfSession object, and
- The context string to write to the trace file.

The function instantiates a DcSessionLock object and calls its `GetLock()` method. However, if it fails to achieve a lock, the subroutine sleeps for one second and tries again. This will continue indefinitely until the lock is achieved. In most cases, this is the behavior you want your code to exhibit. It may seen dangerous to loop indefinitely waiting for a lock, but since most applications and components are synchronous, there is minimal risk that another section of your code will be locking the session at the same time. Using this function saves you the time and effort of implementing similar logic every time you try to lock a session, and centralizes the instantiation of all DcSessionLock objects.

Note this function utilizes another function named `sleep()` when it cannot establish a lock. The `sleep()` function does exactly what its name suggests: sleep. The specifics of the `sleep()` function are discussed in the next section.

Using the `lockSession()` function, the previous example now looks like this:

Source Code A working example of this source code can be found in the "`Chapter5/Lock Session`" directory of the source code archive.

```
Dim sessionLock As DcSessionLock
Dim sObj As IDfSysObject

Set sessionLock = lockSession(session, "Lock 1")
```

```
Set sObj = session.GetObject(cx.getId("0900218d8000d145"))
sObj.setTitle ("Testing 1,2,3")
sObj.save

sessionLock.ReleaseLock
```

5.5 A Non-blocking Visual Basic sleep() Function

It's not often that you want to slow down the execution of your program or perform a no-op, but sometimes it is necessary. I can think of two instances when this might be useful. The first is when you are waiting for a process to complete. For example, the QueryManager, discussed in Chapter 3, *Working with Queries and Collections*, and the Sentinel, discussed later in this chapter, both require the main program to wait for them to complete (or be cancelled) before continuing. The `lockSession()` function, discussed in the previous section, also needs to `sleep()` while waiting for the session to become available. The second instance when a `sleep()` might be used is between screen transitions when a lot of processing is required to paint the screen. For example, I often `sleep()` for a second between establishing a successful login using the Login Manager, and presenting the application's main screen. This gives the Login Manager a chance to hide itself, and the main screen time to paint itself. In both of these cases, it is imperative that the `sleep()` function is non-blocking, that is, it allows other processes to continue in the background while it does nothing.

Visual Basic does not have a non-blocking `sleep()` function, nor does the Win32API. The `sleep()` function that follows is non-blocking and is the one I use when I need a process to wait.

> **Source Code** A working example of this source code can be found in the "`Chapter5/Sleep`" directory of the source code archive.

```
Sub sleep(t As Integer)
    Dim EndTime As Date

    EndTime = DateAdd("s", t, Now)
    Do Until Now > EndTime
       DoEvents
    Loop

End Sub
```

Note the `DoEvents()` function inside the `Do Loop,` it is the key to the whole thing. The `DoEvents()` function relinquishes control back to the operating system and the application to process other events. This is what makes the function non-blocking.

Using the `sleep()` function is simple: call the function and provide the number of seconds to sleep as the argument. For example:

```
' sleep for one second
sleep(1)

' sleep for ten seconds
sleep(10)
```

Note you can only sleep for integer durations, that is, you can't sleep for 0.5 seconds.

5.6 Running Documentum Components

There are times when it is necessary to run a Documentum component from your application or from another component. This is similar to how the Documentum Desktop checkin component runs the Properties component when the **Properties** button is clicked. You might face this situation if you write a custom checkin component that forces the user to enter mandatory attributes before proceeding with a checkin. In this case, your component would run the Documentum checkin component after validating that the mandatory attributes were filled.

Whenever you run a component, use the Component Dispatcher, `DcComponent Dispatcher`. You should never directly call the `Init()`, `Run()`, and `DeInit()` methods on the component, though you are able. Documentum components should always be called via the Component Dispatcher; otherwise, you bypass DART, the Cabinet Manager, and all the other features that Documentum provides for component delivery. See Chapter 2, *Getting Started with Applications and Components* for more a detailed discussion about the Component Dispatcher and DART.

To run a component, use the `DcComponentDispatcher.RunComponent()` method. This method requires ten arguments:

```
rv = compDispatcher.runComponent(functionalClass, _
                                 ApplicationName, _
                                 docbaseName, _
                                 userOSName, _
                                 domain, _
                                 items, _
```

```
                              hWndForDialog, _
                              reporter, _
                              StringForIID, _
                              itemContainer)
```

The purpose of each input argument is discussed in Table 5.2.

Table 5.2—DcComponentDispatcher.RunComponent() Input Arguments

No.	Name	Type	Comment
1.	functionalClass	String	Name of the component to run.
2.	applicationName	String	This is the name of the DocApp containing the component. If this argument is left blank, `RunComponent()` will search the default DocApp for the `functionalClass`.
3.	docbaseName	String	Name of the Docbase containing the component.
4.	userOSName	String	Name of the user to run the component.
5.	domain	String	Name of the user's domain. This variable can be left blank and `RunComponent()` will assume the default domain.
6.	Items	DcItems	This is the collection of objects passed into the component. Usually, the component operates on the objects in this collection. The component may also update or add to the objects in this collection and return it to the calling application.
7.	hWndForDialog	Long	The handle for the dialog or form that is calling the component. This is usually the `Me.hWnd` form variable but could also be the Win32 API command `GetDesktopWindow()`.
8.	reporter	IDcReport	This is a report object that allows `RunComponent()` to report errors back to the calling application.
9.	stringForIID	String	Optional. The item container's interface Id (IID) as a string constant. Only applicable if `itemContainer` is defined.
10.	itemContainer	Variant	Optional. The item container's IUnknown interface from which to access the item container interface specified in `stringForIID`.

The following code snippet demonstrates calling the DcProperties component using the Component Dispatcher. The code assumes the Item Server Type Library and the Component Dispatcher Type Library have been referenced in your project.

The `DcComponentDispatcher.RunComponent()` method expects a DcItems object as its sixth input argument. The first few lines of code in the following snippet create a DcItems object from an object Id string for this purpose. The DcItems object holds a reference to the object upon which the called component will operate. For this example, the object Id is `0900218d8007c4d6`.

Source Code A working example of this source code can be found in the "`Chapter5/RunComponent`" directory of the source code archive.

```
' Win32 API
Public Declare Function GetDesktopWindow Lib "user32" () As Long

Dim rv As Long
Dim compDispatcher As New DcComponentDispatcher
Dim reporter As New DcReport
Dim items As New DcItems
Dim itemObj As New DcObjectItem

' build items object
itemObj.id = "0900218d8007c4d6"
items.Type = DC_OBJECT_ITEM_IID_STRING
items.Add itemObj

rv = compDispatcher.runComponent("DcProperties", _
                    "", _
                    session.getDocbaseName, _
                    session.getUser("").getUserOSName, _
                    "", _
                    items, _
                    GetDesktopWindow, _
                    reporter, _
                    "", _
                    "")

' check for errors
' note the use of GetDesktopWindow Win32 API method
If (reporter.GetEntryCount > 0) Then
    reporter.Display GetDesktopWindow, DC_REPORT_OK_ONLY
End If
```

The `DcComponentDispatcher.RunComponent()` returns a long integer constant indicating its status: DC_COMP_SUCCESS, or DC_COMP_FAILURE. In this snippet, in addition to checking the number of entries in the DcReport object, I could also have checked the return code, `rv`, for success for failure.

5.7 Error Trapping

Error trapping can be extremely useful to both the developer and the end user. Unexpected errors that are not handled (i.e., trapped) can result in ungraceful and frustrating program crashes. The technique that follows is simple to implement and allows errors to be handled gracefully.

Error trapping in Visual Basic is implemented with the `On Error` statement. The construct is simple, but the trap code must be comprehensive enough to trap both Visual Basic errors *and* Documentum errors. The easiest way to do this is to use a combination of Documentum DcReport and IDfException objects, and Visual Basic Err objects. The following code snippet demonstrates this technique.

Source Code A working example of this source code can be found in the "`Chapter5/Error Trap`" directory of the source code archive.

```
' Win32 API
Public Declare Function GetDesktopWindow Lib "user32" () As Long

Dim r As New DcReport
Dim e As IDfException

On Error GoTo HandleError

' lots of hairy code here

HandleError:

If (Len(Err.Description) > 0) Then
    Set e = cx.parseException(Err.Description)
    r.AddException e
    r.Display GetDesktopWindow(), DC_REPORT_OK_ONLY
End If
```

This error trap determines if an error occurred by checking the length of the `Description` property in the Err object. Fortunately, when errors occur in the DFC, they are also manifested as Visual Basic errors.

The Err object is used to instantiate an IDfException object and the IDfException object is then added to the DcReport object for display. The DcReport object provides a standard UI to display error messages and has the added benefit of providing a stack trace. The DcReport object needs a window handle to ensure it displays on top of the window where the error occurred. By using the `GetDesktopWindow()` API method, I ensure the DcReport object is always on the top of the window stack.

Figure 5.2 shows an example of the type of error information this code snippet returns to the user.

Something to consider when trapping errors is whether a collection could be open when an error occurs. If one could be, you must close it in the error trap code. A collection can be closed in the trap code like this:

```
' close an open collection
If (Not col Is Nothing) Then
    If (col.getState <> DF_CLOSED_STATE) Then
        col.Close
    End If
End If
```

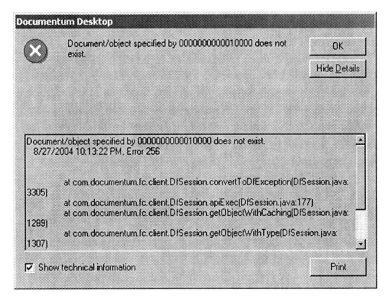

Figure 5.2—DcReport UI Showing Error and Stack Trace

Something else to consider is whether a session lock could be engaged when an error occurs. If one could be, you can release it in the trap code also. For example:

```
' release session lock
If (Not sessionLock Is Nothing) Then
    sessionLock.ReleaseLock
End If
```

Of course, there could be any number of other things that must be closed, released, or otherwise handled in an error trap. Your implementation may vary, but the basic structure and logic demonstrated here provides a base on which to build. You will see this technique put to real use in Chapter 8, *Putting It All Together In A Sample Application*.

Use error trapping judiciously. Remember that errors bubble up through the call stack until they are trapped. Therefore, not every little helper method and subroutine needs an error trap. Little helper methods and subroutines can let their errors bubble up the call stack to their callers.

5.8 Tracing

Tracing is a useful debugging and tuning tool. Tracing is when the server and/or the client records information regarding its actions and interactions to a file. This file can then be reviewed to debug problems or performance issues.

This section discusses three types of tracing: client-side, server-side, and custom. Client-side tracing is provided by Documentum, is enacted on the client, and writes to files on the client. It records the actions of the DFC and the Documentum API as commands are executed on the client. Server-side tracing is also provided by Documentum, is enacted on the server, and writes to files on the server. It records the actions of the server and the database as they execute commands. Custom tracing is implemented on the client by the developer using custom code. It can record whatever information is valuable to the developer, such as execution times of loops, or memory usage. All three types of tracing are valuable, but depending upon your purpose, one may be more useful than another.

5.8.1 Client-Side Tracing

Client-side tracing captures API, DFC, and DQL information, as well as the informational, warning, error, and fatal messages generated by these commands. Client-side tracing can be enabled in three ways:

- From the Properties screen of the Documentum Desktop,
- From the `dmcl.ini` file, and
- Programmatically from an application or component.

I will briefly discuss each of these methods; however, since this book is written for developers, I will give the most attention to the programmatic method. Note the content and format of the trace files produced by Documentum vary depending upon the category and trace level selected. Consult the *Documentum Content Server Administrator's Guide* and *Documentum Desktop User Guide* for details.

5.8.1.1 Properties Screen Of The Documentum Desktop

To enable client-side tracing from the Documentum Desktop icon:

1. Login to the Docbase using the Documentum Desktop.
2. Close the Documentum Desktop window.
3. Right-click the Documentum Desktop icon on the desktop.
4. Choose **Properties**.
5. Click on the **Advanced** tab (see Figure 5.3).
6. Choose a **Category** of event to trace (see Table 5.3 for an explanation of these categories).
7. Choose a severity **Level** (see Table 5.4 for an explanation of these levels). Note that levels are cumulative so choosing severity level 3 will capture levels 1, 2, and 3 messages also.
8. Note the log file name and location is pre-determined: C:\Documentum\logs\trace.log. Also, note that this file is *appended* every time tracing is enabled, so its potential for growth is great.
9. Click **OK**.
10. Restart the Documentum Desktop.

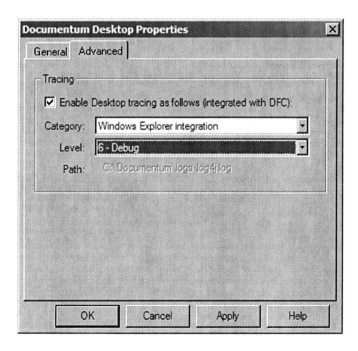

Figure 5.3—Advanced Tab of Documentum Desktop Properties

The categories and levels of tracing are explained in Tables 5.3 and 5.4. Note not all trace levels are applicable to all trace categories.

Table 5.3—Client-Side Trace Categories

Trace Category	Explanation
Component dispatching	Trace dispatching of COM components, including Microsoft Internet Component Delivery (ICD).
Event dispatching	Trace the dispatching of events.
Login management	Trace logins.
Virtual document management	Trace the actions of the Virtual Document Manager.
Windows Explorer integration	Trace the actions of the Documentum Desktop.
Workflow management	Trace workflows.
Enable Desktop tracing as follows (integrated with DFC) checkbox	Enable DFC and API tracing in any of the categories list. Note this checkbox is only active when a Docbase session exists.

Table 5.4—Client-Side Trace Levels

Trace Level	Value	Explanation
None	0	Turns tracing off.
Exceptions	1	Records DFC exceptions.
Errors	2	Records fatal DFC error information.
Interface Entry/Exit	3	Traces all method calls that are members of COM interfaces.
Interface Debug	4	Records detailed trace information about all method calls that are members of COM interfaces.
All Entry/Exit	5	Traces all calls into and out of all methods.
Debug	6	Records more detailed trace information about all method calls.
Object Creation	7	Records Java object creation message.
Object Destruction	8	Records Java object destruction message.
System Memory	10	Records system memory usage.

Following is an excerpt from a log file generated with `Windows Explorer integration` tracing with `Enable Desktop tracing as follows (integrated with DFC)` selected, and the trace level set to `6—Debug` (see Figure 5.3). The event traced was a query for the object named `us_constitution.txt` in the /Temp directory:

```
select r_object_id,object_name from dm_document where FOLDER('/Temp')
and object_name like 'us_con%'
```

With your knowledge of how queries and collections work, you will be able to follow the actions recorded in the log file. I have highlighted a few lines with bold typeface to help you. Note that toward the end of the excerpt I excised some lines to save space.

```
22:19:49,141 [Thread-8] ..djcb::IDfClientX.getQuery() [started]
22:19:49,141 [Thread-8] ..com.documentum.com.DfClientX@12d263f. getQuery()
  [started]
22:19:49,141 [Thread-8] ...com.documentum.fc.client. DfQuery@39ab89.<init>()
  [started]
22:19:49,141 [Thread-8] ...com.documentum.fc.client.DfQuery [finished]
22:19:49,141 [Thread-8] ..getQuery [finished] com.documentum.fc.client.
  DfQuery@39ab89
22:19:49,141 [Thread-8] .djcb::Create Java Object -->com.documentum.fc.
  client.DfQuery (e165c88)
22:19:49,141 [Thread-8] .djcb::IDfClientX.getQuery [finished] com.
  documentum.fc.client.DfQuery@cb84044
22:19:49,141 [Thread-8] ..djcb::IDfQuery.setDQL ('select r_object_id,
  object_name from dm_document where FOLDER('/Temp') and object_name like
  'us_con%') [started]
22:19:49,141 [Thread-8] ..com.documentum.fc.client. DfQuery@39ab89. setDQL
  ('select r_object_id, object_name from dm_document where FOLDER('/Temp')
  and object_name like 'us_con%'') [started]
22:19:49,141 [Thread-8] ..setDQL [finished]
22:19:49,141 [Thread-8] .djcb::IDfQuery.setDQL [finished]
22:19:49,141 [Thread-8] ..djcb::IDfQuery.execute
  ('com.documentum.fc.client.DfSession@cb83ffc, '0) [started]
22:19:49,141 [Thread-8] ..com.documentum.fc.client. DfQuery@39ab89.execute
  ('DfSession@23e5d1', '0') [started]
22:19:49,141 [Thread-8] ...com.documentum.fc.client.
  DfSession@23e5d1.apiGet [SYNCH] ('query_cmd,s0,T,F,,,,,select
  r_object_id, object_name from dm_document where FOLDER('/Temp') and
  object_name like 'us_con%'') [started]
```

```
22:19:49,251 [Thread-8] ...apiGet [finished] q0
22:19:49,251 [Thread-8] ...com.documentum.fc.common. DfId@2cb49d.<init>
  ('q0') [started]
22:19:49,251 [Thread-8] ...com.documentum.fc.common.DfId [finished]
22:19:49,251 [Thread-8] ...com.documentum.fc.client.
  DfTypedObject@105d88a.<init> ('DfSession@23e5d1', 'q0', 'false')
  [started]
22:19:49,251 [Thread-8] ....com.documentum.fc.client.
  DfCollection@105d88a.initialize ('DfSession@23e5d1', 'q0') [started]
22:19:49,251 [Thread-8] ....initialize [finished]
22:19:49,251 [Thread-8] ...com.documentum.fc.client.DfCollection
  [finished]
22:19:49,251 [Thread-8] ...com.documentum.fc.client.
  DfTypedObject@105d88a.<init> ('DfSession@23e5d1', 'q0') [started]
22:19:49,251 [Thread-8] ...com.documentum.fc.client.DfCollection
  [finished]
22:19:49,251 [Thread-8] ...com.documentum.fc.client.
  DfCollection@105d88a.<init> ('DfSession@23e5d1', 'q0', 'true')
  [started]
22:19:49,251 [Thread-8] ....com.documentum.fc.client.
  DfCollection@105d88a.getAttachedSession() [started]
22:19:49,251 [Thread-8] ....getAttachedSession [finished]
  com.documentum.fc.client.DfSession@23e5d1
22:19:49,251 [Thread-8] ....com.documentum.fc.client.
  DfCollection@105d88a.getObjectId() [started]
22:19:49,251 [Thread-8] ....getObjectId [finished] q0
22:19:49,251 [Thread-8] ....com.documentum.fc.common.DfId@ddf. isNull()
  [started]
22:19:49,251 [Thread-8] ....isNull [finished] 'false'
22:19:49,251 [Thread-8] ...com.documentum.fc.client.DfCollection
  [finished]
22:19:49,251 [Thread-8] ..execute [finished]
  com.documentum.fc.client.DfCollection@105d88a
22:19:49,261 [Thread-8] .djcb::Create Java Object --
  >com.documentum.fc.client.DfCollection (e165c90)
22:19:49,261 [Thread-8] .djcb::IDfQuery.execute [finished]
  com.documentum.fc.client.DfCollection@cb8412c
```

```
< snip >
22:19:49,261 [Thread-8] ..djcb::IDfCollection.getAttrCount() [started]
< snip >
22:19:49,281 [Thread-8] .djcb::IDfCollection.getAttrCount [finished] 2
< snip >
22:19:49,291 [Thread-8] ..djcb::IDfCollection.getAttr (0) [started]
< snip >
22:19:49,311 [Thread-8] ..getAttr [finished] DfAttr: name: r_object_id;
   repeating: false; type: DM_STRING; length: 16
```

Obviously, higher trace levels produce more output than lower ones. Be aware of this: Documentum traces are *very* verbose. Not only can you fill up your hard drive, but who wants to wade through megabytes of information looking for a particular trace message? Tracing implemented in this fashion should be used sparingly.

5.8.1.2 DMCL.INI *File*

Client-side tracing can also be enabled from the dmcl.ini file. The tracing level specified in the dmcl.ini file is for API[*] tracing *only*. API tracing can produce very granular trace results since the DFC calls into the API to communicate with the Documentum Server. This trace method produces trace files that contain much different information than ones produced by the Documentum Desktop. In addition to the API calls themselves, these files often contain communication messages between the client and server, as well as the DQL passed between them. You will notice that this trace file's format is a little cleaner than the DFC trace file's format.

To enable tracing in the dmcl.ini file, add the following name-value pairs to the [DMAPI_CONFIGURATION] section of the file.

- trace_file = <full path and name of trace file>
- trace_level = <numeric trace level from Table 5.5>

---

[*] API tracing is also known as DMCL tracing.

Table 5.5—API Trace Levels

Trace Level	Value	Explanation
None	0	Turns tracing off.
Level 1 Messages	1	Records informational messages only.
Level 2 Messages	2	Records informational and warning messages.
Level 3 Messages	3	Records informational, warning, and error messages.
Level 4 Messages	4	Records informational, warning, error, and fatal error messages.
Timing Information	10	Records all messages plus timing statistics.
Load Operation Information	11	Records information regarding loading of data objects during Load operations.

Here is a sample `dmcl.ini` file that enables API tracing:

```
[DOCBROKER_PRIMARY]
host = 192.168.0.1

[DMAPI_CONFIGURATION]
trace_level = 10
trace_file = c:\Documentum\logs\dmcl-trace-10.log
```

The `dmcl.ini` file is read by the Documentum Desktop when it first starts, and then not again—even if you close the Documentum Desktop window. Therefore, if you modify the `dmcl.ini` file while the Documentum Desktop is running, you will need to restart it before the changes will take affect. Chapter 7, *Tips, Tools and Handy Information*, discuss how to do this. When you use the `dmcl.ini` file to trace a custom Documentum Desktop application, it is read every time the application initializes the DFC.

Following is an excerpt from a log file generated with API tracing level 10 enabled through the `dmcl.ini` file. The same query traced in the previous section is also traced here:

```
select  r_object_id,object_name  from  dm_document  where  FOLDER('/Temp')
and object_name like 'us_con%'
```

Again, I highlighted a few lines in bold typeface to help you follow along.

```
# [ 3676 ] 22:50:41 2004 334000 (0.000 sec) (143 rpc) API>
  query_cmd,s0,T,F,select r_object_id, object_name from dm_document where
  FOLDER('/Temp') and object_name like 'us_con%'
# [ 3676 ] 22:50:41 2004 334000 (0.000 sec) (143 rpc) Server RPC: EXEC
  (0000000000000000) select r_object_id, object_name from dm_document
  where FOLDER('/Temp') and object_name like 'us_con%'
# [ 3676 ] 22:50:41 2004 354000 (0.020 sec) (144 rpc) Res: 'q0'
# [ 3676 ] 22:50:41 2004 354000 (0.000 sec) (144 rpc) API> count,s0,q0
# [ 3676 ] 22:50:41 2004 354000 (0.000 sec) (144 rpc) Res: '2'
# [ 3676 ] 22:50:41 2004 354000 (0.000 sec) (144 rpc) API>
  get,s0,q0,_names[0]
# [ 3676 ] 22:50:41 2004 354000 (0.000 sec) (144 rpc) Res: 'r_object_id'
# [ 3676 ] 22:50:41 2004 354000 (0.000 sec) (144 rpc) API>
  get,s0,q0,_repeating[0]
# [ 3676 ] 22:50:41 2004 354000 (0.000 sec) (144 rpc) Res: '0'
# [ 3676 ] 22:50:41 2004 354000 (0.000 sec) (144 rpc) API>
  get,s0,q0,_lengths[0]
# [ 3676 ] 22:50:41 2004 354000 (0.000 sec) (144 rpc) Res: '16'
# [ 3676 ] 22:50:41 2004 354000 (0.000 sec) (144 rpc) API>
  get,s0,q0,_types[0]
# [ 3676 ] 22:50:41 2004 354000 (0.000 sec) (144 rpc) Res: '2'
```

Notice the difference in content between this trace file and the previous one, even though they were tracing the same event. The previous trace file exposed the inner workings of the DFC where this one exposes the API commands generated by the DFC.

5.8.1.3 Programmatically

Programmatically, you can enable both DFC and API client-side tracing, but since the API is not the focus of this book, I will not discuss it in detail. Instead, I will concentrate on how to enable and use tracing from the DFC.

5.8.1.3.1 API

The basic API trace command is:

```
dmAPIExec("trace,c,<trace level>")
```

The value for <trace level> is any API trace value from Table 5.5. Chapter 7, *Tips, Tools and Handy Information,* provides details for using API commands. See the *Documentum Content Server API Reference Manual* for more information about the `trace()` API method.

5.8.1.3.2 DFC

In the DFC, tracing is controlled by the DfClientX class. The following code snippet demonstrates an easy way to start and stop DFC tracing programmatically. Refer to Table 5.4 for the definitions of the different trace levels.

```
Dim cx As New DfClientX

' start tracing
cx.setTraceLevel (10)
cx.setTraceFileName ("c:\Documentum\logs\dfc-trace-10.log")

' your code here

' stop tracing
cx.setTraceLevel (0)
```

The example above is a fine technique to use during development and testing when the source code of your application is available and can be recompiled when needed. However, often you need to debug and troubleshoot problems after your application has gone to testing—or worse, is in production. To do this, a more dynamic technique for controlling tracing is needed. The following code snippet demonstrates a technique for dynamically controlling tracing in your application. It utilizes arguments passed on the command line when the application starts to enable tracing. These arguments can also be encapsulated in the application's shortcut or Start menu item if necessary.

Source Code A working example of this source code can be found in the "`Chapter5/Tracing`" directory of the source code archive.

```
Dim cx As New DfClientX
Dim cmd() As String
Dim cmdLine As String

' to start tracing, start program with:  c:\>tracing.exe debug 10

cmdLine = Command()
If (cmdLine <> "") Then
```

```
    cmd() = Split(cmdLine, " ")
    If (LCase(cmd(0)) = "debug") Then
        cx.setTraceFileName App.EXEName & ".log"
        cx.setTraceLevel cmd(1)
    End If
End If

cx.traceMsg "Start Trace:  " & Time

' your code here

cx.setTraceLevel (0)
```

This code snippet examines the command line arguments, and if they meet the criteria (i.e., the word "debug" followed by a number), sets up tracing in the DFC. The trace level is set to the value passed on the command line, and the trace file is named after the application. This snippet also demonstrates how to write your own debugging messages into the trace file using the `DfClientX.traceMsg()` method.

To initiate tracing for an application using this technique, use command line syntax like this (assume your program is named `tracing.exe`):

```
C:> tracing.exe debug 10
```

The tracing level will be set to DFC Level 10 (`System Memory`) and the trace file will be named `tracing.log`.

5.8.2 Server-Side Tracing

Server-side tracing captures server activity messages, as well as informational, warning, error, and fatal error messages. All server-side tracing information is written to the server log file. Server-side tracing can be enabled in two ways:

- Setting the trace flag on the server startup command line
- Using the `apply()` API method

Remember, server-side trace captures messages not only from your session, but from all sessions. These messages are recorded in the server log, and have the potential for consuming a large amount of disk space very quickly. I recommend that you only enable server-side tracing for short periods of time to minimize the size of the log files.

5.8.2.1 Server Startup Command Line

You can enable server-side tracing by adding the trace flag (-o) at the end of the command line argument list used to start the Documentum Server. The easiest way to do this is by editing the **Service** definition for the Docbase in the Documentum Server Manager utility.

1. Start the **Documentum Server Manager** utility by selecting it from the **Start** menu. The interface for the **Documentum Server Manager** is shown in Figure 5.4

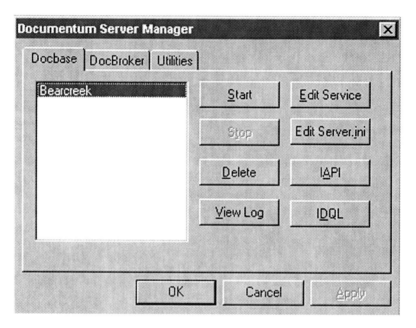

Figure 5.4—Documentum Content Server Manager

2. Select a Docbase and click the **Edit Service** button. The **Edit Service** dialog box is displayed (see Figure 5.5).
3. Add—o and a trace level value from Table 5.6 to the startup parameters in the **Command** field. For example: -odebug
4. Click **OK**.
5. Stop and restart the Docbase for the trace command to take affect.
6. Close the Documentum Server Manager utility.

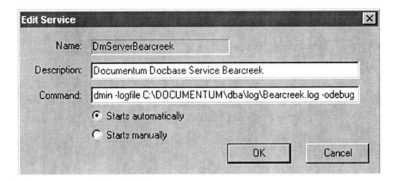

Figure 5.5—Edit Service Dialog

Table 5.6—Server-Side Trace Levels

Trace Level	Explanation
debug	Records session shutdown, change check, launch, and fork messages.
lock_trace	Records Windows NT locking information.
sqltrace	Records SQL queries and commands sent to the RDBMS.
nettrace	Records RPC trace information.
trace_authentication	Records details about user authentication.
net_ip_addr	Records client and server IP addresses.
trace_complete_launch	Records Unix process launch information.
docbroker_trace	Records DocBroker information and messages.

5.8.2.2 API

While the server is running, server-side tracing can be enabled (and disabled) by using the `apply()` API method. This API method can be issued from the API editor in the Documentum Administrator, the `iapi32.exe` command line utility[*], or from within an application. The format of the `apply()` method used to enable tracing is:

    apply,c,NULL,SET_OPTIONS,OPTIONS,S,<option name>,VALUE,B,T

Use one of the trace levels from Table 5.6 in place of <option name>. For example, to enable SQL tracing use:

    apply,c,NULL,SET_OPTIONS,OPTIONS,S,sqltrace,VALUE,B,T

---

[*] See Chapter 7, *Tips, Tools and Handy Information*, for more information regarding the `iapi32.exe` utility.

Changing the trailing T to an F will disable tracing. To discontinue SQL tracing, use:

```
apply,c,NULL,SET_OPTIONS,OPTIONS,S,sqltrace,VALUE,B,F
```

The `apply()` API method is a very powerful administrative tool. You must have at least, System Administrator privileges in the Docbase to use the `apply()` API method. I recommend reviewing the *Documentum Content Server API Reference Manual* to understand its full capabilities.

5.8.3 Custom Tracing

This section discusses how to implement a custom tracing technique. Similar to the tracing techniques discussed previously, this technique writes trace information to a log file. Unlike the previous techniques, it also writes to the Visual Basic IDE **Immediate** window. The beauty of this technique is it only captures and writes the exact information that you need to successfully debug and optimize your application. It is able to accomplish this because you control the information it writes to the log file. Therefore, it is easy to tweak and tune to provide the most valuable output for your situation. There are many other tracing techniques and tools discussed by numerous Documentum resources;[*] I refer you to those resources instead of rehashing them here.

The implementation of this technique is contained in a simple subroutine. This subroutine produces output in an easy to read, standardized format. It assumes the `gDEBUG` Boolean variable is defined globally in your application and the DFC trace level has been set to a value greater than 0 using the `IDfClient.setTraceLevel()` method. Based upon these variables, the subroutine will record trace messages to the log file, the Visual Basic **Immediate** window, one or the other, or neither. Note the use of the Win32 API function `GetTickCount()` to provide millisecond granularity in the trace file.

> **Source Code** A working example of this source code can be found in the "`Chapter5/Debug`" directory of the source code archive.

```
' Win32 API declaration
Private Declare Function GetTickCount Lib "kernel32" () As Long

Sub outputDebugMsg(caller As String, msg As String)

    msg = Now() & " - " & GetTickCount() & " - " & caller _
        & ": " & msg
```

---

[*] See Documentum Technical Support Note #7700 for a discussion of interpreting trace files. Also, the *Documentum Application Performance and Tuning* guide makes extensive use of trace files for performance tuning and does an excellent job of explaining them.

```
    ' ouput to trace file
    If (cx.getTraceLevel > 0) Then
        cx.traceMsg (msg)
    End If

    ' output to immediate window
    If (gDEBUG > 0) Then
        Debug.Print msg
    End If

End Sub
```

The subroutine requires two arguments:

- The name of the subroutine/function/module calling the *outputDebugMsg()* subroutine. Unfortunately, it is necessary to pass this information into the subroutine because Visual Basic does not provide a way to easily glean the caller's name from the IDE, the OS, or the stack.
- The message to be written to the file.

To use the subroutine, simply define the global gDEBUG variable and call the subroutine as illustrated below.

```
Private Const gDEBUG = 1        ' 0 to disable

Sub main()

    Call outputDebugMsg("main", "Start Trace")

' your code here

    Call outputDebugMsg("main", "End Trace")

End Sub
```

The format of the output debug message is:

```
<date/time> - <milliseconds> - <caller name> : <debug message>
```

where:

- `<date/time>` is the date and time the debug message was written.
- `<milliseconds>` are the number of milliseconds since the CPU was last rebooted. This value provides a more granular measure of duration than the date/time stamp does.
- `<caller name>` is the name of the subroutine/function/module calling the subroutine.
- `<debug message>` is the message you passed to the subroutine.

The following is sample output from the **Immediate** window generated by the `outputDebugMsg()` subroutine.

```
6/14/2002 10:27:47 AM - 95689734 - main: Start Trace
6/14/2002 10:27:47 AM - 95689754 - collectionCount1: query count: 1
6/14/2002 10:27:47 AM - 95689774 - collectionCount1: row: 090030398000015c
   TargetSetup.Result
6/14/2002 10:27:47 AM - 95689784 - collectionCount2: row: 090030398000015c
   TargetSetup.Result
6/14/2002 10:27:47 AM - 95689784 - collectionCount2: count = 1
6/14/2002 10:27:47 AM - 95690475 - main: End Trace
```

From this output, it is easy to determine that the `main()` subroutine ran for 741 milliseconds by subtracting the millisecond value recorded with `Start Trace` (95689734) from the millisecond value recorded with `End Trace` (95690475). If DFC tracing was enabled (i.e., `cx.getTraceLevel() > 0`), these messages were written to the Documentum trace file (`c:\Documentum\logs\trace.log`) also.

5.9 Auditing

Auditing captures information about system events and records it in protected objects in the Docbase. This information can then be analyzed to determine access patterns, user activity, or reconstruct security events. Documentum provides the capability to automatically audit over 65 system events. The only requirement to enable auditing of one or all of these events is for a System Administrator to configure it through the Documentum Administrator. For more information on how to set up auditing, see the *Documentum Content Server Administrator's Guide*.

The auditing described in this section is custom auditing. This means that the events audited are not among the 65-plus events Documentum has defined. In this section, I will show you how to programmatically create Documentum audit records for any action that takes place in the Docbase. In addition, this auditing does not require any action from the System Administrator; the code takes care of it all.

Documentum's audit trail is maintained in dm_audittrail objects. The dm_audittrail objects have six named attributes, five generic string attributes, and five generic Id attributes. The six named attributes are mandatory and must contain valid entries. However, only five are mutable; one is maintained by the server. For system-defined events (i.e., one of the more than 65 Documentum has defined), the server provides values for these attributes automatically. The five string and five Id attributes are not mandatory and are provided to hold custom values. The six named attributes are summarized in Table 5.7

Table 5.7—Mandatory dm_audittrail Attributes

Attribute Name	Type	Comment
event_name	String	The name of the event that generated the audit entry.
event_source	String	The name of the source of the event.
user_name	String	The name of the user whose event caused the audit entry.
audited_obj_id	Id	The r_object_id of the object on which the event occurred.
time_stamp	Time	The time and date the event occurred.
r_gen_source	Number	This attribute is automatically set by the server and is immutable. It contains 0 if the event is user-defined, 1 if the event is system-defined.

The five generic string attributes are named string_1 through string_5, and the five generic Id attributes are named id_1 through id_5.

To programmatically create an audit trail entry, simply create a dm_audittrail object as you would any other object; provide values for the five mandatory attributes that you can update; provide values for any of the generic attributes you need; and save the object. The snippet of code below demonstrates this process.

In this example, an event named "New audit entry created" occurs on an object with Id of 090023eb8000015b. The source of the event is a test program and the user is the currently logged in user. After the five mandatory attributes are filled, the code snippet inserts values into two of the generic string attributes.

Source Code A working example of this source code can be found in the "`Chapter5/Audit`" directory of the source code archive.

```
Dim pObj As IDfPersistentObject

' create audit trail object
Set pObj = session.newObject("dm_audittrail")

' enter mandatory attributes
' NOTE: r_gen_source is not an update-able attribute
pObj.setString "event_name", "New audit entry created"
pObj.setString "event_source", "test program"
pObj.setString "user_name", session.getUser("").getUserOSName
pObj.setString "audited_obj_id", "090023eb8000015b "
pObj.setString "time_stamp", Now

' enter optional attributes
pObj.setString "string_1", "The name of the object: " _
    & "090023eb8000015b is in string_2"

pObj.setString "string_2", session.GetObject(cx.getId _
             ("090023eb8000015b ")).getString("object_name")

' save audit record
pObj.save
```

After running this code, you can examine the audit trail using the Documentum Administrator, or use the following code snippet.

Source Code A working example of this source code can be found in the "`Chapter5/Audit`" directory of the source code archive.

```
    Dim q As IDfQuery
    Dim col As IDfCollection
    Dim attr As IDfAttr
    Dim numCols As Integer
    Dim i As Integer
```

```
' query the audit trail object
Set q = cx.getQuery
q.setDQL "select * from dm_audittrail where audited_obj_id" _
    & " = '090023eb8000015b'"
Set col = q.execute(session, DF_READ_QUERY)

' get number of attrs in collection
numCols = col.getAttrCount

' iterate over collection and process each row
While (col.Next = True)

    ' process each column in a row
    For i = 1 To numCols
        Set attr = col.GetAttr(i - 1)
        Debug.Print i & ": " & attr.getName & " = " _
                    & col.getValue(attr.getName).asString
    Next i
Wend
col.Close
```

The output from this code snippet looks like this:

```
1:  r_object_id = 5f0023eb80000901
2:  event_name = New audit entry created
3:  event_source = dm_book tester program
4:  user_name = dmadmin
5:  audited_obj_id = 090023eb8000015b
6:  time_stamp = 12/30/2002 23:56:24
7:  string_1 = The name of the object: 090023eb8000015b is in string_2
8:  string_2 = TargetSetup.Result
9:  string_3 =
10: string_4 =
11: string_5 =
12: id_1 = 0000000000000000
13: id_2 = 0000000000000000
14: id_3 = 0000000000000000
15: id_4 = 0000000000000000
16: id_5 = 0000000000000000
```

As you can see, this query returns all 16 of the `dm_audittrail`'s attributes. Notice how it includes the five generic string attributes, and the five generic Id attributes. You can easily modify the collection-processing loop if a more elegant presentation of this data is needed.

5.10 Using The Progress Sentinel

The progress sentinel is a class you see in action whenever you launch the Documentum Desktop or a component. It's the little window that pops up letting you know the class is initializing or loading, as in Figure 5.7.

The progress sentinel is a class similar to the operation monitor discussed in Chapter 4, *Implementing Core Document Management Functions*. It provides user feedback during an operation, and optionally allows users to cancel the operation. However, unlike the operation monitor class, *all* of the programming work is up to you. The class is simple; it displays and hides itself, updates the percentage complete, and indicates when the **Cancel** button is clicked. Similar to the operation monitor, it runs as its own process so other code in your application can run simultaneously.

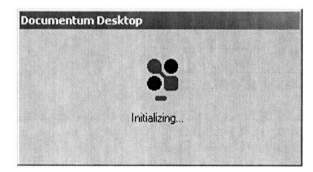

Figure 5.7—The Progress Sentinel

The code snippet below illustrates a very simple implementation of the progress sentinel. While the sentinel is displayed, the code updates the percentage complete property every second as it waits for you to click the **Cancel** button. Your project must reference the Documentum Progress Sentinel Type Library to run this code.

Source Code A working example of this source code can be found in the "`Chapter5/Progress Sentinel`" directory of the source code archive.

```
' Win32 API declares
Public Declare Function GetDesktopWindow Lib "user32" () As Long

Dim sentinel As New DCPROGRESSSENTINELLIB.Progress
Dim i As Integer

' set up the sentinel
sentinel.Message = "This is the Progess Sentinel"
sentinel.Title = "Operation in Progress..."
sentinel.ShowDialog GetDesktopWindow

i = 0
While ((sentinel.Cancelled = False) And (i < 10))
    sleep (1)
    i = i + 1
    sentinel.PercentComplete = (i * 10)
Wend

sentinel.HideDialog

If (sentinel.Cancelled = True) Then
    MsgBox "You clicked cancel on the sentinel when i = " _
            & i, vbInformation, "Sentinel Cancel"
End If
```

This code snippet produces the progress sentinel shown in Figure 5.8

Figure 5.8—Example Sentinel

Though simple, this snippet effectively illustrates how the progress sentinel works. It also shows the programming effort required to make the underlying process aware of the sentinel's cancel event. Unlike the operation monitor class, this class does not undo anything when the cancel event occurs. The progress sentinel is a fun and useful class, and gives your application a professional polish.

5.11 Using The Registry

Like most Microsoft Windows applications, the Documentum Desktop makes use of the registry. Among other things, the Documentum Desktop uses it to persist the identity and location of files checked out for editing, viewing, and deletion. If you haven't browsed the Documentum registry keys, take a look at them. The Documentum root registry key is HKEY_LOCAL_MACHINE\SOFTWARE\Documentum, and the user specific key is HKEY_CURRENT_USER\SOFTWARE\Documentum[*].

Documentum provides several convenient classes in the DFC for accessing the Windows registry. One of the most useful is the DcRegistryKey class and will be discussed in more detail in following sections. At first glance, it would appear that the IDfRegistry class would also be useful. This class appears to provide access to the registry and its contents with methods that return easy-to-use-data structures. Unfortunately, it has some serious limitations that render it all but useless. Not the least of which is, it is generally undocumented and unsupported. As attractive as this class and its methods appear, don't use it. Documentum maintains this class is for *internal use only* and is not supported. If you peruse the source code provided in the Documentum Desktop Component Source archive[**], you will not find one mention of this class, even though several of the components clearly use the registry. In every case where the Windows registry is accessed, Documentum wrote custom code using the Microsoft Win32 API as opposed to using this class.

Fortunately, all the other registry-related DFC classes work fine. This section will use several of them to accomplish three common tasks:

- Accessing the registry and reading/writing key values,
- Enumerating subkeys, and
- Accessing checked out files.

---

[*] Documentum's Windows registry keys changed slightly throughout the 4i and 5 releases, and from operating system to operating system. You might need to make slight adjustments to the registry keys discussed in this section to accommodate your version of Documentum and your operating system.

[**] You can download the Documentum Desktop Component Source archive from the Documentum Download Center (http://documentum.subscribenet.com).

5.11.1 Accessing The Registry

The IDfRegistry class insulates you from much of the ugliness of accessing the Windows registry. It provides the basic functionality and control necessary to effectively and *easily* use the Windows registry in applications. The code snippet below demonstrates how easy this class is to use by opening the `HKEY_CURRENT_USER\Software\Documentum\Common\LastConnectedDocbase` key, reading the `User` value, writing a test value, and closing the key. Your project must reference the Documentum Desktop Client Utilities Manager Type Library to run this code.

Source Code A working example of this source code can be found in the "`Chapter5/Registry`" directory of the source code archive.

```
Dim regObj As New DcRegistryKey
Dim user As String

regObj.open regObj.UserHiveHkey, "Software\Documentum\Common\" _
        & "LastConnectedDocbase"
user = regObj.ReadStringValue("User")
MsgBox "user=" & user, vbInformation, "User"
regObj.WriteStringValue "test", "test"
regObj.Close
```

The DcRegistryKey class makes it easy to read and write Windows registry keys. If you know the key, you can read or write its value with a simple method call. You can use `regedit.exe` to verify the changes this code snippet made to the `HKEY_CURRENT_USER\Software\Documentum\Common\LastConnectedDocbase` key.

Another useful class for dealing with the Windows registry is the IDfClientRegistry class. This class provides easy access to Documentum object and Desktop information stored in the Windows registry. It is used mostly to retrieve and persist information necessary to implement library services. IDfClientRegistry objects are manufactured by the DfClientX class. The next section discusses how to use the class to access checked out files.

5.11.2 Accessing Checked Out Files

If you want to determine if a file is checked out and what its local file path is, you can use the methods of the IDfClientRegistry and IDfCheckedOutObject classes. The following snippet demonstrates this technique. It determines if an object with Id of `0900218d800895eb` is checked out.

Source Code A working example of this source code can be found in the "`Chapter5/Checked Out Files`" directory of the source code archive.

```
Dim reg As IDfClientRegistry
Dim chkObj As IDfCheckedOutObject

Set reg = cx.getClientRegistry

Set chkObj = reg.getCheckedOutObjectById _
    (cx.getId("0900218d800895eb"))

' if not checked out, chkObj will be Nothing
If (Not chkObj Is Nothing) Then
    MsgBox chkObj.getFilePath, vbInformation, "Checked out path"
Else
    MsgBox "Not checked out", vbInformation, "Not checked out"
End If
```

You can similarly access viewed objects in the Windows registry by replacing the chkObj variable with vwObj of type IDfViewedObject, and using the *IDfClientRegistry.getViewedObjectById()* method.

```
Dim reg As IDfClientRegistry
Dim vwObj As IDfViewedOutObject

Set reg = cx.getClientRegistry

Set chkObj = reg.getViewedObjectById _
    (cx.getId("0900218d800895eb"))

' if not viewed, vwObj will be Nothing
If (Not vwObj Is Nothing) Then
    MsgBox vwObj.getFilePath, vbInformation, "Viewed path"
Else
    MsgBox "Not viewed", vbInformation, "Not viewed"
End If
```

5.11.3 Enumerating Subkeys

One capability the DcRegistryKey class does not provide is the ability to enumerate subkeys. That is, it does not provide a method to list or manipulate the subkeys of a known key. For example, you might search the Windows registry to determine whether a document is checked out on the current workstation[*]. This would require enumerating the `HKEY_LOCAL_MACHINE\USER\Software\Documentum\Common\WorkingFiles` key looking for a subkey with a particular value. Wouldn't it be nice to obtain a list of subkeys from the Windows registry, so they could be easily manipulated? The following code snippet demonstrates just how to do that.

This example looks through the Windows registry keys the Documentum Desktop uses to track checked out files to determine if a document with an Id of `0900218d80034cc7` has been checked out on this workstation. Your project must reference the Documentum Desktop Client Utilities Manager Type Library to run this code.

> **Source Code** A working example of this source code can be found in the "`Chapter5/Registry`" directory of the source code archive.

```
Dim regObj As New DcRegistryKey
Dim subKeyList As IDfList
Dim objId As String
Dim filename As String
Dim i As Integer

' call function to get subkeys as list
Set subKeyList = getRegSubKeyList(regObj.UserHiveHkey, _
                "Software\Documentum\Common\WorkingFiles")

' iterate through list object searching for Id
For i = 0 To subKeyList.getCount - 1

    regObj.open regObj.UserHiveHkey, _
        "Software\Documentum\Common\WorkingFiles\" _
        & subKeyList.getString(i)
```

---

[*] You could, of course, determine this using the IDfClientRegistry and IDfCheckedOutObject objects as demonstrated in the previous section.

```
    If (regObj.ReadStringValue("MasterObjectId") = _
               "0900218d80034cc7") Then

        ' now that you found the right subkey, do something
        ' with it

        MsgBox "Found it!"

    End If

    regObj.Close
Next i
```

The key to this example is the *getRegSubKeyList()* function. This function provides the subkey enumeration functionality missing from the DcRegistryKey class. The *getRegSubKeyList()* function returns subkeys in an IDfList object so they can be easily enumerated or otherwise manipulated.

The *getRegSubKeyList()* function follows, and is a good example of the type of programming the DcRegistry class has insulated you from doing. Before you use the function, you need to make a few declarations at the beginning of your code. The following snippet registers the four Win32 API functions necessary to manipulate the registry, as well as the constants and data types they use.[*]

Source Code A working example of this source code can be found in the "**Chapter5/Registry**" directory of the source code archive.

```
' Win32 API Registry Declarations
Private Declare Function RegOpenKeyEx Lib "advapi32.dll" Alias _
        "RegOpenKeyExA" (ByVal hKey As Long, ByVal lpSubKey As _
        String, ByVal ulOptions As Long, ByVal samDesired As _
        Long, ByRef phkResult As Long) As Long

Private Declare Function RegQueryInfoKey Lib "advapi32.dll" _
        Alias "RegQueryInfoKeyA" (ByVal hKey As Long, ByVal _
        lpClass As String, lpcbClass As Long, ByVal lpReserved _
```

---

[*] These Win32 API declaration statements and constant definitions can be easily obtained from the *API Text Viewer* installed as part of the Visual Studio tools.

```
           As Long, lpcSubKeys As Long, lpcbMaxSubKeyLen As Long, _
       lpcbMaxClassLen As Long, lpcValues As Long, _
       lpcbMaxValueNameLen As Long, lpcbMaxValueLen As Long, _
       lpcbSecurityDescriptor As Long, _
       lpftLastWriteTime As FILETIME) As Long

Private Declare Function RegEnumKeyEx Lib "advapi32.dll" Alias _
       "RegEnumKeyExA" (ByVal hKey As Long, ByVal dwIndex As _
       Long, ByVal lpName As String, lpcbName As Long, ByVal _
       lpReserved As Long, ByVal lpClass As String, lpcbClass _
       As Long, lpftLastWriteTime As FILETIME) As Long

Private Declare Function RegCloseKey Lib "advapi32.dll" (ByVal _
       hKey As Long) As Long

' Win32 API Registry Constants
Private Const HKEY_LOCAL_MACHINE = &H80000002
Private Const ERROR_SUCCESS = 0&
Private Const STRING_BUFFER_SIZE = 256
Private Const KEY_ALL_ACCESS = 983103

' Registry Types
Private Type FILETIME
    dwLowDateTime As Long
    dwHighDateTime As Long
End Type
```

In general, the *getRegSubKeysList()* function opens the Windows registry key name passed to it, and determines if it has any subkeys by using the Win32 API *RegQueryInfoKey()* function. If it does, it iterates over the subkeys using the Win32 API *RegEnumKeyEx()* function to collect the subkey names. It then packages the names into an IDfList object and returns it. Note these Win32 APIs return status codes and not the values from the registry. Registry values are returned in arguments passed into the functions by reference.

The *getRegSubKeysList()* function requires two arguments:

- The hive as a long integer. The hive is usually defined as a constant (e.g., HKEY_LOCAL_MACHINE).
- The key's path as a string.

Source Code A working example of this source code can be found in the "**Chapter5/Registry**" directory of the source code archive.

```
Function getRegSubKeyList(hive As Long, Path As String) As _
    IDfList
    Dim hPathKey As Long
    Dim keyList As IDfList
    Dim rc As Long
    Dim keyName As String
    Dim keyNameLen As Long
    Dim keyClassName As String
    Dim keyClassNameLen As Long
    Dim numSubKeys As Long
    Dim numKeyValues As Long
    Dim lastWriteTime As FILETIME
    Dim i As Integer

    Set keyList = cx.getList()

    ' registry APIs want all this stuff pre-set
    keyNameLen = STRING_BUFFER_SIZE
    keyClassNameLen = STRING_BUFFER_SIZE
    keyName = String(keyNameLen, 0)
    keyClassName = String(keyClassNameLen, 0)

    ' open the path key
    If (RegOpenKeyEx(hive, Path, KEY_ALL_ACCESS, hPathKey) = _
        ERROR_SUCCESS) Then

        ' see if there are any subkeys.
        If (RegQueryInfoKey(hPathKey, keyClassName, _
            keyClassNameLen, numSubKeys, 1024, 1024, _
            numKeyValues, 1024, 1024, KEY_ALL_ACCESS, _
            lastWriteTime) = ERROR_SUCCESS) Then

            ' numsubKeys returned by RegQueryInfoKey API function

            ' if there are subkeys, process them
            If (numSubKeys > 0) Then
                For i = 0 To numSubKeys - 1
```

```
                    ' registry APIs want all this stuff pre-set
                    keyNameLen = STRING_BUFFER_SIZE
                    keyClassNameLen = STRING_BUFFER_SIZE
                    keyName = String(keyNameLen, 0)
                    keyClassName = String(keyClassNameLen, 0)

                    ' get the subkey name
                    rc = RegEnumKeyEx(hPathKey, i, keyName, _
                        keyNameLen, keyClassName, _
                        keyClassNameLen, lastWriteTime)

                    ' keyName, keyNameLen returned by
                    ' RegEnumKeyEx API function

                    ' append subkey name to list object
                    keyList.appendString Left(keyName, _
                        keyNameLen)
                Next i

            Else
                Set keyList = Nothing
            End If

        Else
            MsgBox "Error on RegQueryInfoKey for key " _
                & hPathKey, vbExclamation, "RegQueryInfoKey _
                & , "Error"
            Set keyList = Nothing
        End If

        RegCloseKey (hPathKey)

    Else
        MsgBox "Failed to open Registry key " & Path, _
            vbExclamation, "Reg Error"
        Set keyList = Nothing
    End If

    Set getRegSubKeyList = keyList

End Function
```

Note since error/success conditions are determined by the values returned from the Win32 API functions and not Visual Basic Err objects, `On Error` statement cannot be used to trap errors in this function.

5.12 Creating A Documentum Resource Locator

A Documentum Resource Locator (DRL) is similar to a Windows shortcut or Microsoft Internet Explorer bookmark. It is a little file on your hard drive or in an e-mail that contains the address to an object in a Docbase. When this file is opened, the object it refers to is automatically located in the Docbase and retrieved. Depending upon your access to the object, Documentum may ask you if you want to **View**, or **Edit** the object. In addition, if you are not logged in, the Docbase will require you to login.

Creating a DRL for an object is very simple; it's just a matter of writing a text string to a file on your hard drive and giving it a `.DRL` extension. The `.DRL` extension associates the file with the Documentum Desktop. The text string written to the file follows this general format:

```
<docbase>:/<object identifier>?<DRL syntax>
```

Where `<docbase>` is the name of your Docbase, `<object identifier>` is the appropriate object identifier of the object, and `<DRL syntax>` is a string of DRL commands from Table 5.8.

Table 5.8—DRL Commands

Syntax	Explanation
DMS_OBJECT_SPEC	Tells Documentum what the preceding string represented. Valid values are: PATH, PREDICATE, CHRONICLE_ID, or OBJECT_ID.
DMS_METHOD	Specifies a server method to run.
DMS_TYPE	Indicates the type of the object. Valid values are: DM_SYSOBJECT or any dm_sysobject subtype.
DMS_VLAB	Specifies a particular version of the object. Valid values are any symbolic version label in the version tree.
DMS_VNUM	Specifies a particular version of the object by version number. Valid values are any version number in the version tree.
DMS_FORMAT	Specifies the format of the object. Valid values are any existing renditions of the object.
DMS_BRKR	Specifies which DocBroker the specified Docbase is using.

Here is a sample DRL that uses the DMS_OBJECT_SPEC=CHRONICLE_ID syntax:

```
Docbase1:/0900218d8003413e?DMS_OBJECT_SPEC=CHRONICLE_ID&DMS_VLAB=CURRENT
```

This DRL will retrieve the current version of the document whose `i_chronicle_id` is `0900218d8003413e` from the Docbase `Docbase1`.

Here is a sample DRL that uses the DMS_OBJECT_SPEC=OBJECT_ID syntax:

```
Docbase1:/0900218d800c4178?DMS_OBJECT_SPEC=OBJECT_ID
```

This DRL simply retrieves the object with `r_object_id` of `0900218d800c4178` from Docbase `Docbase1`.

The following *makeDRL()* function demonstrates how to create a DRL programmatically. The function takes the object Id of the object as its only argument. The function saves the DRL file in your default, temporary directory[*], and returns its fully qualified name to the function's caller. Your project must reference the Microsoft Scripting Runtime library to run this code.

Source Code A working example of this source code can be found in the "`Chapter5/DRL`" directory of the source code archive.

```
Function makeDRL(objid As String) As String
    Dim sobj As IDfSysObject
    Dim drl As String

    ' Microsoft Scripting Runtime
    Dim drlFile As FileSystemObject
    Dim drlText As TextStream
    Dim drlFolder As folder

    ' get the object
    Set sobj = session.GetObject(cx.getId(objid))
```

---

[*] Your default temporary directory is the value stored in the `TMP` environment variable. To view the value of this variable, type `set` in a command window.

```
    ' build the drl string
    drl = session.getDocbaseName & ":/" _
          & sobj.getChronicleId.toString _
          & "?DMS_OBJECT_SPEC=CHRONICLE_ID&DMS_VLAB" _
          & "=CURRENT&DMS_BRKR=" & session.getDocbrokerMap._
          & getString("host_name")

    ' build the drl file
    Set drlFile = New FileSystemObject

    ' get temp path from the TMP environment variable.
    Set drlFolder = drlFile.GetSpecialFolder(TemporaryFolder)

    ' give it the same name as the object + a DRL extension
    Set drlText = drlFolder.CreateTextFile(sobj.getObjectName _
        & ".drl")

    ' write drl to file
    drlText.Write (drl)
    drlText.Close

    ' return fully qualified filename
    makeDRL = drlFolder.Path & "\" & sobj.getObjectName & ".drl"

End Function
```

This technique was presented as a function because it will be used by other examples in this chapter. If you were to call this function and pass it an object Id, you would find a file in your default temporary directory with an icon and an extension of .DRL. Double-clicking the file would cause the Documentum Desktop to launch and retrieve the object from the Docbase.

5.13 Sending E-Mail From A Documentum Desktop Application

A question I hear frequently is "How can I send e-mail from my Documentum application?" There are several answers to this question. If you want to send e-mail from an application running on a client computer, and that computer uses Microsoft Outlook for its e-mail, you can employ this solution.

This solution demonstrates how to send a Documentum Resource Locator (DRL) in an e-mail message. It takes advantage of Microsoft OLE Automation to send the e-mail using the Microsoft Outlook Object Library. This solution is really more about OLE Automation than Documentum. The only Documentum specific parts of the code are those that compose the content of the e-mail body and generate the DRL file to attach. Note I use the `makeDRL()` function discussed in the previous section to create the DRL file to attach to the message. If possible, you should send DRLs in e-mail as opposed to actual content. This preserves the access control on the content and reduces the load on the network.

This code snippet assumes an object with Id of 0900218d800794d1, and utilizes the Microsoft Outlook Object Library, so make sure it is referenced it in your project file.

Source Code A working example of this source code can be found in the "`Chapter5/E-mail`" directory of the source code archive.

```
Dim sobj As IDfSysObject
Dim drl As String

' Microsoft Outlook Object Library
Dim OLapp As Outlook.Application
Dim eMail As Outlook.MailItem
Dim drlFile As Attachments

' get the object - assume you already know the object id
Set sobj = session.GetObject(cx.getId("0900218d800794d1"))

' create email
Set OLapp = New Outlook.Application
Set eMail = OLapp.CreateItem(olMailItem)
Set drlFile = eMail.Attachments

' build email
eMail.To = "someone@microsoft.com"
eMail.Subject = "DRL to Docbase object '" & sobj.getObjectName _
    & "'"
eMail.Body = "Attached is the Documentum Resource Locator " _
    & "(DRL) to '" & sobj.getObjectName & "'.  Click it to " _
    & "retrieve the object."
```

```
' attach DRL file to email-call makeDRL
drlFile.Add makeDRL(sobj.getObjectId.toString)

' send the email
' Note:  Windows will warn you before programmatically sending
' e-mail!

eMail.Send
```

Windows will display a message when you run this code warning that an application is sending e-mail. Click **Yes** to send the email. Alternatively, you can use the `Outlook.MailItem.Display()` method to send the e-mail instead of `Outlook.MailItem.Send()`. The `Display()` method will display the e-mail message in Outlook, and require the user to click the **Send** button to send the message.

5.14 Finding The Folder Path From An Object Id

A common practice is to display an object's folder path, or location, in the Docbase when you are displaying a list of objects from which a user needs to choose (e.g., search results). The more context you can give the user, the easier their choices. Often, simply knowing which folder an object is in can be enough context. Unfortunately, the folder path is not included as part of a document object's attributes. To obtain it, you have to determine which folder contains the object and return the path information from the folder object. There are two easy ways to do this: one using DQL, and one using the DFC. This section will discuss the DFC technique. The DQL technique was discussed in Chapter 3, *Working with Queries and Collections*.

The following code snippet assumes the document is only contained in one folder. The ramifications of this assumption are discussed later. It also supposes the document in question has an object Id of `0900218d80034d35`.

Source Code A working example of this source code can be found in the "`Chapter5/Folder Path`" directory of the source code archive.

```
Dim fObj As IDfFolder
Dim sObj As IDfSysObject
Dim folder As String

Set sObj = session.GetObject(cx.getId("0900218d80034d35"))
```

```
Set fObj = session.GetObject(sObj.getFolderId(0))
folder = fObj.getFolderPath(0)
MsgBox folder, vbInformation, "Folder Path 0"
```

Notice the only folder path retrieved from the IDfFolder object is the first one (index position 0). Though this is probably OK in most situations, it really limits this code's usability. What would happen if the document was linked to two folders? You would not know using this technique. A more general solution would be to put all the folder paths into an IDfList object. This would allow the rest of the application code to easily manipulate them. The following snippet demonstrates this idea.

Source Code A working example of this source code can be found in the "`Chapter5/Folder Path`" directory of the source code archive.

```
Dim fObj As IDfFolder
Dim sObj As IDfSysObject
Dim folders As IDfList
Dim i As Integer
Dim tmp As String

Set folders = cx.getList()
Set sObj = session.GetObject(cx.getId("0900218d80034d35"))

' get all folder paths
For i = 0 To sObj.getFolderIdCount - 1

    ' !! EXPENSIVE !!
    Set fObj = session.GetObject(sObj.getFolderId(i))

    folders.appendString fObj.getFolderPath(0)
Next i

' display folder paths
For i = 0 To folders.getCount - 1
    tmp = tmp & vbCrLf & folders.getString(i)
Next i

MsgBox tmp, vbInformation, "Folder Path List"
```

This code snippet puts all the object's folder paths into the IDfList object where they can be easily accessed and used by other parts of the code. Though more thorough, this code snippet does not perform well because it fetches each dm_folder object only to retrieve an attribute (r_folder_path[i]). You will recall that this practice was discussed in Chapter 3, *Working with Queries and Collections*. A better approach is to use a query to retrieve just the r_folder_path attribute from the folder object. This idea is demonstrated below.

```
Dim fObj As IDfFolder
Dim sObj As IDfSysObject
Dim folder As String
Dim folders As IDfList
Dim i As Integer
Dim tmp As String
Dim q As IDfQuery
Dim col As IDfCollection
Dim j As Integer

Set folders = cx.getList()
Set sObj = session.GetObject(cx.getId("0900218d80034d35"))

' get all folder paths
For i = 0 To sObj.getFolderIdCount - 1
    Set q = cx.getQuery
    q.setDQL ("select r_folder_path from dm_folder where " _
        & "r_object_id = '" & sObj.getFolderId(i) & "'")
    Set col = q.execute(session, 0)

    While (col.Next)

        ' get each value of repeating string
        For j = 0 To col.getValueCount("r_folder_path") - 1
            folders.appendString col.getRepeatingString _
                ("r_folder_path", j)
        Next j
    Wend
Next i

' display folder paths
For i = 0 To folders.getCount - 1
    tmp = tmp & vbCrLf & folders.getString(i)
Next i

MsgBox tmp, vbInformation, "Folder Path List"
```

Though this code is a bit longer and is not as straightforward to read as the first example, it does perform much better, especially when high volumes are involved.

5.15 Creating Docbase Paths

Creating folder paths programmatically, based upon an object's attributes (or any other data), can be tricky. Paths have to be created incrementally, one folder at a time. There is no DFC method equivalent of mkdir -p*, which takes a long folder path, parses it, and creates the necessary folders along the way. That is the reason I created the *dmMkDir()* function. This function takes a folder path as a string argument (e.g., "/News/2004/Jan/01") and creates each cabinet or folder that is necessary until it can return the object Id of the folder with r_folder_path(0) equal to "/News/2004/Jan/01."

For example, suppose you have a program reading live news stories from the Internet. Your program captures the content, parses it, processes it, and extracts data that it assigns to the object's attributes. To simplify the management of these thousands of stories, you decide to store them in the Docbase according to their date. Your folder hierarchy might look like this.

```
/News/2004/Jan/01
/News/2004/Jan/02
  . . .
/News/2004/Dec/30
/News/2004/Dec/31
```

The program that captures the stories from the Internet knows where to save them based upon the stories' metadata. But, what if the folder doesn't exist yet? Suppose that during the processing of a story, the clock moved from Jan 31, 2004 to Feb 1, 2004. The program needs to create the Feb folder as well as the /01 folder (i.e.,/News/2004/Feb/01). That is were the *dmMkDir()* function comes in, you feed it a path and it creates it in the Docbase.

The *dmMkDir()* function requires two arguments:

- A session object used to create the cabinet and folder objects, and
- The complete path as a string.

The first thing this function does is determine if the folder path already exists. If it does, it exits the function and returns the folder's object Id. For example, if the folder /News/2004/Jan/02 exists,

---

* mkdir is a Unix command that allows you to create deep directory structures. For example, you could say: mkdir -p /News/2004/Jan/01 and the mkdir command would make all the necessary directories automatically instead of forcing you to create News, and then 2004, and then Jan, and then 01.

dmMkDir() returns the `r_object_id` for the `/02 dm_folder` object. If the folder doesn't exist, it parses the path and processes each folder sequentially. If any folder in the path already exists, that folder is skipped. Ultimately, the `r_object_id` for the `/02 dm_folder` object is returned.

For example, assume `/News/2004/Jan/01` exists, but `/News/2004/Jan/02` does not. *dmMkDir()* functions like this:

1. `/News/2004/Jan/02` does not exist, so continue
2. `/News` exists, skip it
3. `/News/2004` exists, skip it
4. `/News/2004/Jan` exists, skip it
5. `/News/2004/Jan/02` does not exist. Create folder named `/02`, and link it to folder `/Jan`.
6. Return object Id for folder `/02`.

The function returns the object Id of the deepest folder created or the null object Id (0000000000000000) if an error occurs. Note that since *dmMkDir()* uses the error trapping code discussed earlier in this chapter, the Win32 API method *getDesktopWindow()* must be declared prior to calling this function.

Source Code A working example of this source code can be found in the "`Chapter5/dmMkdir`" directory of the source code archive.

```
' Win32 API
Public Declare Function GetDesktopWindow Lib "user32" () As Long

Function dmMkDir(session As IDfSession, docPath As String) As String
    Dim dirs() As String
    Dim dm_path As String
    Dim i As Integer
    Dim j As Integer
    Dim tmp_path As String
    Dim reporter As New DcReport
    Dim fObj As IDfFolder

    ' init to null obj id
    dmMkDir = "0000000000000000"
```

```
On Error GoTo HandleError

' check if path already exists
Set fObj = session.getObjectByPath(docPath)

' if path doesn't exist, continue
If (fObj Is Nothing) Then

    ' chop off leading /
    If (Left(docPath, 1) = "/") Then
        docPath = Right(docPath, Len(docPath) - 1)
    End If
```

An easy way to parse the directory path into its constituent folders is to use the Visual Basic *Split()* function, and split the path on the "/" character. *Split()* returns an array that you can then process sequentially.

```
        ' create array of dir names
        dirs = Split(docPath, "/", -1, vbTextCompare)

        ' Test each hierarchical path for existence
        For i = 0 To UBound(dirs)
            dm_path = dm_path & "/" & dirs(i)

            ' does partial path exist?
            Set fObj = session.getObjectByPath(dm_path)

            ' if not, create it
            If (fObj Is Nothing) Then

                ' if first dir, create cabinet
                If (i = 0) Then
                    Set fObj = session.newObject("dm_cabinet")
                Else
                    Set fObj = session.newObject("dm_folder")
                End If
                'Set sObj = pObj

                ' set object name to dir name
                fObj.setObjectName dirs(i)
```

If the folder isn't a cabinet (cabinets can only exist at the root level), it is linked to its parent folder.

```
                    ' link it to the path above it
                    tmp_path = dm_path

                    ' if first dir, its a cabinet and doesn't get
                    ' linked
                    If (i > 0) Then
                        j = Len(dirs(i)) + 1
                        tmp_path = "'" & Left(dm_path, _
                            & (Len(dm_path) - j)) & "'"
                        fObj.link tmp_path
                    End If

                    ' save new object
                    fObj.save

                    ' return obj id of created object
                    dmMkDir = fObj.getObjectId.toString

            End If
        Next i
    Else
        ' return obj id of passed in path
        dmMkDir = fObj.getObjectId.toString
    End If
```

The *dmMkDir()* function assumes it is operating in the context of an application that uses forms. This is manifest in the fact that the error trapping code makes use of the DcReporter and the *getDesktopWindow()* Win32 API method. To operate in a non-form or non-UI environment, you will need to change the error trapping code.

```
HandleError:
    ' assume GUI environment and Win32 API GetDesktopWindow() is
    ' declared
```

```
    Dim r As New DcReport
    Dim e As IDfException

    If (Len(Err.Description) > 0) Then
        Set e = cx.parseException(Err.Description)
        r.AddException e
        r.Display GetDesktopWindow(), DC_REPORT_OK_ONLY
    End If

End Function
```

To use *dmMkDir()*, call it with a session and path, like this:

```
Dim folder_id As String
folder_id = dmMkDir(session, "/News/2004/Jan/02")
```

5.16 Working With The Inbox

A handy feature of Documentum is the Inbox. It is used for many things, one of which is notifications. Notifications are similar to e-mails in the Docbase. You may receive notification that a job completed or a workitem completed—or is past due. If you have played with events in the Docbase, you have noticed that the Docbase can send you a notification when an event occurs. It's a very handy communication tool and easy to use, yet often the subject of many questions. This section will help familiarize you with the Inbox and how to manipulate it using the DFC.

Notifications are sent to the Inbox using the *IDfSysObject.queue()* method, and are removed from the Inbox using the *IDfSession.dequeue()* method. Making the *queue()* method specific to an IDfSysObject allows the object to include a lot of information about itself in the notification, for example: its object Id, object type, and content type. If it didn't, you would have to set these attributes manually every time you created a notification. Conversely, the *dequeue()* method is not specific to any object but rather a user's session. Therefore, objects can be deleted on a per-session basis, en masse, as opposed to singularly from their originating dm_sysobject objects.

The following code snippet demonstrates three things: sending a notification to a user's Inbox; displaying a notification in a user's Inbox; and deleting a notification from a user's Inbox.

To begin, this code fetches a document object from the Docbase. This example assumes the document's Id is 0900218d80034d35. One of the input arguments for the *queue()* method is the due date of the contained workitem. Though this notification isn't associated with a workflow or specific activity, it could be.

Therefore, to satisfy the required argument, create an IDfTime object and initialize it for five days in the future. Then, send the notification by calling the *queue()* method and passing the required arguments.

Source Code A working example of this source code can be found in the "`Chapter5/Inbox`" directory of the source code archive.

```
Dim sObj As IDfSysObject
Dim timeObj As IDfTime
Dim idObj As IDfId
Dim q As IDfQuery
Dim col As IDfCollection
Dim answer As Long

' get the object
Set sObj = session.GetObject(cx.getId("0900218d80034d35"))

' set due date 5 days in the future
Set timeObj = cx.getTime(DateAdd("d", 5, Now), "mm/dd/yyyy")

' send notification (queue item) to inbox
Set idObj = sObj.queue("dmadmin", "Sub sendNotification", 1, _
    & False, timeObj, "This is a test message generated by the" _
    & " test program.")
```

Once a notification is in the Inbox, a simple query can be used to retrieve it. This code displays a message box containing some of the notification's attribute data.

```
' query for inbox items
Set q = cx.getQuery
q.setDQL "select * from dmi_queue_item where name = user and " _
        & "delete_flag = false"
Set col = q.execute(session, DF_READ_QUERY)

' display inbox item attributes
While (col.Next = True)
    answer = MsgBox("Item in Inbox:" & vbCrLf & vbCrLf _
```

```
            & "Sent: " & col.getString("date_sent") & vbCrLf _
            & "Due : " & col.getString("due_date") & vbCrLf _
            & "Event: " & col.getString("event") & vbCrLf _
            & "Message: " & col.getString("message") & vbCrLf _
            & vbCrLf & "Would you like to DeQueue it?", _
            & vbYesNo, "Inbox")
```

This last portion of code removes notifications from the inbox using the *dequeue()* method.

```
        ' dequeue item?
        If (answer = vbYes) Then
            session.dequeue cx.getId(col.getString("r_object_id"))
        End If

Wend
col.Close

End Sub
```

The result of running this code snippet is a Yes/No dialog box as shown in Figure 5.9. Depending upon which button is clicked, the notification is removed from the Inbox.

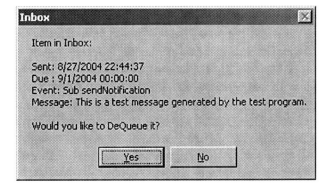

Figure 5.9—Inbox Queue Item Attributes

5.17 Dumping And Loading The Docbase

Documentum supplies the Dump and Load operations to meet two needs. The first is to easily backup and restore a Docbase. The second is to copy and/or move a Docbase from one sever to another. Whichever is your need, Dump and Load is the built-in answer.

Historically, Dump and Load have received a bad rap because they are not user-friendly operations, and not always reliable. In addition, not all objects in a Docbase can be Dumped and Loaded (e.g., workflow instances). So, a successful Dump and Load operation can also be incomplete. Therefore, take the following discussions and examples with caution.

The following sections demonstrate how to execute Dump and Load programmatically by building a simple wizard, which walks you through the process of creating the required objects and executing the operations.

5.17.1 Dump

The Dump operation is used to archive, or export objects and content from a Docbase to a file on the file system. This file can be kept for archival purposes, used as a backup, or used to migrate objects from one Docbase to another. The Dump operation is governed by a `dm_dump_record` object. To execute a Dump, you simply create a `dm_dump_record`, set its attributes and save it. The action of saving the `dm_dump_record` object executes the Dump.

Here are a few general rules to keep in mind while using the Dump operation:

- You can choose to Dump the entire Docbase or only selected objects.
- You can include the content or only dump the metadata.
- If you choose to include content in the Dump, you can compress it.
- Dump files are only forwardly compatible. This means you cannot create a Dump file on a Documentum 5 Content Server and Load it into a 4i eContent Server™. However, you can Load a 4i eContent Server Dump file into a Documentum 5 Content Server.
- You should always run the `dm_DMClean` job before doing a Dump operation. This will prevent outdated files from unnecessarily being archived.
- You can Dump registered table objects but not their underlying RDBMS tables.
- If an object type has no instantiated objects in the scope of the Dump, the definition of the object type is not included in the Dump unless specifically declared. This means if you have a custom object type in your Docbase, but none of those objects are in the scope of your Dump, the archive will not contain your custom type's definition.
- Object ACLs are included in the Dump file.
- Usually, you can restart a failed Dump operation by fetching and re-saving the Dump object.

The attributes of the dm_dump_record object and an explanation of their values are contained in Table 5.9.

Table 5.9—dm_dump_record Attributes To Configure Dump Operation

dm_dump_record Attribute	Explanation
`file_name`	Holds the fully qualified name of the file on the file system to which the dump will be written. This file must be a new file (i.e., it cannot currently exist), and its path is relative to the *server*, not the client.
`dump_operation`	Set this attribute to `full_docbase_dump` to execute a full Dump of the Docbase. The Content Server will ignore the values of `type`, `predicate`, and `predicate2` attributes when this value is set. If you do not want to Dump the entire Docbase, leave this attribute blank.
`include_content`	Set this attribute to `true` if you want the Content Server to include the content files in the Dump file. You should always choose to include content if you are making a backup of the Docbase. The default value of this attribute is `false`.
`dump_parameter`	Set this attribute to one of three string expressions, or leave it blank. Note that these attributes are all name-value pairs. • `compress_content = T/F` – this expression causes the content to be compressed, thus saving space in the archive file. Possible values are `T` (true) or `F` (false) • `cache_size = ###` – this expression sets the size of the cache in megabytes. Possible values are 1 – 100; the default value is 1. Increasing the cache size can improve performance on large Dumps. • `restartable = T/F` – this expression toggles the restartable nature of a Dump: on (`T`) or off (`F`). In case of failure, restartable Dumps can be restarted at the point of failure. Setting `restartable = F` can improve performance.

The next three attributes are all repeating attributes that work together. The value at each index position of each attribute work together to qualify objects for inclusion. These attributes are discussed in Table 5.10.

Table 5.10—dm_dump_record Attributes to Select Objects

dm_dump_record Attribute	Explanation
type	A repeating attribute that contains a list of all object types to Dump. It works in conjunction with the `predicate` and `predicate2` attributes to determine which objects to Dump. The Dump operation will dump all of the object types–as qualified by `predicate` and `predicate2`–listed in the type attribute as well as all of their subtypes and referenced objects.
predicate	A repeating attribute that contains WHERE clauses that qualify each of the associated object types listed in the type attribute. Each type listed in the type attribute *must* have an associated predicate. To ensure all objects of a particular type are Dumped, you can use a predicate that always evaluates to true, like 1 = 1.
predicate2	A repeating attribute that contains continuations of the WHERE clauses started in the `predicate` attribute and exceed 255 characters in length.

To illustrate this idea of three repeating attributes working together to determine which objects to include in the Dump file, consider the Table 5.11. The table shows the seven attributes of a dm_dump_record object and their values.

From this table we can determine this is not a full Docbase dump (the dump_operation attribute is empty); the content files will be included in the Dump file (the include_content attribute is set to T); and the content will be compressed (the dump_parameter attribute contains compress_content= T). Examining the values in the 0th position of the three repeating attributes we can determine that all of the dm_folder objects in, and below, the /Temp folder will be included. Similarly, looking at the values in the 1st positions, the dm_documents will also be included. Finally, looking at the values in the 2nd positions we see all of the regional_docs in the Docbase will be Dumped since the predicate in the 2nd position will always be true. Note it was not necessary to use the predicate2 attribute because the predicate statements were shorter than 255 characters.

Table 5.11—dm_dump_record Dump

Attribute Name	Index	Attribute Value
file_name		D:\Documentum\data\dump1.dmp
dump_operation		
include_content		T
dump_parameter		compress_content = T
type	[0]	dm_folder
	[1]	dm_document
	[2]	regional_doc
predicate	[0]	FOLDER('/Temp',DESCEND)
	[1]	FOLDER('/Temp',DESCEND)
	[2]	1=1
predicate2	[0]	
	[1]	
	[2]	

If we combine the content of the three repeating attributes into DQL predicates, it becomes much clearer how they work together, and what their intent is:

- dm_folder where FOLDER('/Temp',DESCEND)
- dm_document where FOLDER('/Temp',DESCEND)
- regional_doc where 1=1

Dump scripts are usually written as text files using the Documentum API. In fact, all of the Dump examples in the *Documentum Content Server Administrator's Guide* are given as API scripts. This is by far the easiest and most effective way to create these scripts. However, API code is not object-oriented and not much fun to write. Instead, I will demonstrate the Dump operation using Visual Basic and the DFC to implement a very simple *Dump Wizard*. The Dump Wizard will prompt you to enter values for each of the seven necessary attributes, save them, display the dm_dump_record, and save it (execute the Dump). Afterward, the wizard will display the number of records Dumped and destroy the dm_dump_record object.

This example begins by logging into the Docbase using the Login Manager as discussed in Section 5.2, *Login Using the Login Manager*, and then prompting you for the name of the Dump file to create.

Source Code A working example of this source code can be found in the "Chapter5/dumpWiz" directory of the source code archive.

```
Private loginMgr As DcLoginManager
Private cx As DfClientX
```

```
Private client As IDfClient
Private session As IDfSession
Private sessionID As String

Private pObj As IDfPersistentObject
Private rv As Long

Sub Main()

    ' login
    Set loginMgr = New DcLoginManager

    ' if no session, login
    If (sessionID = "") Then
        sessionID = loginMgr.Connect("", "", "", "", 0)
    End If

    ' if still no session, error out
    If (sessionID = "") Then
        MsgBox "Could not Log In.", vbCritical, "Could Not Login"
        Set loginMgr = Nothing
        End
    Else
        ' set up dfc
        Set cx = New DfClientX
        Set client = cx.getLocalClient
        Set session = client.findSession(sessionID)
    End If

    ' create dump record object
    Set pObj = session.newObject("dm_dump_record")

    ' get file name
    pObj.setString "file_name", InputBox("Enter fully " _
        & "qualified dump filename.  Remember, this path is " _
        & "in relation to the server, not the client.", "File " _
        & "Name")
```

Remember the path and filename you enter are relative to the server. For example, if you enter `C:\dump1.dmp`, this file will be written on the server's root directory, and not your workstation's. This is especially important to remember if you are writing to a network share. The server must be able to reach the network share. Next, you are prompted for a full Docbase dump, followed by prompts for the remaining attributes.

```
' full docbase dump
rv = MsgBox("Is this a full Docbase dump?", vbYesNo, _
        & "Full Docbase Dump")
If (rv = vbYes) Then
    pObj.setString "dump_operation", "full_docbase_dump"
End If
```

Of course, answering yes to the "Is this a full Docbase dump?" question renders the rest of the inputs unnecessary, but the wizard forces you to answer them anyway.

```
' include content
rv = MsgBox("Include Docbase content?", vbYesNo, "Docbase " _
        & "Content")
If (rv = vbYes) Then
    pObj.setBoolean "include_content", True

    ' compress content
    rv = MsgBox("Compress Docbase content?", vbYesNo, _
            & "Compress Content")
    If (rv = vbYes) Then
        pObj.setString "dump_parameter", "compress_content=T"
    End If

Else
    pObj.setBoolean "include_content", False
End If
```

In the following loop, the wizard doesn't check the length of the predicate string to see if it is longer than 255 characters. It assumes it's not, and never prompts for the `predicate2` attribute.

```
    ' loop to create predicates
    rv = vbYes
    While (rv = vbYes)

        ' type
        pObj.appendString "type", InputBox("Enter object type " _
            & "to dump",.Object Type")

        ' predicate
        pObj.appendString "predicate", InputBox("Enter " _
            & " predicate (less than 255 chars).", "Predicate")

        rv = MsgBox("Enter another type to dump?", vbYesNo, _
                & "Another Type")

    Wend
```

Saving the dm_dump_record executes the Dump operation. Depending on your inputs, this could be a lengthy operation. This example provides no feedback during the Dump. However, the dm_dump_record object is updated periodically during the Dump operation with statistics regarding its progress. It is possible to provide feedback during the Dump, but the Dump operation blocks the thread, so the the feedback mechanism must run outside of the thread running the Dump. One possibility is to use the Sentinel class described in Section 5.10, *Using the Progress Sentinel*.

```
    ' save and do dump
    rv = MsgBox("SUMMARY OF DUMP OBJECT" & vbCrLf & vbCrLf _
            & pObj.dump & vbCrLf & vbCrLf _
            & "SAVE DUMP OBJECT?", vbYesNo, "Save")
    If (rv = vbYes) Then

        ' saving the dm_dump_record executes the Dump!
        Screen.MousePointer = vbHourglass
        pObj.save
        Screen.MousePointer = vbDefault
```

The last few steps in the wizard check for errors, display a message, and destroy the dm_dump_record object. You should always destroy these objects when the Dump is completed to clean up the Docbase and remove object records and state information that is no longer needed.

```
            ' report messages
            If (Len(session.getMessage(3)) > 0) Then
                MsgBox "MESSAGES:" & vbCrLf & vbCrLf _
                    & session.getMessage(3), vbInformation, "Messages"
            End If

            ' total dumped
            MsgBox "Successfully Dumped: " _
                & pObj.getInt("r_current_object_count") _
                & " objects", vbInformation, "Count"
        End If

        ' destroy the dump record object
        pObj.destroy
End Sub
```

This example demonstrated once you understand the dm_dump_record object and its attributes, performing a Dump is a rather easy task. For a more information regarding Dump, see the *Documentum Content Server Administrator's Guide*.

5.17.2 Load

The counterpart of the Dump operation is Load. The Load operation reads objects and content from a Dump file and recreates them in a new or existing Docbase.

Here are a few general rules to keep in mind while using the Load operation:

- You should *always* run the Documentum preload.exe utility with the script_file argument on Dump files before Loading them. See the *Documentum Content Server Administrator's Guide* for more details regarding preload.
- Run the script generated by preload or otherwise ensure all of the necessary storage locations exist before executing a Load operation.
- By default, the Load operation does not overwrite any pre-existing objects in the Docbase. This is a safety feature to prevent corruption of key Docbase objects, which could render the Docbase unusable (e.g., everything in the /System cabinet).
- The server will not allow a Load operation to execute within an explicit transaction.
- Usually, you can restart a failed Load operation by fetching and re-saving the Load object.

The Load operation is very similar to the Dump operation. It is governed by a dm_load_record object and the values of its attributes. Like Dump, to execute a Load, you simply create a dm_load_record, set its attributes and save it. The action of saving the object executes the operation. The `dm_load_record`'s three key attributes and an explanation of their values are contained in Table 5.12.

Table 5.12—dm_load_record Attributes To Configure Load Operation

dm_load_record Attribute	Explanation
`file_name`	Holds the fully qualified name of the file on the file system to Load. This file must to be accessible by the server.
`load_parameter`	Set this attribute to `preserve_replica = T/F` or leave it blank. When set to `T (true)`, the `preserve_replica` parameter ensures the server loads objects marked as replicas in the Dump file, as replicas in the new Docbase. Note the value of this attribute is a name-value pair.
`relocate`	Set this attribute to `true` if you want the server to assign new object Ids to all of the objects it loads. Set this attribute to `false` if you want the server to use each object's original Id. Setting this attribute to `false` can result in invalid object Ids and duplicate objects. The default is `true`.

Because of their simplicity, Load scripts are usually written as text files using the Documentum API. In fact, all of the examples in the *Documentum Content Server Administrator's Guide* are given as API scripts. This is by far the easiest and most effective way to create Load scripts. But, as with the Dump scripts, where's the fun in that? So, instead, I will demonstrate the Load operation using Visual Basic and the DFC to implement a very simple *Load Wizard*. The Load wizard will prompt you to enter values for each of the three necessary attributes, save them, display the `dm_load_record`, and save it (execute the Load). Afterward it will display the number of records Loaded and destroy the `dm_load_record` object.

This example begins by logging into the Docbase using the Login Manager as discussed in Section 5.2, *Login Using the Login Manager*, and then prompting you for the name of the file to Load.

Source Code A working example of this source code can be found in the "`Chapter5/loadWiz`" directory of the source code archive.

```
Private loginMgr As DcLoginManager
Private cx As DfClientX
Private client As IDfClient
Private session As IDfSession
Private sessionID As String
```

```
Private pObj As IDfPersistentObject
Private rv As Long

Sub Main()

    ' login
    Set loginMgr = New DcLoginManager

    ' if no session, login
    If (sessionID = "") Then
        sessionID = loginMgr.Connect("", "", "", "", 0)
    End If

    ' if still no session, error out
    If (sessionID = "") Then
        MsgBox "Could not Log In.", vbCritical, "Could Not Login"

        Set loginMgr = Nothing
        End
    Else
        ' set up dfc
        Set cx = New DfClientX
        Set client = cx.getLocalClient
        Set session = client.findSession(sessionID)
    End If

    ' first, warn about preload utility
    MsgBox "You must run the preload.exe program on your dump " _
        & "file prior to Loading.  The preload.exe syntax is:" _
        & vbCrLf & vbCrLf & "preload <docbase> -U<username> " _
        & "-P<password> -dump_file <dump file> -script_file " _
        & "<script file>" & vbCrLf & vbCrLf & "Then run " _
        & "<script file> in the iAPI32.exe editor", _
        & vbInformation, "Run preload.exe"

    ' create load record object
    Set pObj = session.newObject("dm_load_record")
```

```
' get file name
pObj.setString "file_name", InputBox("Enter fully " _
    & "qualified dump filename.  Remember, this path is " _
    & "in relation to the server, not the client.", "File " _
    & "Name")
```

Remember the path and filename you enter are relative to the *server*. For example, if you enter C:\dump1.dmp, the server will search its root directory for this file—*not* your workstation's. This is especially important to remember if you are reading from a network share, the server must be able to reach the network share. Next, you are prompted for values for the remaining attributes.

```
' set load parameters
pObj.setString "load_parameter", InputBox("Enter the load " _
    & "parameter: preserve_replica = true/false", "Load " _
    & "Parameter")

' set relocate
rv = MsgBox("Set the relocate attribute to TRUE?",vbYesNo, _
        "Relocate")

If (rv = vbYes) Then
    pObj.setBoolean "relocate", True
Else
    pObj.setBoolean "relocate", False
End If
```

Saving the dm_load_record executes the Load operation. Depending upon the size of the Dump file you are processing, this could be a lengthy operation. This example provides no feedback to you during the Load. Like the dm_dump_record, the dm_load_record object is updated periodically during the Load operation with statistics regarding its progress. Again, it is possible to use the Sentinel class to provide feedback during the Load operation.

```
    ' save and do load
    rv = MsgBox("SUMMARY OF LOAD OBJECT" & vbCrLf & vbCrLf _
            & pObj.dump & vbCrLf & vbCrLf & "SAVE LOAD " _
            & "OBJECT?", vbYesNo, "Save")
    If (rv = vbYes) Then

        ' saving the dm_load_record executes the Load!
        Screen.MousePointer = vbHourglass
        pObj.save
        Screen.MousePointer = vbDefault
```

The last few steps in the wizard check for errors, display a message, and destroy the dm_load_record object. You should always destroy these objects when the Load is completed to clean up the Docbase, and remove object records and state information that is no longer needed.

```
        ' report messages
        If (Len(session.getMessage(3)) > 0) Then
            MsgBox "MESSAGES:" & vbCrLf & vbCrLf _
                & session.getMessage(3), vbInformation, _
                "Messages"
        End If

        MsgBox "Loaded completed " _
            & pObj.getString("r_end_time"), vbInformation, _
            "Completed"

    End If

    ' destroy the load record object
    pObj.destroy
End Sub
```

If the Load operation fails and you want to start over cleanly, you can remove the objects added before the failure using the Documentum API. Issue a *fetch()* command and then a *revert()* command in the API editor. Like this:

```
API> fetch,c,<load_object_id>
API> revert,c,<load_object_id>
```

Where `<load_object_id>` is the `r_object_id` of the `dm_load_record`.

This example demonstrates that once you understand the `dm_load_record` object and its attributes, performing a Load is a rather easy task. For a more information regarding Load, see the *Documentum Content Server Administrator's Guide*.

I encourage you to run the Dump and Load wizards presented here and take careful note of which objects can and cannot be Dumped and Loaded. Dump and Load can be a useful utility, but you must be aware of its limitations.

5.18 Implementing A Simple Search Form

In the final section of this chapter, I demonstrate how to implement a simple search form. I call it *simple* because it's not as comprehensive as Documentum's Find component, but it is more sophisticated than just a single field used in a full-text search. Implementation of a search form like this is common, and a frequent topic of discussion.

This search form will provide three specific fields to search against: **Name**, **Author**, and **Content Size**. The user can **AND/OR** the fields together and select equal (=), greater than (>), or less than (<) operators for the **Content Size** field. To provide a more complete example, I did not use the IDfQueryMgr, but instead used the IDfQuery and IDfCollection classes, and explicitly coded all of the logic. As discussed earlier, it is easy to use the IDfQueryMgr and would be a simple task to map input values from the form to properties in the IDfQueryMgr object. However, I don't like how the IDfQueryMgr returns its results.

5.18.1 The Form

The form for this example is shown in Figure 5.10. The top section of the form contains TextBoxes for the entry of **Name** and **Author** values, as well as radio buttons to toggle the **And/Or** conjunction between them. It also contains a ComboBox to select a comparison operator and a TextBox to enter **Content Size**. You can search on one, two, or all three attributes by entering values in the fields.

One interesting feature of this form is that by selecting the **Display?** CheckBox next to either the **Name** or **Author** field, will cause that field to appear in the results, but not be used as search criteria. For example, you can search for all objects named "Constitution" with content size greater than 0, and return their authors by entering "constitution" in the **Name** field, > 0 in the **Content Size** fields, and selecting the **Display?** CheckBox next to the **Author** field (see Figure 5.10).

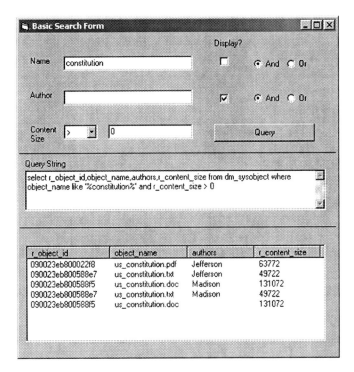

Figure 5.10—Simple Search Form

The middle section of the form is just a large TextBox. When the query button is clicked, the form will post the DQL query string it generates to this TextBox. This doesn't serve any purpose other than allowing you to observe how the query string was constructed based upon your inputs.

The bottom section of the form contains a ListView control. The results of the query are displayed in the ListView control, similar to a spreadsheet.

Table 5.13 lists the screen controls used in the form. Knowing the names and types of these controls will help you read the code more easily.

Table 5.13—Form Controls

Control Name	Control Type	Purpose
txt_Name	TextBox	Name field
cb_name	CheckBox	Display name in results?
rb_And1	Radio Button	"And" radio button for conjunction set 1
rb_Or1	Radio Button	"Or" radio button for conjunction set 1
txt_Author	TextBox	Author field
cb_author	CheckBox	Display author in results?
rb_And2	Radio Button	"And" radio button for conjunction set 2
rb_Or2	Radio Button	"Or" radio button for conjunction set 2
cbx_Operator	ComboBox	Comparison operator for content size
txt_Size	TextBox	Content size
btn_doQuery	Button	Button to run query
txt_QueryString	TextBox	TextBox to display DQL string
lv_Results	ListView	ListView to display results

5.18.2 The Code

The code for this form starts in the typical fashion. It assumes a login occurred in the main program and the `sessionID` variable is passed into the form. The `Form_Load()` subroutine then creates local instances of the DFC client and session variables. Since this code snippet uses the session locking and error trapping routines discussed earlier in this chapter, your project must reference the Documentum Desktop Client Utilities Manager Type Library and include the `DcSessionLock.cls` class file.

Source Code A working example of this source code can be found in the "`Chapter5/Simple Search`" directory of the source code archive.

```
' frm_Search

' passed in
Public sessionID As String

' global to form
Private client As IDfClient
```

```
Private cx As DFCLib.DfClientX
Private session As IDfSession

Private Sub Form_Load()

    ' setup DFC client vars
    If (sessionID = "") Then
        MsgBox "You must set the sessionID property of the " _
            & "form before showing it", vbExclamation, _
            "No Session"
        Exit Sub
    End If

    Set cx = New DFCLib.DfClientX
    Set client = cx.getLocalClient
    Set session = client.findSession(sessionID)

End Sub
```

Clicking the **Query** button is when all the action in this form happens, so let's look at the code that handles that event.

In the `btn_DoQuery_Click()` subroutine, three strings are built: `strSelect`, `strWhere`, and `strDQL`. `strSelect` will contain the select portion of the query, `strWhere` will contain the predicate of the query, and `strDQL` will contain the finished query statement. The code starts by adding `r_object_id` to the `strSelect` variable so every query will return the objects' Ids. Then it processes each of the form's input fields sequentially, from top to bottom, starting with the **Name** field.

If the **Name** field isn't blank, or the `cb_name` CheckBox was selected, then `object_name` is added to the `strSelect` string. If the **Name** field isn't blank then a condition clause is created for the `strWhere` string that uses the `like` operator and the value of the **Name** field. The final bit of processing is to determine what the conjunction should be: AND/OR. Note the conjunction is only added to the `strWhere` string if the **Name** field isn't blank.

```
Private Sub btn_DoQuery_Click()
    Dim strSelect As String
    Dim strWhere As String
```

```
Dim strDQL As String
Dim strTmp As String
Dim col As IDfCollection
Dim q As IDfQuery

On Error GoTo HandleError

' always select the r_object_id
strSelect = "r_object_id,"

' process name
If ((Me.txt_Name.Text <> "") Or _
    (Me.cb_name.Value = 1)) Then
    strSelect = strSelect & "object_name,"

    If (Me.txt_Name.Text <> "") Then
        strWhere = "object_name like '%" _
            & Me.txt_Name.Text & "%' "

        ' process conjunction 1
        If (Me.rb_And1.Value = True) Then
            strWhere = strWhere & "and "
        Else
            strWhere = strWhere & "or "
        End If

    End If
End If
```

The processing for the **Author** field is similar to the processing for the **Name** field.

```
' process author
If ((Me.txt_Author.Text <> "") Or _
    (Me.cb_author.Value = 1)) Then
    strSelect = strSelect & "authors,"

    If (Me.txt_Author.Text <> "") Then
        strWhere = strWhere & "any authors like '%" _
```

```
                & Me.txt_Author.Text & "%' "

        ' process conjunction 2
        If (Me.rb_And2.Value = True) Then
            strWhere = strWhere & "and "
        Else
            strWhere = strWhere & "or "
        End If

    End If
End If
```

Processing the fields for the **Content Size** are a little different from the previous two fields. There has to be values in both the **Operator** field and the **Size** field; otherwise, the input is ignored. If both fields contain an entry, the attribute name is appended to the strSelect string, and a condition clause is created using the values of the **Operator** field and the **Content Size** field. The condition clause is then appended to the strWhere string. If either or both fields are empty, nothing is appended to the strWhere string and we have to clean up the unnecessary conjunction and punctuation in the strings.

```
    ' process content size
    If ((Me.cbx_Operator.Text <> "") And
        (Me.txt_Size.Text <> "")) Then
        strSelect = strSelect & "r_content_size"

        ' process operator and size value
        strWhere = strWhere & "r_content_size " _
            & Me.cbx_Operator.Text & " " & Me.txt_Size.Text
```

Cleaning up the query strings happens in the content size else block. First, the code deletes the trailing comma in the strSelect string by testing for its existence and then shortening the strSelect by one character. Next, it tests for the existence of a conjunction at the end of the strWhere string, and deletes it by shorting the strWhere string by the appropriate amount.

```
    Else
        ' trim trailing comma
        If (Right(strSelect, 1) = ",") Then
            strSelect = Left(strSelect, (Len(strSelect) - 1))
        End If

        ' trim trailing conjunction
        strTmp = Right(strWhere, 4)

        If (strTmp = "and ") Then
            strWhere = Left(strWhere, Len(strWhere) - 4)
        Else
            strWhere = Left(strWhere, Len(strWhere) - 3)
        End If

    End If
```

Finally, the `strDQL` variable is assembled with the entire query string, the query executed, and the results displayed.

```
    strDQL = "select " & strSelect & " from dm_sysobject " _
                & "where " & strWhere

    Set q = cx.getQuery
    q.setDQL (strDQL)

    Me.txt_QueryString.Text = strDQL

    Set sessionLock = lockSession(session, "Simple Query")
    Set col = q.execute(session, DF_READ_QUERY)
    sessionLock.ReleaseLock

    If (Not col Is Nothing) Then
        Call doResults(col)
        col.Close
    Else
        MsgBox "Query " & strDQL & " returned no results."
    End If
```

Note the use of the session locking code and the error handler. Both of these code features were discussed previously in this chapter.

```
HandleError:
    Dim r As New DcReport
    Dim e As IDfException

    If (Len(Err.Description) > 0) Then
        Set e = cx.parseException(Err.Description)
        r.AddException e
        r.Display GetDesktopWindow(), DC_REPORT_OK_ONLY
    End If

    ' close an open collection
    If (Not col Is Nothing) Then
        If (col.getState <> DF_CLOSED_STATE) Then
            col.Close
        End If
    End If

' release session lock
If (Not sessionLock Is Nothing) Then
    sessionLock.ReleaseLock
End If

End Sub
```

The *doResults()* subroutine simply iterates over the contents of the IDfCollection object passed into it, and builds the contents of the `lv_results` control. The logic used to iterate over the collection is the same as introduced in Chapter 3, *Working with Queries and Collections*. The only difference is that this code loads the results into a ListView control.

```
Private Sub doResults(col As IDfCollection)
    Dim attr As IDfAttr
    Dim colName As String
    Dim colValue As String
    Dim li As ListItem
```

```
    Dim numCols As Integer
    Dim i As Integer

    ' clear lv
    Me.lv_Results.ListItems.Clear
    Me.lv_Results.ColumnHeaders.Clear

    ' get number of attrs in collection
    numCols = col.getAttrCount

    ' get column names from attrs in collection
    For i = 1 To numCols
        Me.lv_Results.ColumnHeaders.Add , , _
            col.GetAttr(i - 1).getName
    Next i

    ' iterate over collection and process each row
    While (col.Next = True)

        ' process each column in a row
        For i = 1 To numCols
            Set attr = col.GetAttr(i - 1)

            ' get value in column
            Select Case attr.getDataType
                Case DF_BOOLEAN
                    colValue = col.getBoolean(attr.getName)
                Case DF_DOUBLE
                    colValue = col.getDouble(attr.getName)
                Case DF_ID
                    colValue = col.getId(attr.getName).toString
                Case DF_INTEGER
                    colValue = col.getInt(attr.getName)
                Case DF_STRING
                    colValue = col.getString(attr.getName)
                Case DF_TIME
                    colValue = col.getTime(attr.getName).toString
            End Select
```

```
                ' load listview control
                If (i = 1) Then
                    Set li = Me.lv_Results.ListItems.Add _
                             (, , colValue)
                Else
                    li.ListSubItems.Add , , colValue
                End If

            Next i
        Wend

End Sub
```

Using this form is as simple as instantiating it and passing it a session Id. For example:

```
Set frm = New frm_Search
frm.sessionId = sessionId
frm.Show vbModal
```

5.18.3 The Results

Figure 5.10 shows the result of searching the Docbase for `dm_sysobjects` with a name that contains "`constitution`," and has content greater than 0. Notice **Authors** appears in the results even though no search criterion was entered for it.

5.19 Chapter Summary

This chapter demonstrated a variety of proven techniques and solutions. It has focused on things as basic as login techniques and session passing, to things as complicated as using the Windows registry and Dump and Load. These *staples of the trade* are invaluable techniques, which all Documentum developers should have in their repertoire. The techniques presented here, and demonstrated in real-world solutions, give you a good taste of the many pieces and parts that go into a successful Documentum application. You will no doubt find—as I have—these solutions are implemented in nearly every application you build.

6

Working With Screen Controls

A key component of any application is its user interface, or UI, and key components of the UI are screen controls (e.g., ListBoxes, ComboBoxes, TextBoxes). When developing UIs, Documentum developers have two options: use the Documentum-provided ActiveX screen controls that are *Docbase-aware*, or use the Microsoft ActiveX screen controls and write your own *Docbase-awareness* into them.

The Documentum screen controls come in two flavors: validation controls, and Docbase-aware controls. Validation controls are used to validate user input against constraints in the data dictionary. Docbase-aware controls use the Docbase as the source for the controls' contents. The validation controls are very object-specific, where the Docbase-aware controls are more general. Of course, the basic Microsoft ActiveX controls offer the most flexibility but require the most work to implement.

This chapter will explore both validation controls and Docbase-aware controls by creating simple forms, which demonstrate the abilities of each type of control. Following these examples, the chapter demonstrates what is necessary to emulate certain validation controls and Docbase-aware controls using Microsoft ActiveX controls. The chapter concludes with a mini-project that builds a new Docbase-aware control from a mixture of Docbase-aware and Microsoft ActiveX controls. This control can be used in other projects, and in fact is used in the sample application discussed in Chapter 8, *Putting It All Together in a Sample Application*.

6.1 Documentum Validation Controls

Documentum validation controls are ActiveX controls that can display, manipulate, and save object attributes. These controls use the data dictionary to validate their contents and are bound to an object's attributes with little effort on your part. Although these controls are called validation controls, validation doesn't happen automatically, it requires you to explicitly call the object's validation routines. Even so, there are advantages to using these controls:

- They automatically retrieve value assistance values from the data dictionary to populate control options.
- Saving a control's value to its corresponding attribute is accomplished with one method call: *SaveValue()*.

However, these controls suffer from two problems:

- They are not complete extensions of their Microsoft ActiveX counterparts so not all of the controls' properties, methods, and event handlers are available.
- They are mostly undocumented.

Documentum's validation controls come in six types. Table 6.1 contains a summary of each control. The example later in this chapter will demonstrate each.

Table 6.1—Documentum Validation Controls

Control Name	Description
DfwAttributeLabel	Displays text that a user cannot change directly.
DfwCheckBox	Displays a CheckBox for the input of true/false or yes/no values.
DfwComboBox	Displays a ComboBox for the selection or input of values.
DfwListBox	Displays a list of values from which one or more can be selected.
DfwRepeating	Displays a control comprised of a ListBox and a ComboBox for the selection or input of values to a repeating attribute.
DfwTextBox	Displays a TextBox for input of string values.

The key to making these controls work is the Documentum Validation Event Dispatcher (DfwEventDispatcher) control. This control is invisible to the user, but must be on each form using validation controls. The event dispatcher automatically updates validation control selections from the data dictionary. It also manages controls that contain attributes linked through conditional value assistance.

Conditional value assistance is a construct implemented through the Documentum Application Builder, which allows the content of one attribute to affect the content of another. For example, one attribute, named `state`, might contain the names of the 50 Unites States. Another attribute, named `county`, might contain the names of all the counties in each state. Conditional value assistance allows the developer to stipulate that when a state name is chosen in the `state` attribute, the control containing the `county` attribute is updated to display only county names for the selected state. Conditional value assistance allows you to *link* controls and attributes together.

6.1.1 Referencing Validation Controls In Your Visual Basic Project

To use validation controls in your project, you must add three component libraries and one reference to your Visual Basic project. Choose **Components** from the **Project** menu in Visual Basic and add the following component libraries to your project:

- Documentum Validation Widgets,
- Documentum Validation Event Dispatcher, and
- Documentum Repeating Attribute Validation Control.

You will also need to add a reference to Documentum Widget Logic. Choose **References** from the **Project** menu in Visual Basic and add:

- Documentum Widget Logic.

6.1.2 Example Of Documentum Validation Controls

The following example uses an object type named `regional_doc`. This document type is a custom type designed to demonstrate Documentum's validation controls. `regional_doc` is a subtype of `dm_document` and has two unique attributes: `region` and `us_state` as described in Table 6.2. To implement this example, you will need to create the `regional_doc` object type using the Documentum Application Builder, and then instantiate a few of them in your Docbase.

Source Code This object type is implemented in a DocApp found in the "`Chapter6/regional_doc DocApp`" directory of the source code archive.

Table 6.2—regional_doc Attribute Definitions

Attribute	Data Type and Size	Value Assistance
region	STRING(32)	North East, Mid-Atlantic, South East
us_state	STRING(32)	Maine, New Hampshire, Maryland, Virginia, Georgia, Florida

The value assistance for each attribute is a simple fixed list. However, `us_state` is linked to `region` by a conditional value assistance clause. The pseudo code for that clause is:

```
if region = "North East" then
    us_state = "Maine, New Hampshire"
else if region = "Mid-Atlantic" then
    us_state = "Maryland, Virginia"
else if region = "South East" then
    us_state = "Georgia, Florida"
else
    us_state = "None"
```

The Documentum Application Builder provides a UI to help you enter value assistance clauses such as this one.

The effect of the conditional value assistance clause is that when the `region` attribute is set to "North East", the only available values for `us_state` are "Maine" and "New Hampshire". Similarly, when `region` is "Mid-Atlantic", the only values available to `us_state` are "Maryland" and "Virginia". When `region` is "South East", `us_state` is "Georgia" and "Florida". However, if any other value than "North East", "Mid-Atlantic", or "South East" is chosen for `region`, the only value available for the `us_state` attribute is "None".

Conditional value assistance can greatly reduce data entry errors, and is a great benefit if used properly. Though this example is simple, value assistance can be quite complicated and utilize parameterized queries to provide and validate control data. For more information on conditional value assistance, see the Documentum Developer website.

In this example, I create a simple form that contains one instance of each of the six validation controls, plus the Event Dispatcher (see Figure 6.1). For simplicity, I use the default name for each control as described in Table 6.3.

When the form loads, each control is initialized with a reference to an IDfSysObject. The control automatically displays the value of the IDfSysObject's attribute associated with it. Clicking the **Save Attributes** button saves the value of each control back to the Docbase.

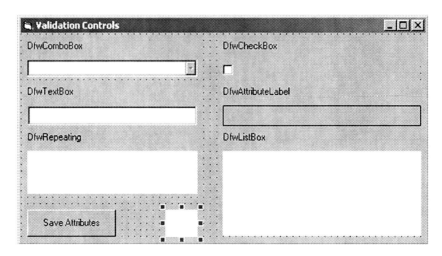

Figure 6.1—Designer View of Validation Controls Plus the Event Dispatcher

Table 6.3—Form Controls

Control Name	Control Type	Control Purpose
DfwComboBox1	DfwComboBox	This control is initialized with the region attribute.
DfwTextBox1	DfwTextBox	This control is initialized with the us_state attribute.
DfwRepeating1	DfwRepeating	This control is initialized with the r_version_label attribute that regional_doc inherits from dm_document.
Command1	CommandButton	The **Save Attributes** button will save all the values selected in the controls.
DfwEventdispatcher1	DfwEventDispatcher	This is the invisible, yet very important, event dispatcher control.
DfwCheckBox1	DfwCheckBox	This control is initialized with the Boolean value of the a_full_text attribute.
DfwAttributeLabel1	DfwAttributeLabel	This control is initialized with the r_object_type attribute.
DfwListBox1	DfwListBox	This control is initialized with the us_state attribute.

To fully appreciate validation controls, study the code behind this form. For simplicity, this code assumes an object with Id of `0900218d8006124b`, and that a login has occurred elsewhere in the application.

Source Code A working example of this source code can be found in the "`Chapter6/Validation Ctrls`" directory of the source code archive.

```
'Validation Controls Form
Public sessionId as String    ' passed in

Private Sub Form_Load()
    Dim sobj As IDfSysObject

    ' set up dfc client vars
    Set cx = New DfClientX
    Set client = cx.getLocalClient
    Set session = client.findSession(sessionId)

    ' get a regional_doc
    Set sobj = session.GetObject(cx.getId("0900218d8006124b"))

    ' combo box of region values
    Me.DfwComboBox1.initWithObj session, DfwEventDispatcher1, _
        sobj, "region"
    Me.DfwComboBox1.ValidateOnLostFocus = True
    Me.DfwComboBox1.Refresh

    ' text box with us_state value
    Me.DfwTextBox1.initWithObj session, DfwEventDispatcher1, _
        sobj, "us_state"
    Me.DfwTextBox1.ValidateOnLostFocus = True
    Me.DfwTextBox1.Refresh

    ' repeating attribute of version labels
    Me.DfwRepeating1.initWithObj session, DfwEventDispatcher1, _
        sobj, "r_version_label"
    Me.DfwRepeating1.ValidateOnLostFocus = True

    ' checkbox on full-text flag
    Me.DfwCheckBox1.initWithObj session, DfwEventDispatcher1, _
```

```
            sobj, "r_version_label"
    Me.DfwRepeating1.ValidateOnLostFocus = True

    ' checkbox on full-text flag
    Me.DfwCheckBox1.initWithObj session, DfwEventDispatcher1, _
        sobj, "a_full_text"
    Me.DfwCheckBox1.ValidateOnLostFocus = True
    Me.DfwCheckBox1.Refresh

    ' label for object type
    Me.DfwAttributeLabel1.initWithObj session, sobj, _
        "r_object_type"
    Me.DfwAttributeLabel1.Caption = Me.DfwAttributeLabel1. _
        TypeName
    Me.DfwAttributeLabel1.Refresh

    ' list of all us_states
    Me.DfwListBox1.initWithObj session, DfwEventDispatcher1, _
        sobj, "us_state"
    Me.DfwListBox1.ValidateOnLostFocus = True
    Me.DfwListBox1.Refresh
End Sub


Private Sub Command1_Click()
    ' save all attribute values
    Me.DfwComboBox1.SaveValue True
    Me.DfwTextBox1.SaveValue True
    Me.DfwRepeating1.SaveValue True
    Me.DfwCheckBox1.SaveValue True
    Me.DfwListBox1.SaveValue True
    MsgBox "Saved"
End Sub
```

This form contains two simple subroutines. The *Form_Load()* subroutine runs when the form is loaded and establishes the local DFC client objects for the form, retrieves the `regional_doc` object, and initializes the validation controls. After initialization, the `ValidateOnLostFocus` property of each control (except DfwAttributeLabel) is set to `true`, and the *Refresh()* method is called. Setting the `ValidateOnLostFocus` property to `true` forces the Event Dispatcher to validate the control's contents against the data dictionary when the control losses focus. The call to `Refresh()` is necessary to update the screen with the contents of the newly initialized control.

The `Command1_Click()` subroutine responds to a click of the **Save Attributes** button and calls the `SaveValue()` method on all the controls, except the DfwAttributeLabel control, which doesn't have one. `SaveValue()` causes each control to save its currently selected values to the Docbase.

Experiment with this form. Notice as the value in the **DfwComboBox** ComboBox changes, the values displayed in the **DfwListBox** ListBox change (see Figure 6.2). This change is in accordance with the conditional value assistance established for the attributes in the Documentum Application Builder. The value displayed in the **DfwTextBox** TextBox is the current value of the us_state attribute. If you select a different value from the **DfwListBox** ListBox and click **Save Attributes**, this value will change.

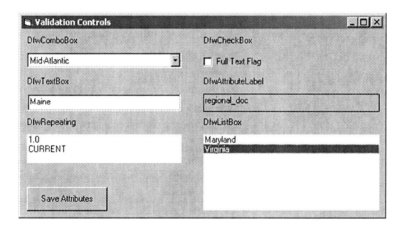

Figure 6.2—Form of Validation Controls

Note that client-side caching can defeat the use of conditional value assistance. You may need to clear the client-side caches before using the code in this section. For information on how to clear client-side caches, see Chapter 7, *Tips, Tools and Handy Information*.

You can see the advantages of using validation controls in this example. I didn't write the code to find and retrieve the value assistance values from the data dictionary, or the code to populate the control. Nor did I write the code to retrieve the value for each attribute and automatically select that value in the control. All of this work is automatically performed when the controls are initialized and refreshed. The elegance of this solution will become more apparent in the following sections when you see how to build this functionality using Microsoft ActiveX controls.

6.2 Docbase-Aware Controls

In addition to validation controls, Documentum provides screen controls that are Docbase-aware. These controls look and behave (mostly) like their Microsoft ActiveX counterparts, but are aware of Docbase objects, values, and events. For the most part, these controls are pre-configured to perform certain common tasks for you, such as: listing users in the Docbase; listing object types in the Docbase; listing format types defined in the Docbase; etc. Docbase-aware controls generally come with two faces: ListBox and ComboBox. In addition, there are a few Docbase-aware controls that encapsulate advanced operations, such as: browsing the Docbase, importing objects into the Docbase, and opening objects in the Docbase. Table 6.4 summarizes the Docbase-aware controls.

Table 6.4—Docbase-Aware Controls

Control Name	Description
DfwAttrCombo	Displays the names of attributes for an object type in a ComboBox. You can specify which attribute to display as default at design-time or run-time.
DfwAttrList	Displays the names of attributes for an object type in a ListBox. You can specify which attribute to display as default at design-time or run-time.
DfwAvailableDocbasesCombo	Displays the names of the Docbases the user can connect to using the current DocBroker in a ComboBox.
DfwConnectedDocbasesCombo	Displays the names of the Docbases to which the user is connected in a ComboBox.
DfwFormatsCombo	Displays the document formats available in the current Docbase in a ComboBox.
DfwFormatsList	Displays the document formats available in the current Docbase in a ListBox.
DfwGroupsCombo	Displays the names of all the groups defined in the Docbase, in a ComboBox.
DfwGroupsList	Displays the names of all the groups defined in the Docbase, in a ListBox.
DfwOperatorCombo	Displays the names of relational operators that are applicable to an attribute in a ComboBox. These operators are obtained from the data dictionary.

Control Name	Description
DfwOTCombo	Displays the names of the object types defined in a Docbase in a ComboBox.
DfwOTList	Displays the names of the object types defined in a Docbase in a ListBox.
DfwUsersCombo	Displays the names of all the users defined in the Docbase in a ComboBox.
DfwUsersList	Displays the names of all the users defined in the Docbase in a ListBox.
BrowserControl	Allows you to navigate a Docbase using a tree view similar to that used by the Documentum Desktop. Double clicking a document object will initiate a checkout. This control does not have any public methods.
Import Tree	Allows you to import documents and folders into the Docbase.
OpenDialog	Provides an open/save dialog that allows you to navigate the Docbase to open/save objects.
QueryListCombo	Displays the results of a query in a ComboBox. You can specify the query at design-time or run-time.
QueryListList	Displays the results of a query in a ListBox. You can specify the query at design-time or run-time.

You can see these specialized controls at work in many of Documentum's components. For example, the Login Manager uses the DfwAvailableDocbasesCombo control to list available Docbases, and the Properties component uses the DfwCheckbox, DfwRepeating, and DfwTextbox controls to display object attributes.

6.2.1   Referencing Docbase-Aware Controls In Your Visual Basic Project

To use Docbase-aware controls, you must add three component libraries to your Visual Basic project. Choose **Components** from the **Project** menu in Visual Basic, and add the following component libraries to your project:

- Documentum Docbase Browser Control,
- Documentum Docbase-Aware Controls, and
- Documentum Open Dialog Control.

6.2.2 Example Of Docbase-Aware Controls

In this example, I create a simple form which contains one instance of four Docbase-aware controls: DfwUserList, QueryListList, Docbase Browser, and Open Dialog (see Figure 6.3). This example also makes use of the `regional_doc` object type introduced in the previous section, Section 6.1.2, *Example of Documentum Validation Controls*.

For simplicity, I use the default name for each control as described in the Table 6.5. The only control that has a special property set is the `QueryListList1` control. Its `query` property contains the DQL string:

    select r_object_id from dm_document where folder('/Temp').

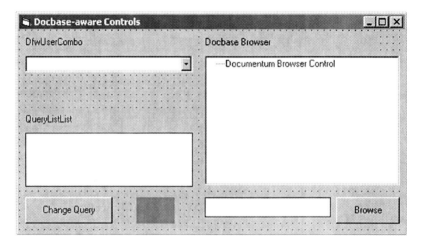

Figure 6.3—Designer View Of Form With Docbase-Aware Controls

Table 6.5—Form Controls

Control Name	Control Type	Control Purpose
DfwUsersCombo1	DfwUsersCombo	This control is initialized with the names of all the users in the Docbase.
QueryListList1	QueryListList	This control is initialized with the results of the query contained in its `query` property.
Command2	CommandButton	The **Change Query** button toggles the `query` property of the QueryListList1 control between two predefined queries.
OpenDialog1	OpenDialog	This is the Documentum Open Dialog control. It is a hidden control.
BrowserControl1	BrowserControl	This control is initialized to contain the list of Docbases available to the DocBroker. The Docbases are displayed in a tree view.
DfwTextBox1	DfwTextBox	This control receives the name and path of the object returned by the Documentum Open Dialog control.
Command1	CommandButton	The **Browse** button launches the Documentum Open Dialog control.

As with the validation controls discussed earlier, these controls perform a large amount of work just by initializing them. Once the form is initialized, clicking the **Change Query** button toggles the `query` property of the `QueryListList1` control between two pre-defined queries, and refreshes its display. Clicking the **Browse** button opens the Documentum Open Dialog. The name of the object selected in the Documentum Open Dialog is transferred to the DfwTextBox adjacent to the **Browse** button, when the Open Dialog is closed.

For the amount of functionality demonstrated on this form, there is very little code. The `Form_Load()` subroutine runs when the form is loaded and establishes the local DFC client objects for the form, and initializes the Docbase-aware controls. Notice there are no object-specific initializations needed for these controls. In fact, there is no reference to any specific object in the code. These controls are initialized by sending them a session object, and calling their `Refresh()` methods.

> **Source Code** A working example of this source code can be found in the "`Chapter6/Docbase-aware Ctrls`" directory of the source code archive.

```
' Docbase-aware control form

Public sessionId as String   ' passed in

Private Sub Form_Load()

    ' set up dfc client vars
    Set cx = New DfClientX
    Set client = cx.getLocalClient
    Set session = client.findSession(sessionId)

    ' init user listbox
    Me.DfwUsersCombo1.setSession session
    Me.DfwUsersCombo1.Refresh

    ' init query listbox
    Me.QueryListList1.setSession session
    Me.QueryListList1.Refresh

    ' hide open dialog control
    Me.OpenDialog1.Visible = False
End Sub
```

The *Command2_Click()* subroutine responds to a click of the **Query** button by changing the query string assigned to the `query` property of the `QueryListList1` control, and refreshing the control's display.

```
Private Sub Command2_Click()
    ' toggle query for query listbox
    If (Me.QueryListList1.query = "select r_object_id from " _
        & "dm_document where folder('/Temp')") Then

        Me.QueryListList1.query = "select object_name from " _
            & "dm_document where folder('/Temp')"
    Else
```

```
            Me.QueryListList1.query = "select r_object_id from " _
                & " dm_document where folder('/Temp')"
        End If
        Me.QueryListList1.Refresh
End Sub
```

The *Command1_Click()* subroutine responds to a click of the **Browse** button. It creates, configures, and displays the Documentum Open Dialog control. The Documentum Open Dialog is an interesting control and is discussed in more detail in Section 6.2.3, *The Documentum Open Dialog*. You can get the general idea of how the Documentum Open Dialog control works by reading through the following code snippet.

```
Private Sub Command1_Click()
    ' create, config, display dctm open dialog
    With Me.OpenDialog1
        .CreateOpenDialog
        .ChgTitle "Documentum Open Dialog Example"
        .SetActionButtonCaption "Open"
        .VersioinComboEnable True   ' note misspelling!
        .DefaultTypeFilter = 0
        .ShowDetail

        .CreateNewFilter (0)
        .TypeName(0) = "regional_doc"
        .TypeDisplayName(0) = "Regional Doc"
        .SingleSelectionOnly(0) = True
        .IsSysObject(0) = True
        .AddColumn 0, "Name", "object_name"
        .AddColumn 0, "Type", "r_object_type"
        .AddColumn 0, "Version", "r_version_label"

        .CreateNewFilter (1)
        .TypeName(1) = "dm_document"
        .TypeDisplayName(1) = "Document"
        .SingleSelectionOnly(1) = False
        .IsSysObject(1) = True
        .AddColumn 1, "Name", "object_name"
        .AddColumn 1, "Type", "r_object_type"
        .AddColumn 1, "Size", "r_content_size"
```

```
        .Path = "/Temp"
        .ChgSession session.getSessionId
        .DoModal
    End With
    
    ' get selected object name in textbox
    If (Me.OpenDialog1.HasSelectedObject = True) Then
        Me.DfwTextBox1.Text = _
            Me.OpenDialog1.GetSelectedObjName(0)
    Else
        MsgBox "No selected objects"
    End If
End Sub
```

Figure 6.4 shows that just by instantiating the form, the controls are populated with data from the Docbase.

The advantage of using these controls should be evident: a large amount of functionality with little code. However, some of these controls' shortcomings should also begin to be evident. What happens if you double-click on an object in the **Docbase Browser**? What if you want to change this behavior? What if you want to display a two-column result in the **QueryListList** control? What if you want to trap an ActiveX event in the control? What if you want to change the control's appearance? The incomplete implementation of these controls makes these ideas impossible. Solutions for some of these problems are addressed in the Section 6.3, *Visual Basic Controls*.

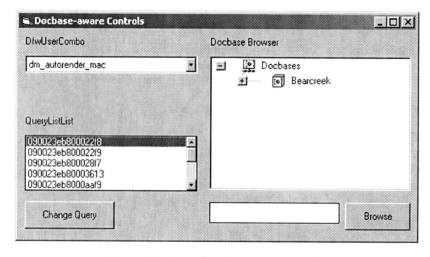

Figure 6.4—Form of Docbase-aware Controls

6.2.3 The Documentum Open Dialog

The Documentum Open Dialog control provides access to the Docbase for object selection. It looks like a standard Microsoft open dialog, but targets the Docbase instead of the file system. It is a very useful control, but largely undocumented. I am not going to discuss or try to document all of the Documentum Open Dialog's methods and properties here, but I will familiarize you with the more common ones. This discussion references the code in the `Command1_Click()` subroutine from the previous example. It is reproduced here for context. The Documentum Open Dialog resulting from this code is shown in Figure 6.5.

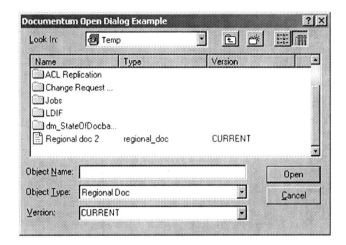

Figure 6.5—Documentum Open Dialog

You create a new instance of the Documentum Open Dialog with a call to the `CreateOpenDialog()` method. This method is the constructor for the control and creates a new instance of the control. However, the control is not yet visible to the user.

```
With Me.OpenDialog1
    .CreateOpenDialog
    .ChgTitle "Documentum Open Dialog Example"
    .SetActionButtonCaption "Open"
    .VersioinComboEnable True   ' note misspelling!
    .DefaultTypeFilter = 0
    .ShowDetail
```

Most of the customization of this control is done through the definition of filters for particular object types. The Documentum Open Dialog contains an array of filters but when you create a new filter, instead of returning a filter object for you to manipulate, it simply adds it to the array. As you see in the sample code, this requires that you use awkward syntax to address filter objects. Essentially, you have to indicate which filter object's methods or properties you are manipulating by passing the filter's array index.

```
.CreateNewFilter (0)
.TypeName(0) = "regional_doc"
.TypeDisplayName(0) = "Regional Doc"
.SingleSelectionOnly(0) = True
.IsSysObject(0) = True
.AddColumn 0, "Name", "object_name"
.AddColumn 0, "Type", "r_object_type"
.AddColumn 0, "Version", "r_version_label"

.CreateNewFilter (1)
.TypeName(1) = "dm_document"
.TypeDisplayName(1) = "Document"
.SingleSelectionOnly(1) = False
.IsSysObject(1) = True
.AddColumn 1, "Name", "object_name"
.AddColumn 1, "Type", "r_object_type"
.AddColumn 1, "Size", "r_content_size"
```

You end your definition of the Documentum Open Dialog with a call to its `DoModal()` method, which causes the dialog to display itself.

```
       .ChgSession session.getSessionId
       .DoModal
   End With
```

After the dialog is closed, but not destroyed, you can access the control's properties using one of several `GetSelectedXXX()` methods where *XXX* is a property of the control. Table 6.6 and Table 6.7 describe these methods and properties.

```
       If (Me.OpenDialog1.HasSelectedObject = True) Then
           Me.DfwTextBox1.Text =
               Me.OpenDialog1.GetSelectedObjName(0)
       Else
           MsgBox "No selected objects"
       End If
```

The Documentum Open Dialog is your only option for allowing users to select objects in the Docbase, unless you want to write your own, which is what I do later in this chapter. It is undocumented and somewhat non-intuitive to use, but with a little experimentation and the explanations provided here, you should find it simple to implement.

Table 6.6—Commonly Used Documentum Open Dialog Methods

Method	Description
`AddColumn (index,"header","attribute")`	Defines columns for the detail view. The columns are added to the display in order of definition, left to right. `index` is the index of the filter this column applies to; `header` is the name that appears at the top of the column; and `attribute` is the name of the object's attribute that will be displayed in the column.
`ChgSession("sessionId")`	Sets the session Id for the dialog. You must call this method before calling the `DoModal()` method. Note `sessionId` is a string and *not* an IDfSession object.
`ChgTitle("title")`	Changes the title bar of the dialog.
`CreateNewFilter(index)`	Creates a new filter for the dialog contents. `index` indicates which filter position receives the new filter. An index of 0 always forces the filter into the first position and causes the other filters to shift downward.
`CreateOpenDialog()`	This is the Documentum Open Dialog constructor and must be called before any method or property of the dialog can be used.
`DoModal()`	Displays the Documentum Open Dialog in modal mode.
`GetSelectedCount()`	Returns the number of objects selected in the dialog.
`GetSelectedFilterIndex()`	Returns the index of the filter used when the selection of the object was made.
`GetSelectedObjID(index)`	Returns the `r_object_id` of the selected object in a particular index position.

Method	Description
`GetSelectedObjName(index)`	Returns the `object_name` of the selected object in a particular index position.
`GetSelectedObjType(index)`	Returns the `r_object_type` of the selected object in a particular index position.
`GetSelectedVersionLabelIndex()`	Returns the index of the version label filter used when the selection of objects was made.
`HasSelectedObject()`	Returns `true` if an object was selected in the dialog. Otherwise, returns `false`.
`SetActionButtonCaption("caption")`	Sets the caption for the only action button on the form.
`SetSelectedVersionLabel(index)`	For a filter at a particular index position, concatenates the selected object's version label to its object name in the dialog's content view.
`ShowDetail()`	Shows the content of the dialog in detail mode.
`ShowList()`	Shows the content of the dialog in list mode.

Table 6.7—Commonly Used Documentum Open Dialog Properties

Property	Value	Description
`DefaultTypeFilter`	`index`	Holds the index of the default filter as defined in the **Object Type** ComboBox.
`IsSysObject`	`true/false`	Causes the filter to display cabinets and folders in addition to your filtered type. I recommend that you always set this property to `true` if you want to allow users to navigate the cabinet/folder structure of your Docbase. If this property is set to false, the **parent folder** (🗁) and **new folder** (🗀) buttons are disabled.

Property	Value	Description
`SingleSelectionOnly(index)`	`true/false`	Controls whether or not more than one object can be selected in the dialog using the filter at position `index`.
`TypeDisplayName(index)`	`"name"`	Defines a natural language name for the filter at position `index` to be displayed in the **Object Type** ComboBox.
`TypeName(index)`	`"type"`	Defines a Docbase object type for the filter at position `index`.
`VersioinComboEnabled`	`true/false`	*Note misspelling of property name!* Controls whether the **Version** ComboBox on the Documentum Open Dialog is enabled.

6.3 Visual Basic Controls

Up until now, this chapter has discussed two types of Documentum-supplied screen controls: validation controls, and Docbase-aware controls. Each of these types of controls offers certain capabilities and features out of the box, but each also suffers from some deficiencies in event handling, properties, and flexibility. In this section, I demonstrate how to make Microsoft Visual Basic ActiveX controls behave like Documentum validation and Docbase-aware controls, including how to utilize value assistance and link the controls together to emulate the functionality of the DfwEventDispatcher. In general, this approach requires more work, but can provide better results depending your needs. The following section discusses three basic Microsoft ActiveX control types: ComboBoxes, ListBoxes, and TreeView controls. It will show you how to transform these ordinary controls into controls with Docbase awareness. During the process, I'm sure you will gain a greater appreciation for the validation and Docbase-aware controls provided by Documentum.

6.3.1 Referencing Microsoft Controls In Your Project

By default, most of the common Microsoft ActiveX controls are probably already part of your Visual Basic project. However, the TreeView control and its accompanying ImageList are contained in an auxiliary component library. To add this library to your project, choose **Components** from the **Project** menu in Visual Basic, and add the following component library to your project:

- Microsoft Windows Common Controls.

6.3.2 Example Of Emulating Validation And Docbase-Aware Controls

In this example, I create a form with two ComboBoxes, two TextBoxes, a ListBox, a TreeView, and two buttons (see Figure 6.6). This example also makes use of the `regional_doc` object type developed in Section 6.1.2, *Example of Documentum Validation Controls*.

For simplicity, I use the default name for each control as described in Table 6.8.

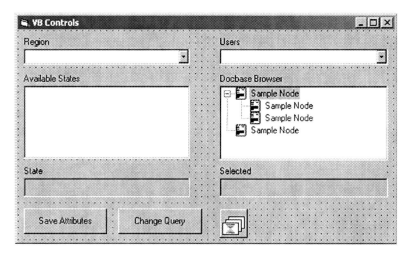

Figure 6.6—Designer View Of Form With Microsoft Visual Basic Controls

Table 6.8—Form Controls

Control Name	Control Type	Control Purpose
Combo2	ComboBox	The **Region** ComboBox emulates the functionality of the DfwComboBox by presenting the value assistance values defined for the region attribute.
List1	ListBox	The **Available States** ListBox emulates the functionality of the DfwListBox by evaluating the conditional value assistance for the us_state attribute, and presenting the resulting values.
Text1	TextBox	The **State** TextBox emulates the functionality of the DfwTextBox by displaying (in read-only format) the value of the object's us_state attribute. The TextBox is not tied to the value assistance for the attribute; it simply shows the value of the attribute.
Combo1	ComboBox	The **Users** ComboBox emulates the functionality of the DfwUserCombo, which is to list all of the users defined in the Docbase.
TreeView1	TreeView	The **Docbase Browser** TreeView approximates the Docbase Browser control. However, unlike the Docbase Browser control, the TreeView allows you to capture the Click() event and process it. Remember, with the Docbase Browser control, a click on a document object caused it to open.
Text2	TextBox	The **Selected** TextBox control simply displays the name of the document selected in the TreeView control.
Command1	CommandButton	The **Save Attributes** button saves the attributes selected in each control to the Docbase. This button emulates the SaveValue() method of the validation controls.
Command2	CommandButton	The **Change Query** button changes the query used by the Combo1 (**Users**) control. It emulates the query property of the QueryListCombo Docbase-aware control.

I won't spend a lot of time discussing the ActiveX controls—I assume you know how to use them or can read a book about them. Rather, I will concentrate on how to make them *Documentum-aware*.

This example is discussed in two parts. The first part concentrates on everything except the TreeView control. The second part concentrates on just the TreeView control. I split this example because the TreeView control requires four separate subroutines to implement it, and I didn't want it to distract you from the other controls. The other controls' implementations are shorter and easier to discuss as a whole.

To begin, examine the `Form_Load()` subroutine. It establishes the local DFC client objects and retrieves a `regional_doc` from the Docbase. The object Id for this `regional_doc` is 0900218d80069fc1. After getting the `regional_doc` object, the form's controls are initialized by calling four subroutines: `loadtxtStates()`, `loadcbxUsers()`, `loadcbxRegions()` and `loadTreeView()`. These initialization subroutines are analogous to the `initWithObject()` methods on the Documentum validation controls and the `setSession()` and `Refresh()` methods on the Docbase-aware controls, though not as elegant. It is in these subroutines where you will gain an understanding of how the validation and Docbase-aware controls work, and what they are doing.

Source Code A working example of this source code can be found in the "`Chapter6/VB Controls`" directory of the source code archive.

```
Public sessionId As String    ' passed in

Private cx As DfClientX
Private client As IDfClient
Private session As IDfSession
Private sObj As IDfSysObject

Private Sub Form_Load()

    ' set up dfc client vars
    Set cx = New DfClientX
    Set client = cx.getLocalClient
    Set session = client.findSession(sessionId)

    ' get a region_doc
    Set sobj = session.GetObject(cx.getId("0900218d80069fc1"))

    ' load state textbox
    Call loadtxtState
```

```
    ' load user combo
    Call loadcbxUsers("select user_name from dm_user order " _
        & "by user_name")

    ' load regions combo
    Call loadcbxRegions

    ' init tree view
    Call loadTreeView

End Sub
```

6.3.2.1 State *TextBox*

The shortest and easiest to understand of the initialization subroutines, is `loadtxtStates()`, which simply copies the value of the `us_state` attribute from the `regional_doc`, to the `Text` property of the `Text1` TextBox (**State**).

```
Private Sub loadtxtState()

    Me.Text1.Text = sObj.getString("us_state")
    Me.Text1.Enabled = False

End Sub
```

6.3.2.2 Users *ComboBox*

The next subroutine is `loadcbxUsers()`, which loads the `ComboBox1` ComboBox (**Users**) with a list of all users in the system. This subroutine is also straightforward and implements the query and collection processing technique discussed in Chapter 3, *Working with Queries and Collections*. The difference here is that within the `while` loop, the collection contents are added to the `Combo1` ComboBox (**Users**).

```
Private Sub loadcbxUsers(query As String)
    Dim q As IDfQuery
    Dim col As IDfCollection

    ' clear current contents
    Me.Combo1.Clear
```

```
    ' query docbase
    Set q = cx.getQuery
    q.setDQL (query)
    Set col = q.execute(session, DF_READ_QUERY)

    ' set label
    Me.Label6.Caption = col.GetAttr(0).getName

    ' load combobox control
    While (col.Next)
        Me.Combo1.AddItem col.getString(col.GetAttr(0).getName)
    Wend
    col.Close

    ' select first combobox list element
    Me.Combo1.ListIndex = 0

End Sub
```

This control is actually emulating two controls. While it is true that the Combo1 ComboBox displays the names of the users of the Docbase, it is only because that is what the query passed into it returns. In that respect, this control also functions similarly to the QueryListCombo (or QueryListList) Docbase-aware control where the query string that populates the control is set as a property of the object. This allows the content of the control to be changed dynamically (e.g., when the **Change Query** button is clicked). Note that like the QueryListCombo Docbase-aware control, only the first attribute in the SELECT list is inserted into the ComboBox.

6.3.2.3 Region *ComboBox*

The `loadcbxRegions()` loads the Combo2 ComboBox (**Region**) and is the first control that deals with value assistance. To emulate the functionality of a DfwComboBox control, this subroutine loads the Combo2 ComboBox with the values listed in the regional_doc's value assistance for the region attribute.

To get these values, the code obtains an IDfValidator object from the regional_doc's IDfSysObject. From that object, it gets an IDfValueAssistance object. Then it tells the IDfValidator to fetch the IDfValueAsssistance object, indicates the attribute for value assistance, and passes Nothing for the second argument. The Nothing argument tells IDfValueAssistance that this attribute does not have any conditional value assistance. Once an instance of IDfValueAssistance is obtained, the code uses the `getActualValues()` method to retrieve the list of values for the region attribute.

```
Private Sub loadcbxRegions()
    Dim validator As IDfValidator
    Dim valAssist As IDfValueAssistance
    Dim regionList As IDfList
    Dim i As Integer
    Dim default As String

    ' get current value
    default = sobj.getString("region")

    ' get list of values from value assistance object
    Set validator = sobj.getValidator
    Set valAssist = validator.getValueAssistance _
        ("region", Nothing)
    Set regionList = valAssist.getActualValues

    ' load combobox control
    For i = 0 To regionList.getCount - 1
        Me.Combo2.AddItem regionList.getString(i)

        ' set combobox default to current attr value
        If (default = regionList.getString(i)) Then
            Me.Combo2.ListIndex = i
        End If
    Next i
End Sub
```

Instead of iterating over a collection like in the `loadcbxUsers()` subroutine, this subroutine iterates over a list to populate the ComboBox. Notice on each iteration it checks if the current list value is equal to the attribute's current value. If it is, it is set as the default value for the ComboBox.

To emulate conditional value assistance, we need to link two controls such that one control's content relies on the value selected in the other. This is the functionality provided by the DfwEventDispatcher when used with Documentum validation controls. To emulate this, we establish a link between the List1 ListBox (**Available States**) and the Combo2 ComboBox (**Region**) by capturing and processing the Click event on the Combo2 ComboBox, and using its content to affect the values in the List1 ListBox. When the Combo2 ComboBox is clicked, the `Combo2_Click()` subroutine determines the conditional value assistance for the us_state attribute and populates the List1 ListBox. The `Combo2_Click()`

subroutine utilizes IDfValidator and IDfValueAssistance objects to access the value assistance data in the data dictionary.

```
Private Sub Combo2_Click()    ' region combobox
    Dim validator As IDfValidator
    Dim valAssist As IDfValueAssistance
    Dim prop As IDfProperties
    Dim list As IDfList
    Dim i As Integer
    Dim stateList As IDfList

    ' clear the state list
    Me.List1.Clear

    ' get list of values from value assistance object
    Set validator = sobj.getValidator

    ' get the property that us_state depends on (i.e., region)
    Set prop = validator.getValueAssistanceDependencies _
        ("us_state")

    ' create a list of values to add to the property obj
    Set list = cx.getList
    list.setElementType DF_STRING
    list.appendString Me.Combo2.Text

    ' add list of values to propery obj
    prop.putList "region", list
```

After instantiating an IDfValidator object, the *getValueAssistanceDependencies()* method retrieves the name of the attribute the conditional value assistance for us_state depends upon. This information is returned as an IDfProperties object. In this case, the IDfProperties object only contains one property name, region, with no value. The value for region is obtained from the Combo2 ComboBox (**Region**) and added to the IDfProperties object as an IDfList of string values. Using an IDfList of strings to set this value is not intuitive, unless you consider that conditional value assistance could depend upon multiple attributes with multiple values. It seems a little odd in this example because the conditional value assistance only depends upon one attribute.

After the IDfProperties object is properly populated, a call to IDfValidator's *getValueAssistance()* method evaluates the conditional value assistance, and returns an IDfValueAssistance object for the us_state attribute.

```
    ' evaluate value assistance for us_state using current
    ' setting of region
    Set valAssist = validator.getValueAssistance _
        ("us_state", prop)
    Set stateList = valAssist.getActualValues

    ' update display
    If (Not stateList Is Nothing) Then
        For i = 0 To stateList.getCount - 1
            Me.List1.AddItem stateList.getString(i)
        Next i
    End If
End Sub
```

Notice this time when the *getValueAssistance()* method is called, we pass the attribute name, us_state, *and* the IDfProperties object containing the value of region. The IDfProperties object contains the critical information that makes the conditional value assistance work. A call to *getActualValues()* returns the list of available states for the region selected, and the remainder of the code loads these values into the List1 ListBox control.

6.3.2.4 Command Buttons

The final snippet of code implements the buttons' actions. The **Save Attributes** button saves the region and us_state values selected in the controls to the Docbase. The **Change Query** button changes the query attached to the Combo1 ComboBox (**User**). Saving attribute values with these controls is not as elegant as with the Documentum validation controls. You have to actually set the attribute values and save the IDfSysObject. Changing the query attached to the Combo1 ComboBox control is almost as easy in this implementation as with the Documentum validation controls, but only because of the way *loadcbxUsers()* was implemented.

```
Private Sub Command1_Click()      ' save
    ' save region and us_state attributes
    sobj.setString "region", Me.Combo2.Text
```

```
    sobj.setString "us_state", Me.List1.Text
    sobj.save

    MsgBox "Saved"
End Sub


Private Sub Command2_Click()      ' change query
    Call loadcbxUsers("select r_object_id from dm_document " _
        & "where folder('/Temp')")
End Sub
```

Figure 6.7 shows an example of the form when it runs.

One last note about this code: when I set the default selection for the Combo1 ComboBox (**Region**) in the loadcbxRegions() subroutine, that action fired a Click event making the value assistance code run. Therefore, when the form loads, the controls are already in sync.

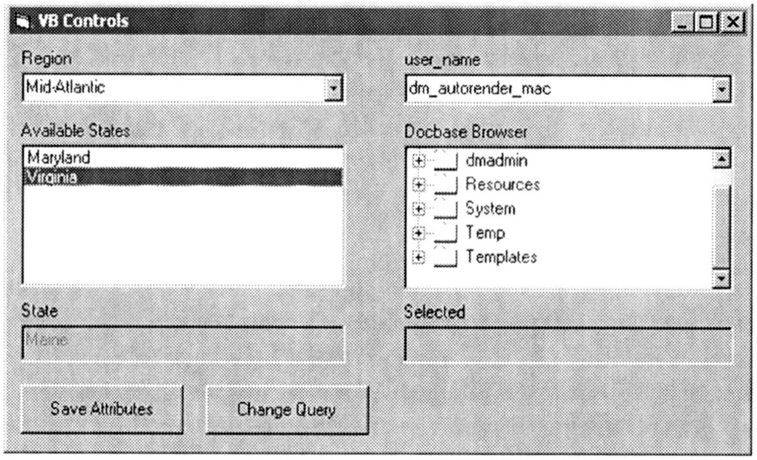

Figure 6.7—Form Of Visual Basic Controls Emulating Validation And Docbase-Aware Controls

6.3.2.5 *Docbase Browser TreeView*

Now that you have seen how to emulate validation controls and Docbase-aware controls with Microsoft ActiveX controls, I will show you how to create a Docbase Browser control, which provides more utility than its Docbase-aware counterpart. Remember, the problems with the Documentum Docbase Browser control were it had no public methods, and it didn't allow you to trap the `Click` event. When an object was clicked in the Documentum Docbase Browser control, it was automatically opened, and this was not always the desired result.

This Docbase Browser control is implemented using an ActiveX TreeView control. There are four, interactive subroutines required to implement the Docbase Browser control:

- `loadTreeView`—subroutine initializes the control and loads it with default content.
- `TreeView1_Expand`—event handler to expand a closed folder and show its contents.
- `TreeView1_Collapse`—event handler to collapse an open folder, thus hiding its contents.
- `TreeView1_Click`—event handler for the `Click` event when a document is selected in the control.

I listed these subroutines before starting the discussion to give you an idea how the control works. I am not going to explain the details of each subroutine as they relate to the TreeView control itself—any good Visual Basic book can teach you that—but rather, how and where to hook Documentum into the code to allow browsing of the Docbase.

Another bit of information I should give you before I start, is the configuration of the ImageList control associated with this TreeView control. The icons displayed in the TreeView control for each node (folder) are stored in an ImageList control. The ImageList is associated with the TreeView control through its properties page. Again, any Visual Basic book will explain how this works. The information I want to give you is where to find the icons to load the ImageList. The Documentum icons are found in the `Images` directory of the Documentum Desktop Component Source code archive*. You will find a variety of icons in the `Images` directory, including the three used here. The ImageList control for this example is shown in Figure 6.8.

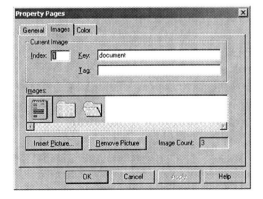

Figure 6.8—Properties Page For The ImageList Used By The Docbase Browser TreeView

---

* You can download the Documentum Desktop Component Source archive from the Documentum Download Center (`http://documentum.subscribenet.com`).

Table 6.9 describes the images contained in the ImageList.

Table 6.9—ImageList Icon Enumeration

Index	Key	Image File Name
1	document	document.ico
2	closed	FolderClosed.ico
3	open	FolderOpen.ico

To use the Docbase Browser control, it must be initialized and loaded. This is accomplished when the *Form_Load()* subroutine calls *loadTreeView()* (see the code listing in Section 6.3.2, *Example of Emulating Validation And Docbase-Aware Controls*).

The *loadTreeView()* subroutine begins by querying the Docbase for all of its cabinets. The cabinets represent the root nodes in the tree. The subroutine iterates over the collection returned by the query and inserts each cabinet as a node at the root level of the tree. The cabinet's *r_object_id* is saved as the node's *Key* property, and the cabinet's *object_name* is saved as the node's *Text* property. Additionally, I use the node's *Tag* property to store the object's type, in this case dm_cabinet. This paradigm is followed throughout the TreeView code, and as you will see, turns out to be a handy technique.

```
Private Sub loadTreeView()
    Dim docbaseNode As Node
    Dim q As IDfQuery
    Dim col As IDfCollection

    ' don't allow changes to root name
    Me.TreeView1.LabelEdit = False

    ' get info from Docbase for root
    Set q = cx.getQuery
    q.setDQL ("select r_object_id,object_name from dm_cabinet " _
        & "order by object_name")
    Set col = q.execute(session, DF_READ_QUERY)
    While (col.Next = True)

        ' build root cabinets
        Set docbaseNode = Me.TreeView1.Nodes.Add _
            (, , col.getString("r_object_id"), _
            col.getString("object_name"), "closed")
```

```
            docbaseNode.Tag = "dm_cabinet"

            ' this gives every node an empty child so that it gets
            ' the '+' icon in the tree view. Expanding this node must
            ' remove this node!

            Set docbaseNode = Me.TreeView1.Nodes.Add _
                (docbaseNode.Index, tvwChild, , "***", "closed")

    Wend
    col.Close
End Sub
```

As each cabinet (root node) is inserted into the tree, they are given *dummy* child nodes. You will notice their names are "***" and they do not have a unique `Key` property. These children are added to force the cabinets to display the "+" sign and allow them to be expanded. You will see later where these dummy children nodes are removed when the cabinets are expanded. This is a common technique used with TreeView controls.

6.3.2.5.2 Expand TreeView Node

When a node is expanded, the `Expand` event is fired and handled by the `TreeView1_Expand()` subroutine. The node that was clicked is automatically passed to this subroutine as an argument.

The first thing this subroutine does is figure out what state the node is in by examining the node's children. If the node has more than one child, it is already expanded and the subroutine exits. If the node only has one child, and that child's name is "***", then the dummy child node is removed. Then the subroutine adds the node's real children. This is done in a manner similar to that described previously for adding the cabinets to the root node. However, since a cabinet or folder can contain documents or more folders, this logic is implemented twice: once for folders, and again for documents. It is necessary to keep folders and documents separate so the tree is built with the folders appearing first; otherwise, the folders and documents would be mixed. Notice that dummy child nodes are added to folders and that each time a node is added—folder or document—to the tree, its type is saved in the node's `Tag` property, and the appropriate icon is assigned from the ImageList.

```
Private Sub TreeView1_Expand(ByVal Node As MSComctlLib.Node)
    Dim docbaseNode As Node
    Dim q As IDfQuery
    Dim col As IDfCollection
```

```
' already expanded
If (Node.Children > 1) Then
    Exit Sub
' check for empty child node
ElseIf (Node.Children = 1) Then
    If (Node.Child.Text = "***") Then
        ' if the only node is the empty node, remove before
        ' continuing
        Me.TreeView1.Nodes.Remove Node.Child.Index
    End If
End If

' set node icon to open
Node.Image = "open"

' add sub folders
Set q = cx.getQuery
q.setDQL ("select r_object_id,object_name from dm_folder " _
    & "where FOLDER(ID('" & Node.Key & "')) order by " _
    & "object_name")
Set col = q.execute(session, DF_READ_QUERY)
While (col.Next = True)
    Set docbaseNode = Me.TreeView1.Nodes.Add _
        (Node.Index, tvwChild, _
        col.getString("r_object_id"), _
        col.getString("object_name"), "closed")
    
    docbaseNode.Tag = "dm_folder"
    
    ' this gives every node an empty child so that it gets
    ' the '+' icon in the tree view. Expanding this node must
    ' remove this node!
    
    Set docbaseNode = Me.TreeView1.Nodes.Add _
        (docbaseNode.Index, tvwChild, , "***", "closed")
Wend
col.Close
```

```
    ' add documents
    Set q = cx.getQuery
    q.setDQL ("select r_object_id,object_name from " _
        & "dm_document where FOLDER(ID('" & Node.Key & "')) " _
        & "order by object_name")
    Set col = q.execute(session, DF_READ_QUERY)
    While (col.Next = True)
        Set docbaseNode = Me.TreeView1.Nodes.Add _
            (Node.Index, tvwChild, _
            col.getString("r_object_id"), _
            col.getString("object_name"), "document")

        docbaseNode.Tag = "dm_document"
    Wend
    col.Close
End Sub
```

The key to the implementation of this subroutine is the use of the Node.Key value (highlighted in the code listing with bold typeface). The queries in this subroutine use the value stored in the Node.Key property to quickly and easily gather the folders and documents subordinate to the expanded folder. Remember, the Node.Key property contains the r_object_id of the object represented by the tree node, in this case, a folder. Notice during the processing of each collection in this subroutine that as a node is added to the TreeView, its Node.Key property is populated with a corresponding r_object_id so that this technique can be repeated when the next node is expanded.

6.3.2.5.3 Collapse TreeView Node

When a node is collapsed, all of its child nodes are removed. The *Nodes.Remove()* method is used to repeatedly remove the first child of the node until no children are left. Afterward, a dummy child node is added so the node can be expanded again. I added some code to the while loop to check whether the name of the selected object on the form in the Text2 TextBox should be cleared because its parent node is collapsing. If so, the Text2 TextBox on the form is cleared. There is nothing Documentum-specific in this subroutine.

```
Private Sub TreeView1_Collapse(ByVal Node As MSComctlLib.Node)
    Dim docbaseNode As Node

    ' show closed icon
    Node.Image = "closed"
```

```
    ' remove all child nodes
    While (Node.Children > 0)

        ' clear selected textbox
        If (Node.Child.Text = Me.Text2.Text) Then
            Me.Text2.Text = ""
        End If

        ' remove it
        Me.TreeView1.Nodes.Remove Node.Child.FirstSibling.Index
    Wend

    ' add empty child so it can be re-expanded
    Set docbaseNode = Me.TreeView1.Nodes.Add _
        (Node.Index, tvwChild, , "***", "closed")
End Sub
```

6.3.2.5.4 Click Event Handler

The Click event is fired when a node in the TreeView is clicked. The Click event handler checks to see whether the selected node is a dm_document by checking the Tag property. If it is, its title is displayed in the Text2 TextBox (**Selected**) on the form. This Click event handler is very simple, but in a real application, this is where the power of using the TreeView control reveals itself. If you recall from the discussion of the Docbase-aware Docbase Browser control, clicking on a leaf node (a document object), only allowed you to open the object. Here, because we can trap the Click event, you can do anything you want. For example, instead of displaying its name in the Text2 TextBox, you could check it out, view it, or start it in a workflow.

```
Private Sub TreeView1_Click()

    If (Me.TreeView1.SelectedItem.Tag = "dm_document") Then
        Me.Text2.Text = Me.TreeView1.SelectedItem.Text
    End If

End Sub
```

This section focused on how to use Microsoft ActiveX controls to emulate both Documentum validation controls and Docbase-aware controls. In all cases, it involved writing more code than using the Documentum controls. However, the result was a form with much finer control and more flexibility.

6.4 The Object Selector Form

To close this chapter, I present a real-world example of a form used to navigate a Docbase and select an object. This form is analogous to the Documentum Open Dialog control discussed earlier, but with a different look and more flexibility. The flexibility manifests itself in the way you can trap and process any and all events on the form, unlike the Documentum Open Dialog control. Therefore, you can easily modify the form to save objects instead of select them, add a button to create a new folder, or change the way the files are displayed.

Before I discuss the form, I want to mention that the code for the Object Selector form is more robust than what has previously been presented. Up to now, most of the code presented has been bare bones—intentionally so. I wanted to concentrate on the specifics of what was discussed and demonstrated, and not get distracted by a lot of error processing code, or session locking code. This source code is different. It's much more representative of how real application source code should look, and implements error trapping and session locking.

I also want to mention I'm not going to explain all of this code. Much of it is representative of techniques and source code you have already seen. Instead, I will provide some general context and let you read the source code yourself. If you wanted to convert this form to an ActiveX control, the conversion should be fairly simple. I leave that as an exercise for you.

6.4.1 The Form

Figure 6.9 show an example of the Object Selector form. It allows the user to select a cabinet in the **Cabinets** ComboBox and navigate its folder hierarchy using a TreeView control. As each folder is expanded in the **Folders** TreeView control, the documents it contains are displayed in the **Files** ListView control on the right. When an object in either the **Folders** TreeView control or the **Files** ListView control is clicked, the **Object** label is updated with the path and name of the object selected. When the **OK** button is clicked, the name, path, and object Id of the selected object are saved to variables that can be returned to the calling subroutine.

This form is built using a combination of Microsoft ActiveX controls and Documentum Docbase-aware controls. The **Cabinets** ComboBox is a QueryListCombo Docbase-aware control, while the **Folders** TreeView control, **Files** ListView control, and the **Object** label are Microsoft ActiveX controls.

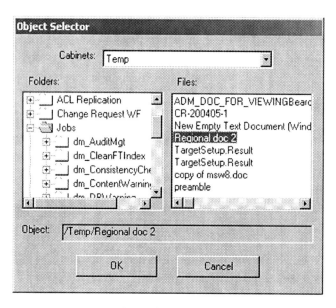

Figure 6.9—Object Selector Form

Figure 6.10 depicts a view of the form in design mode, and Table 6.10 offers a brief description of each control. Note this form does not use default names for controls. Instead, it uses more realistic, descriptive names.

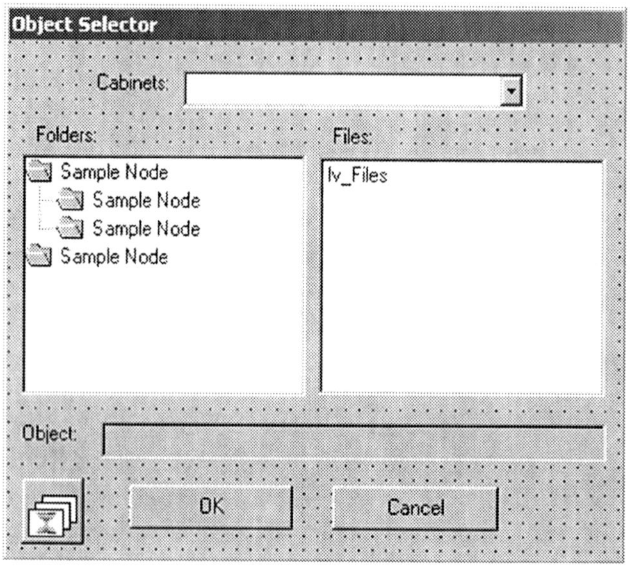

Figure 6.10—Designer View of Object Selector Form

Table 6.10—Form Controls

Control Name	Control Type	Control Purpose
`frm_ObjectSelector`	Form	This is the main form.
`cbx_Cabinets`	QueryListCombo	This is the **Cabinets** ComboBox. It is a QueryListCombo Docbase-aware control.
`tv_Docbase`	TreeView	This is the **Folders** TreeView control that allows you to navigate the Docbase.
`lv_Files`	ListView	This is the **Files** ListView control that displays the contents of a selected folder. Set the `View` property = `lvwList`.
`lbl_ObjName`	Label	This is the **Object** Label that displays the full path of the object selected.
`ImageList1`	ImageList	This is the TreeView's associated ImageList.
`btn_OK`	CommandButton	This is the OK button.
`btn_Cancel`	CommandButton	This is the Cancel button.

6.4.2 The Code

To build this form, you will need to add a reference to your Visual Basic project. Choose **References** from the **Project** menu in Visual Basic, and add:

- Documentum Desktop Client Utilities Manager Type Library

You will also need to add two component libraries to your project. Choose **Components** from the **Project** menu in Visual Basic, and add:

- Documentum Docbase-Aware Controls
- Microsoft Windows Common Controls

Finally, you will need to add the `DcSessionLock.cls` class file to your project. The `DcSessionLock.cls` file is found in the `/Utilities` folder of the Documentum Desktop Component Source code archive[*].

The key to understanding the code for the Object Selector form is to realize that all the screen controls are linked together, so that a change in one control propagates to the others. This is accomplished by trapping

---

[*] You can download the Documentum Desktop Component Source archive from the Documentum Download Center (`http://documentum.subscribenet.com`).

events on the controls and using their selections to affect the others. For example, a change in the **Cabinets** ComboBox selected value is propagated to the **Folders** TreeView control as the root folder. A click on a folder in the **Folders** TreeView propagates three ways: First, the clicked folder is expanded or collapsed; second, the folders path is displayed in the **Object** Label; and third, the content of the folder is displayed in the **Files** ListView control. Figure 6.11 depicts this interaction.

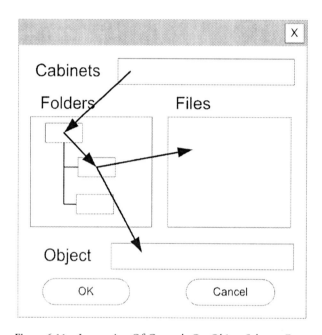

Figure 6.11—Interaction Of Controls On Object Selector Form

The code for the Object Selector form begins with variable declarations. `sessionId`, `cabinet`, and `objType` are public variables set by the calling subroutine. The `sessionId` is the session ID string used many times previously in this book. `cabinet` is the name of the cabinet you want the control to open. `objType` is the name of the Docbase object type you want displayed in the **Files** ListView. `cabinet` and `objType` are optional variables, and will be discussed in more detail later. `objectId`, `objectPath`, `objectName`, and `bCancel` are the variables the form makes available to the calling subroutine. `objectId` contains the `r_object_id` of the selected object; `objectPath` contains the folder path of the selected object; `objectName` contains the `object_name` of the selected object, and `bCancel` returns `true` if the **Cancel** button was clicked.

The remaining four variables are used to establish local references to the DFC client, and enable error reporting. This should be standard fare by now.

> **Source Code** A working example of this source code can be found in the "`Chapter6/Object Selector`" directory of the source code archive.

```
' Object Selector form

Option Explicit

' passed in
Public sessionId As String
Public cabinet As String      ' optional
Public objType As String      ' optional

' result values returned via these variable
Public objectId As String
Public objectPath As String
Public objectName As String
Public bCancel As Boolean

' global to form
Private client As IDfClient
Private cx As DFCLib.DfClientX
Private session As IDfSession
Private r As New DcReport

' Win32 API
Private Declare Function GetDesktopWindow Lib "user32" () As Long
```

The *Form_Load()* subroutine confirms the form has a `sessionId` and then creates the local DFC client objects. After the local DFC client objects are created, it initializes the Docbase-aware ComboBox and calls the *loadCabinets()* subroutine with `cabinet` as an argument. Notice `bCancel` is set to True, and the **OK** button is disabled. `bCancel` is set to `false` when the **OK** button is clicked. The **OK** button is never enabled until an object in the **Files** ListView control is selected. This prevents a user from clicking the **OK** button without selecting an object.

```
Private Sub Form_Load()

    ' setup DFC client vars
    If (sessionId = "") Then
```

```
            MsgBox "You must set the sessionID property of the " _
                & "form before showing it", vbExclamation, _
                "No Session"
            Exit Sub
        End If
        
        Set cx = New DFCLib.DfClientX
        Set client = cx.getLocalClient
        Set session = client.findSession(sessionId)
        
        ' init dctm controls
        Me.cbx_Cabinets.setSession session
        
        ' assume cancel until OK clicked
        bCancel = True
        
        ' disble OK button
        Me.btn_OK.Enabled = False
        
        ' load cabinets into combobox
        Call loadCabinets(cabinet)
        
End Sub
```

When the **OK** button is clicked, the form's return values are populated, the `bCancel` variable is set to `False`, and the form is unloaded. A quick and easy way to obtain the object's path and object Id is through clever use of TreeView item's `Tag` and the ListView item's `Key` properties. I'll explain these in more detail later.

```
Private Sub btn_Cancel_Click()

    ' clear return values
    objectPath = ""
    objectName = ""
    objectId = ""
    bCancel = True
    Unload Me
    
End Sub
```

The `loadCabinets()` subroutine loads all the names of the cabinets in the Docbase, into the **Cabinets** ComboBox. It then searches the ComboBox's items for the name of the cabinet passed in, and sets it as the default. The last thing it does is call the event handler for the `SelectionChanged` event on the ComboBox. As you will see in a moment, the `SelectionChanged` event handler loads the TreeView control with the folders in the selected cabinet. By calling this subroutine directly, we emulate a selection change in the ComboBox and cause the **Folders** TreeView to initialize.

```
Private Sub loadCabinets(cabinet As String)
    Dim sessionLock As DcSessionLock
    Dim i As Integer

    On Error GoTo HandleError

    Set sessionLock = lockSession(session, "Load Cabinets")

    ' load cbx control
    Me.cbx_Cabinets.query = "select object_name from " _
        & "dm_cabinet order by object_name"
    Me.cbx_Cabinets.Refresh

    ' set default cabinet
    i = Me.cbx_Cabinets.findString(0, cabinet)
    If (i > -1) Then
        Me.cbx_Cabinets.ListIndex = i
    End If

    ' force first event
    Call cbx_Cabinets_SelectionChanged

HandleError:

    If (Len(Err.Description) > 0) Then
        Dim e As IDfException
        Set e = cx.parseException(Err.Description)
        reporter.AddException e
        reporter.Display GetDesktopWindow, DC_REPORT_OK_ONLY
    End If
```

```
        If (Not sessionLock Is Nothing) Then
            sessionLock.ReleaseLock
        End If
End Sub
```

The event handler for the `SelectionChanged` event is really a thin wrapper around the subroutine that loads the TreeView control. It is wrapped like this for one reason, which is to do some preprocessing before the TreeView control is actually called. First, it ensures that the **OK** button is disabled to protect against a user having selected an object in the **File** ListView and then clicking on the **Folders** TreeView again. Second, it displays the name of the selected cabinet in the **Object** Label. Finally, the call to *loadTVNode()* is made and the name of the selected cabinet in the **Cabinets** ComboBox is passed as an argument.

```
Private Sub cbx_Cabinets_SelectionChanged()

    ' disable OK button
    Me.btn_OK.Enabled = False

    ' update text box with cabinet path
    Me.lbl_ObjName.Caption = _
        Me.cbx_Cabinets.List(Me.cbx_Cabinets.ListIndex)

    ' load TV with cabinet
    Call loadTVNode(Me.cbx_Cabinets.List _
                    (Me.cbx_Cabinets.ListIndex))

End Sub
```

The TreeView subroutines (load, expand, and collapse) are generally the same as those discussed in Section 6.3.2.5, *Docbase Browser TreeView*. Noted exceptions are: the queries are different, and the value assigned to each node's `Tag` property is the object's full Docbase path as opposed to its object type. Assigning the object's Docbase path to the node's `Tag` property makes it much easier to retrieve and display it later. Notice the object's `r_object_id` is used for the node's `Key` property. This also expedites its retrieval later.

```
Private Sub loadTVNode(currentPath As String)
    Dim tempNode As Node
    Dim q As IDfQuery
```

```
    Dim col As IDfCollection
    Dim sessionLock As DcSessionLock

    On Error GoTo HandleError

    ' clear the tv
    Me.tv_Docbase.Nodes.Clear

    ' get folders with currentpath in r_folder_path attr
    Set q = cx.getQuery
    q.setDQL ("select r_object_id,object_name from dm_folder " _
        & "where any r_folder_path = '/" & currentPath _
        & "' order by object_name")

    ' get session lock
    Set sessionLock = lockSession(session, "Load TV Node")

    Set col = q.execute(session, DF_READ_QUERY)
    While (col.Next = True)
        Set tempNode = Me.tv_Docbase.Nodes.Add _
            ( , , col.getString("r_object_id"), _
            col.getString("object_name"), "closed")

        tempNode.Tag = "/" & col.getString("object_name")

        ' Give every node an empty child so that it gets the
        ' + icon in the tree view.  Expanding this node must
        ' remove this node!

        Set tempNode = Me.tv_Docbase.Nodes.Add(tempNode.Index, _
            tvwChild, , "***", "closed")

        ' selecting the node generates an 'Expand' event
        tempNode.Selected = True
    Wend
    col.Close
```

```vb
        If (Len(Err.Description) > 0) Then
            Dim e As IDfException
            Set e = cx.parseException(Err.Description)
            r.AddException e
            r.Display GetDesktopWindow(), DC_REPORT_OK_ONLY
        End If
        
        If (Not col Is Nothing) Then
            If (col.getState <> DF_CLOSED_STATE) Then
                col.Close
            End If
        End If

End Sub


Private Sub tv_Docbase_Expand(ByVal Node As MSComctlLib.Node)
    Dim newNode As Node
    Dim q As IDfQuery
    Dim col As IDfCollection
    Dim sessionLock As DcSessionLock
    
    On Error GoTo HandleError
    
    ' already expanded
    If (Node.Children > 1) Then
        Call updateNodeFiles
        Exit Sub
    ' check for empty child node
    ElseIf (Node.Children = 1) Then
        If (Node.Child.Text = "***") Then
            ' if the only node is the empty node, remove before
            ' continuing
            Me.tv_Docbase.Nodes.Remove Node.Child.Index
        End If
    End If
    
    ' set node icon to open
    Node.Image = "open"
```

```
' get session lock
Set sessionLock = lockSession(session, "Expand Node")

' add folders
Set q = cx.getQuery
q.setDQL ("select r_object_id,object_name from dm_folder " _
    & "where FOLDER(ID('" & Node.Key & "')) order by " _
    & "object_name")
Set col = q.execute(session, DF_READ_QUERY)
While (col.Next = True)
    Set newNode = Me.tv_Docbase.Nodes.Add _
        (Node.Index, tvwChild, _
        col.getString("r_object_id"), _
        col.getString("object_name"), "closed")

    newNode.Tag = Node.Tag & "/" _
        & col.getString("object_name")

    ' this gives every node an empty child so that it gets
    ' the '+' icon in the tree view.  Expanding this node
    ' must remove this node!

    Set newNode = Me.tv_Docbase.Nodes.Add(newNode.Index, _
        tvwChild, , "***", "closed")
Wend
col.Close

' release lock before entering sub
If (Not sessionLock Is Nothing) Then
    sessionLock.ReleaseLock
End If

' update the file list control
Call updateNodeFiles

' update path in text box
Me.lbl_ObjName.Caption = Node.Tag
```

```
HandleError:

    If (Not sessionLock Is Nothing) Then
        sessionLock.ReleaseLock
    End If

    If (Len(Err.Description) > 0) Then
        Dim e As IDfException
        Set e = cx.parseException(Err.Description)
        r.AddException e
        r.Display GetDesktopWindow(), DC_REPORT_OK_ONLY
    End If

    If (Not col Is Nothing) Then
        If (col.getState <> DF_CLOSED_STATE) Then
            col.Close
        End If
    End If

End Sub



Private Sub tv_Docbase_Collapse(ByVal Node As MSComctlLib.Node)
    Dim dumbNode As Node

    ' show closed icon
    Node.Image = "closed"

    ' remove all child nodes
    While (Node.Children > 0)
        Me.tv_Docbase.Nodes.Remove Node.Child.FirstSibling.Index
    Wend

    ' add empty child so it can be re-expanded
    Set dumbNode = Me.tv_Docbase.Nodes.Add(Node.Index, _
        tvwChild, , "***", "closed")

End Sub
```

Forcing the **Files** ListView to update every time a folder is expanded or collapsed is accomplished by trapping the `Click` event for the TreeView control. The `Click` event fires after the expand or collapse. The `Click` event handler calls *updateNodeFiles()* to update the **Files** ListView control.

```
Private Sub tv_Docbase_Click()

    ' disble OK button
    Me.btn_OK.Enabled = False

    ' update file list box
    Call updateNodeFiles

    ' update result text box
    Me.lbl_ObjName.Caption = Me.tv_Docbase.SelectedItem.Tag

End Sub
```

The *updateNodeFiles()* subroutine populates the **Files** ListView control with the names of the objects in the folder selected in the **Folders** TreeView that are of type `objType`. Remember, `objType` was passed into the form from the calling subroutine. If `objType` is the empty string, the subroutine defaults it to `dm_sysobject`. The trick to easily obtaining the objects in the selected folder is to use the selected node's (folder's) `Key` property in the query. Remember, we saved the folder's `r_object_id` in the node's `Key` property when we built the TreeView. The same technique is used when we build the ListView: the object's `r_object_id` is saved in the ListItem's `Key` property. This expedites retrieving an item's `r_object_id` when it is selected in the ListView control.

Notice the code filters out folders while adding the results of the query to the ListView control by checking if an object's `r_object_id` begins with `0b`. Displaying folders in the **Files** ListView could be confusing in this interface.

```
Private Sub updateNodeFiles()
    Dim q As IDfQuery
    Dim col As IDfCollection
    Dim sessionLock As DcSessionLock

    On Error GoTo HandleError
```

```vb
    ' get session lock
    Set sessionLock = lockSession(session, "Update Node Files")

    ' clear files in control
    Me.lv_Files.ListItems.Clear

    ' default object type
    If (objType = "") Then
        objType = "dm_sysobject"
    End If

    Set q = cx.getQuery
    q.setDQL ("select r_object_id,object_name from " _
        & objType & " where FOLDER(ID('" _
        & Me.tv_Docbase.SelectedItem.Key & "')) order by " _
        & "object_name")
    Set col = q.execute(session, DF_READ_QUERY)
    While (col.Next = True)

        ' if it's not a folder, add it to lv
        If (InStr(1, col.getString("r_object_id"), "0b", _
            vbTextCompare) <> 1) Then
                Me.lv_Files.ListItems.Add , _
                    col.getString("r_object_id"), _
                    col.getString("object_name")
        End If
    Wend
    col.Close

HandleError:

    If (Not sessionLock Is Nothing) Then
        sessionLock.ReleaseLock
    End If

    If (Len(Err.Description) > 0) Then
        Dim e As IDfException
        Set e = cx.parseException(Err.Description)
```

```
            r.AddException e
            r.Display GetDesktopWindow(), DC_REPORT_OK_ONLY
        End If

        If (Not col Is Nothing) Then
            If (col.getState <> DF_CLOSED_STATE) Then
                col.Close
            End If
        End If

End Sub
```

The final subroutine, `lv_Files_Click()`, traps the Click event on the ListView control. Once activated, this subroutine updates the **Object** Label by assessing both the TreeView and the ListView controls. Most importantly, it enables the **OK** button.

```
Private Sub lv_Files_Click()

    ' if nothing to select in control, exit
    If (Me.lv_Files.ListItems.Count = 0) Then
        Exit Sub
    End If

    ' update textbox with object selected
    Me.lbl_ObjName.Caption = Me.tv_Docbase.SelectedItem.Tag _
        & "/" & Me.lv_Files.SelectedItem.Text

    ' enable OK button
    Me.btn_OK.Enabled = True

End Sub
```

Though present in the example, I will not discuss the `lockSession()` and `sleep()` subroutines; they are the same ones presented in Chapter 5, *Proven Solutions for Common Tasks*.

6.4.3   Using The Form

To use the Object Selector form, simply declare it, set the appropriate variables, and Show() it, as demonstrated below.

```
Dim frm As New frm_ObjectSelector

frm.sessionId = sessionId
frm.cabinet = "Temp"
frm.Show vbModal

If (Not frm.bCancel) Then
    MsgBox "Choosen file: " & frm.objectName & vbCrLf _
        & "Path: " & frm.objectPath & vbCrLf & "Object Id: " _
        & frm.objectId, vbInformation, "Object Selected"
Else
    MsgBox "Form Canceled", vbInformation, "form Canceled"
End If

Set frm = Nothing
```

The results of this code are shown in Figure 6.12 and Figure 6.13.

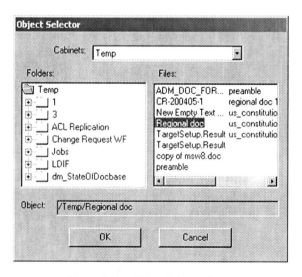

Figure 6.12—Object Selector Form

Figure 6.13—Object Selector Result

6.5 Chapter Summary

This chapter examined three types of screen controls: Documentum validation controls, Documentum Docbase-aware controls, and Microsoft ActiveX controls. Each of these types of controls are useful in their own way. Documentum validation controls are very object-specific. These controls are initialized with an object and draw all of their information from objects or the data dictionary. These controls can be linked together using conditional value assistance so a change in one control affects the content of another control. The Documentum Event Dispatcher control manages these linkages.

Documentum Docbase-aware Controls are controls with broader application. These controls often use DQL queries as the source of their content and are used to display information such as the names of all the users in the Docbase, or to implement the Docbase Browser Control and Open Dialog.

The third set of controls examined was the Microsoft ActiveX controls. With these controls, you saw how to emulate the Documentum validation and Docbase-aware controls. The advantage to fashioning your own Docbase controls out of Microsoft ActiveX controls is you have much greater control over how the controls reacted (i.e., event handlers). The disadvantage is you have to write a lot more code than with the Documentum-provide controls.

The final portion of the chapter was an example called the Object Selector form. With it, I demonstrated how to use a combination of Docbase-aware controls and Microsoft ActiveX controls to create a replacement for the Documentum Open Dialog control. The advantage to this form over the Documentum Open Dialog is you can easily change it to look and act as you need. You will see the Object Selector form again in Chapter 8, *Putting It All Together in a Sample Application*.

7

Tips, Tools and Handy Information

This chapter contains an assortment of tips, tools and information that didn't fit well into the earlier chapters. For example, this chapter discusses how to use the Documentum API, where to find some valuable *hidden* tools on the server, and tables of frequently used values and constants. Many of these topics were referenced in earlier chapters, but the inclusion of the information at those points seemed awkward. Therefore, I collected it all here, in one big eclectic chapter. Enjoy.

7.1 The Documentum API

The Documentum API is a set of parameterized, command-style methods. The DFC is really an object-oriented wrapper around the API. The API has remained relatively unchanged over time, and that's good news because it means Documentum has maintained a high degree of backward compatibility with customers' customizations.

The Documentum API consists of more than 140 server and client methods that are all accessed through three functions: `dmAPIGet()`, `dmAPISet()`, and `dmAPIExec()`. Use of the API, as described in this section, is usually reserved for programming languages that cannot take advantage of the DFC's object-oriented interfaces, or for API scripts specifically written for the iAPI32 command line utility discussed in Section 7.4, *The iAPI32 and iDQL32 Command Line Utilities*. For more information regarding the API methods, see the *Documentum Content Server API Reference Manual*. Note that all arguments in section are strings.

7.1.1   dmAPIExec()

The `dmAPIExec()` function executes server and client methods. `dmAPIExec()` returns TRUE (1) or FALSE (0) based upon the success or failure of the method it executes. The basic syntax is:

```
success = dmAPIExec("<method name>, <session id>,
                    <method args>")
```

where `<method name>` is a Documentum method name, `<session id>` is a Documentum session identifier*, and `<method arguments>` are arguments required by `<method name>`.

For example:

```
rv = dmAPIExec("close,c,q0")
```

where q0 is the Id of an open collection.

7.1.2   dmAPIGet()

The `dmAPIGet()` function retrieves information from the server. `dmAPIGet()` returns a string containing the information that was requested. The basic syntax is:

```
value = dmAPIGet("<method name>, <session id>, <method args>")
```

where `<method name>` is a Documentum method name, `<session id>` is a Documentum session identifier, and `<method arguments>` are arguments required by `<method name>`.

For example:

```
title = dmAPIGet("get,c,0900218d800554f6,title")
```

where `0900218d800554f6` is the Id of a `dm_sysobject`, and `title` is the name of an attribute of that object.

---

* This session identifier is *not* an IDfSession object, or session Id as discussed previously in this book. It is usually the letter 'c' (for 'current'), or an 's' followed by a number assigned by the server. Most often the 'c' notation is used.

7.1.3 dmAPISet()

The `dmAPISet()` function sets the value of an attribute on an object. `dmAPISet()` returns TRUE (1) or FALSE (0) based upon the success or failure of setting the indicated value. The basic syntax is:

```
success = dmAPISet("<method name>, <session id>,
                  <method args>", "<value>")
```

where `<method name>` is a Documentum method name, `<session id>` is a Documentum session identifier, `<method arguments>` are arguments required by `<method name>`, and `<value>` is the value of the attribute to set.

For example:

```
rv = dmAPISet("set,c,0900218d800554f6,title","The Three
              Bears")
```

where `0900218d800554f6` is the Id of a `dm_sysobject`, `title` is the name of the attribute to set, and *The Three Bears* is the value of the `title`.

7.2 The Documentum API from the DFC

The Documentum API is also directly accessible from the DFC, although the syntax is slightly different. The IDfSession class contains the accessor methods `apiExec()`, `apiGet()`, and `apiSet()`, which are analogous to `dmAPIExec()`, `dmAPIGet()`, and `dmAPISet()`. The primary difference in syntax between the API functions and their DFC counterparts is the absence of the session identifier in the latter. Since the accessor methods belong to the IDfSession class, they are already aware of the session so don't require it to be passed with each method call. There is rarely any reason to call the API directly from the DFC, and Documentum recommends not doing it. In some instances (e.g., the Business Object Framework), direct API calls do not function properly. Note, once again, that all of the arguments are strings.

7.2.1 apiExec()

The `apiExec()` method returns a Boolean variable, `true` for success and `false` for failure. Its basic syntax is:

```
success = session.apiExec("<method name>", "<method args>")
```

where `session` is an IDfSession object, `<method name>` is a Documentum method name, and `<method arguments>` are arguments required by `<method name>`.

For example:

```
rv = session.apiExec ("close","q0")
```

where q0 is the Id of an open collection.

7.2.2   apiGet()

The *apiGet()* method returns a String variable. Its basic syntax is:

```
value = session.apiGet("<method name>", "<method args>")
```

where `session` is an IDfSession object, `<method name>` is a Documentum method name, and `<method arguments>` are arguments required by `<method name>`.

For example:

```
title = session.apiGet("get","0900218d800554f6,title")
```

where `0900218d800554f6` is the Id of a `dm_sysobject`, and `title` is the name of an attribute.

7.2.3   apiSet()

The *apiSet()* method returns a Boolean variable, `true` for success and `false` for failure. Its basic syntax is:

```
success = session.apiSet ("<method name>", "<method args>,
                          <value>")
```

where `<method name>` is a Documentum method name, `<method arguments>` are arguments required by `<method name>`, and `<value>` is the value of the attribute to set.

For example:

```
rv = session.apiSet ("set","0900218d800554f6,title,The Three
                     Bears")
```

where `0900218d800554f6` is the Id of a `dm_sysobject`, `title` is the name of the attribute to set, and *The Three Bears* is the value of the `title`.

7.3 The Interactive Message Tester

The Interactive Message Tester (IMT) is a quick and dirty API editor built into the Documentum Desktop. Actually, it's a hold over from an older version of the Desktop named *WorkSpace*. Nonetheless, it is a handy tool that allows you to obtain information about selected items in the Desktop, and execute API commands against them.

To use the IMT in Documentum 5, you must specifically enable the deprecated WorkSpace capabilities. To enable them, simply create an empty dm_document object named Enable_EDMS98_Client in the /System/Desktop Client folder of your Docbase. To access the IMT, click **Documentum Help** on the **Help** menu while holding down the control key (Ctrl). The IMT user interface is shown in Figure 7.1.

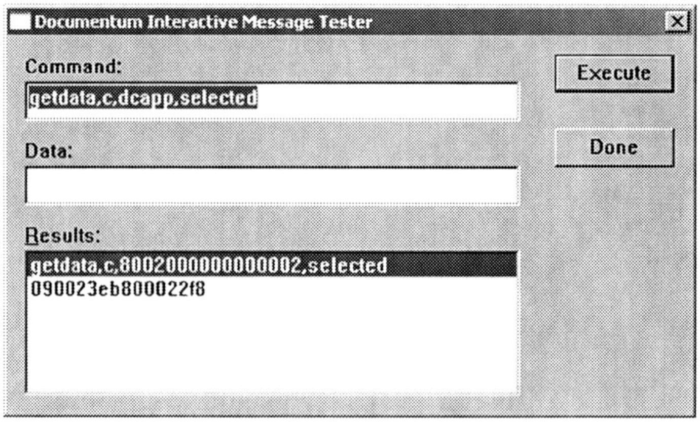

Figure 7.1—Interactive Message Tester

To obtain information about the selected item in the Documentum Desktop, enter:

```
getdata,c,dcapp,selected
```

This will return the selected object's, r_object_id. Once you have it, you can execute any API method on the object, including set(). One very useful API method is dump(). You execute dump() like this (assuming your r_object_id is 090023eb800022f8 as above):

```
dump,c,090023eb800022f8
```

Unfortunately, the output format in the IMT is not the greatest (it doesn't word wrap); however, the output can easily be cut and pasted into a text editor for further analysis.

Another terrific use of the IMT is to quickly enable and disable tracing (tracing was discussed in Chapter 5, *Proven Solutions to Common Problems*). To enable tracing, simply enter:

```
trace,c,10,"c:\temp\trace-10.log"
```

To disable tracing, enter:

```
trace,c,0
```

7.4 The iAPI32 and iDQL32 Command Line Utilities

The iAPI32 and iDQL32 are invaluable tools, but difficult to find because they are buried on the server. Both of these tools are located on the server in the `%DM_HOME%\bin` directory. I usually copy them (`iapi32.exe and idql32.exe`) to my workstation for quick, easy access.

The iAPI32 utility is an interactive API editor. It allows you to interactively enter API commands to affect the Docbase, or run API script files. Its use is fully documented in the *Documentum Content Server Administrator's Guide*.

Similarly, the iDQL32 utility is an interactive DQL editor. It allows you to interactively enter DQL commands to affect the Docbase, or run DQL script files. It, too, is fully documented in the *Documentum Content Server Administrator's Guide*.

7.5 Samson

Samson is an unsupported tool distributed with the Documentum Server. It puts a Windows UI on the iAPI32 and iDQL32 tools and calls them iAPIPlus and iDQLPlus, respectively. Besides just the UI aspects of the tool, it also includes numerous canned queries useful for administrative tasks. Samson is also buried on the server. It is located in the `%DM_HOME%\unsupported\win\samson` directory. I usually copy this entire folder to my workstation for quick, easy access to Samson. Samson is fully documented in the `SAMSON.doc` file also located in that directory.

7.6 Resetting The Documentum Desktop

During the development, debugging, and testing process, it is often necessary to point the Documentum Desktop at a different DocBroker, or re-initialize its local settings. To accomplish this, simply switch to offline mode by choosing **Work Offline** from the **File** menu. Then, switch to online mode by selecting

Work Offline again from the **File** menu. When you switch from offline mode to online mode, the Documentum Desktop re-reads the `dmcl.ini` file and reinitializes all of its local settings.

This technique can be employed whenever you need the Documentum Desktop to re-read the `dmcl.ini` file, not just to switch DocBrokers. For example, you may want to change the cache query setting (as described in Chapter 3, *Working with Queries and Collections*), or any of the other settings described in Section 7.8, *Anatomy of the `dmcl.ini` File*.

7.7 Clearing The Client-Side Caches

Occasionally, it is necessary to manually clear the client-side caches. You may have done this in Chapter 6, *Working with Screen Controls*, if the conditional value assistance was not working. Documentum applications have two caches that may need to be cleared. The first is the Docbase cache. This is usually found in a folder in the `%DOCUMENTUM%` directory with the same name as the Docbase. To clear it, delete the folder and all of its contents. The Documentum Desktop will automatically re-create it.

The second cache is the DMCL cache. This cache is usually in a folder named `dmcl` in the `%DOCUMENTUM%` directory. To delete this cache, open the `dmcl` folder and delete its contents—do not delete the actual folder.

7.8 Anatomy Of The dmcl.ini File

The `dmcl.ini` file is the client-side configuration file. It is located in your `c:\Windows` directory. The `dmcl.ini` file is automatically read every time your application starts. Generally, this file is simple in content as illustrated in the following example.

```
#Default DMCL.INI. Refer to DMCLFULL.INI for other options

[DOCBROKER_PRIMARY]
host = 192.168.0.1
port = 1489

[DMAPI_CONFIGURATION]
cache_queries = T
```

However, the `dmcl.ini` file can be much more complicated and control a wide range of features affecting how your client functions. Documentum provides the `dmclfull.ini` file as an example and documentation of the full capabilities of the dmcl.ini file. The dmclfull.ini file can also be found in your c:\Windows directory. The following discussion highlights some of the more commonly used features controlled by this file.

7.8.1 Backup DocBroker

The DOCBROKER_BACKUP section lists alternate DocBrokers the client should try if the DOCBROKER_PRIMARY is unavailable. Each backup DocBroker entry must use both the host and the service keys.

```
[DOCBROKER_BACKUP_<n>] where <n> is 1-8
host = <string>
service = dmdocbroker
```

7.8.2 Client-Side Cache Size

The size of the client-side cache can be controlled by the client_cache_size key in the DMAPI_CONFIGURATION section. The default value of -1 causes the cache size to be infinite.

```
[DMAPI_CONFIGURATION]
client_cache_size = -1
```

7.8.3 Local Path

The local_path key of the DMAPI_CONFIGURATION section indicates where the client should store its local temporary files. For example, files fetched from the Content Server for viewing. If this value is not set, the client automatically uses your default working directory on Windows, and the /tmp directory on Unix.

```
[DMAPI_CONFIGURATION]
local_path = c:\windows\temp
```

7.8.4 Batch Hint Size

The batch_hint_size key of the DMAPI_CONFIGURATION section suggests an optimal size for data transported across the network. This value affects both client to Content Server and Content Server to RDBMS traffic. It is only a suggestion, there is no guarantee it will be respected. The default value is 20; however, on high-latency networks, a larger value may improve performance.

```
[DMAPI_CONFIGURATION]
batch_hint_size = 20
```

7.8.5 Compression

Compression of content on low-bandwidth networks can improve performance. By default, compression is disabled.

```
[DMAPI_CONFIGURATION]
use_compression = F
```

7.8.6 Cached Queries

Cached queries were discussed in Chapter 3, *Working with Queries and Collections*. Setting the `cache_queries` key is only one of two steps required to enable query caching. The default value is F.

```
[DMAPI_CONFIGURATION]
cache_queries = T
```

7.8.7 Tracing

Enabling tracing through the `dmcl.ini` file was discussed in Chapter 5, *Proven Solutions to Common Tasks*. These are the default values.

```
[DMAPI_CONFIGURATION]
trace_level = 0
trace_file = ""
```

7.9 Anatomy Of The r_object_id

`r_object_id`s are not just random numbers, they are composed of three distinct parts: the type identifier, the Docbase Id, and the object Id. Understanding the anatomy of the `r_object_id` can give you greater insight to objects in your Docbase. For example, consider this `r_object_id`:

0900218d80034cc7

If you think of it in its three parts, you might conceptualize it like this:

09-00218d-80034cc7

The first two digits of the `r_object_id` represent the type identifier. A complete list of these identifiers can be found in Section 7.10, *Object Type Identifiers*. Custom object types do *not* receive custom type identifiers; rather they inherit the same type identifier as their parent (supertype). For example, a custom object type, `regional_doc`, that inherits from `dm_document` will be represented by 09, the same as the `dm_document`. Knowing object type codes can be a handy coding and debugging tool.

The next six digits of the `r_object_id` are the Docbase Id of the Docbase where the object was created. In this case, 00218d, which is the hexadecimal representation of the Id I assigned to my development Docbase. Docbase Ids help ensure the global uniqueness of an `r_object_id`. Production Docbases should always use Docbase Ids assigned by Documentum (the company). These Ids are never reused and are assigned to customers in blocks. Knowing your Docbase Id can help you quickly identify objects that were replicated or loaded into your Docbase as opposed to originating in it.

The final eight digits of the `r_object_id` represent the object's unique identifier in the Docbase. This number is generated by the Content Server and is a sequential number. Therefore, it is a safe bet that an object with a greater unique identifier was created after one with a lesser identifier. For example, it is safe to assume 0900218d80034cc7 was created before 0900218d80034cc8, based upon the value of the last eight digits of the `r_object_id`.

7.10 Object Type Identifiers

As mentioned in Section 7.9, *Anatomy of the r_object_id*, the first two characters of the `r_object_id` represent the type identifier. Table 7.1 lists the most common object types with their hexadecimal identifiers. The left table is sorted by type name, and the right table is sorted by hex id.

Table 7.1—Object Type Identifiers

Type Name	Hex Id	Type Name	Hex Id
dm_acl	45	dm_auth_config	00
dm_activity	4c	dm_state_type	00
dm_aggr_domain	51	dmi_audittrail_attrs	00
dm_alias_set	66	dm_session	01
dm_app_ref	07	dm_type	03
dm_application	08	dmr_containment	05
dm_assembly	0d	dmr_content	06
dm_audittrail	5f	dm_app_ref	07
dm_audittrail_acl	5f	dm_application	08
dm_audittrail_group	5f	dm_cache_config	08
dm_auth_config	00	dm_category_class	08
dm_blobstore	40	dm_ci_config	08
dm_builtin_expr	54	dm_component	08
dm_ca_store	6a	dm_job	08
dm_cabinet	0c	dm_ldap_config	08
dm_cache_config	08	dm_locator	08
dm_category	0b	dm_media_profile	08
dm_category_assign	37	dm_procedure	08
dm_category_class	08	dm_qual_comp	08
dm_ci_config	08	dm_script	08
dm_component	08	dm_smart_list	08
dm_cond_expr	56	dm_sysobject	08
dm_cond_id_expr	57	dm_webc_config	08
dm_dd_info	4e	dm_webc_target	08
dm_display_config	6b	dm_docset	09
dm_distributedstore	2c	dm_docset_run	09
dm_docbase_config	3c	dm_document	09
dm_docbaseid_map	44	dm_email_message	09
dm_docset	09	dm_esign_template	09
dm_docset_run	09	dm_xml_config	09
dm_document	09	dm_xml_custom_code	09

Type Name	Hex Id	Type Name	Hex Id
dm_dump_record	2f	dm_xml_zone	09
dm_email_message	09	dm_query	0a
dm_esign_template	09	dm_category	0b
dm_expression	52	dm_folder	0b
dm_extern_file	61	dm_taxonomy	0b
dm_extern_free	63	dm_xml_application	0b
dm_extern_store	60	dm_cabinet	0c
dm_extern_url	62	dm_assembly	0d
dm_federation	5e	dm_store	0e
dm_filestore	28	dm_method	10
dm_folder	0b	dm_user	11
dm_foreign_key	65	dm_group	12
dm_format	27	dm_outputdevice	17
dm_fulltext_index	3b	dm_router	18
dm_func_expr	55	dm_registered	19
dm_group	12	dmi_queue_item	1b
dm_job	08	dmi_tdk_collect	1c
dm_key	59	dmi_vstamp	1e
dm_ldap_config	08	dmi_index	1f
dm_linkedstore	2a	dmi_sequence	20
dm_literal_expr	53	dmi_otherfile	23
dm_load_record	31	dmi_tdk_index	24
dm_location	3a	dmi_registry	26
dm_locator	08	dm_format	27
dm_media_profile	08	dm_filestore	28
dm_method	10	dm_linkedstore	2a
dm_mount_point	3e	dmi_linkrecord	2b
dm_nls_dd_info	4f	dm_distributedstore	2c
dm_note	41	dmi_replica_record	2d
dm_outputdevice	17	dm_type_info	2e
dm_plugin	67	dm_dump_record	2f
dm_policy	46	dmi_dump_object_record	30
dm_procedure	08	dm_load_record	31
dm_process	4b	dmi_load_object_record	32

Type Name	Hex Id	Type Name	Hex Id
dm_qual_comp	08	dmi_change_record	33
dm_query	0a	dm_category_assign	37
dm_reference	47	dm_relation	37
dm_registered	19	dm_state_extension	37
dm_relation	37	dm_relation_type	38
dm_relation_type	38	dm_location	3a
dm_router	18	dm_fulltext_index	3b
dm_scope_config	6c	dm_docbase_config	3c
dm_script	08	dm_server_config	3d
dm_server_config	3d	dm_mount_point	3e
dm_session	01	dm_blobstore	40
dm_smart_list	08	dm_note	41
dm_state_extension	37	dm_docbaseid_map	44
dm_state_type	00	dm_acl	45
dm_store	0e	dm_policy	46
dm_sysobject	08	dm_reference	47
dm_taxonomy	0b	dmi_package	49
dm_type	03	dmi_workitem	4a
dm_type_info	2e	dm_process	4b
dm_user	11	dm_activity	4c
dm_value_assist	5a	dm_workflow	4d
dm_value_func	5d	dm_dd_info	4e
dm_value_list	5b	dm_nls_dd_info	4f
dm_value_query	5c	dm_domain	50
dm_webc_config	08	dm_aggr_domain	51
dm_webc_target	08	dm_expression	52
dm_workflow	4d	dm_literal_expr	53
dm_xml_application	0b	dm_builtin_expr	54
dm_xml_config	09	dm_func_expr	55
dm_xml_custom_code	09	dm_cond_expr	56
dm_xml_style_sheet	09	dm_cond_id_expr	57
dm_xml_zone	09	dmi_expr_code	58
dmi_audittrail_attrs	00	dm_key	59
dmi_change_record	33	dm_value_assist	5a

Type Name	Hex Id	Type Name	Hex Id
dmi_dd_attr_info	6a	dm_value_list	5b
dmi_dd_common_info	68	dm_value_query	5c
dmi_dd_type_info	69	dm_value_func	5d
dmi_dump_object_record	30	dm_federation	5e
dmi_expr_code	58	dm_audittrail	5f
dmi_index	1f	dm_audittrail_acl	5f
dmi_linkrecord	2b	dm_audittrail_group	5f
dmi_load_object_record	32	dm_extern_store	60
dmi_otherfile	23	dm_extern_file	61
dmi_package	49	dm_extern_url	62
dmi_queue_item	1b	dm_extern_free	63
dmi_registry	26	dmi_subcontent	64
dmi_replica_record	2d	dm_foreign_key	65
dmi_sequence	20	dm_alias_set	66
dmi_subcontent	64	dm_plugin	67
dmi_tdk_collect	1c	dmi_dd_common_info	68
dmi_tdk_index	24	dmi_dd_type_info	69
dmi_vstamp	1e	dm_ca_store	6a
dmi_workitem	4a	dmi_dd_attr_info	6a
dmr_containment	05	dm_display_config	6b
dmr_content	06	dm_scope_config	6c

Notice that many object types have an identifier of 08 or 09 (dm_sysobject or dm_document, respectively), demonstrating that even Documentum's basic object types use inheritance.

7.11 Attribute Data Types

All object attributes must be one of the six data types list in Table 7.2. As you can see from the middle column, these data types are implemented differently in different RDBMS. However, the Documentum API and the DFC normalize these differences for you, as long as you refer to, and operate on, the Documentum defined data types.

Table 7.2—Documentum Attribute Types

Documentum Attribute Data Type	Type Code	Database Data Type (Oracle/ SQL Server)	Range of Values
dm_boolean	0	number(6)/integer	1 (true), 0 (false)
dm_integer	1	number(10)/integer	-2147483647 to 2147483647
dm_string	2	char(2000)/varchar(7000)	0 – RDBMS maximum
dm_id	3	char(16)/char(16)	There is no range of values for this data type, however, all Ids are 16 characters in length.
dm_time	4	date/datetime	1/1/1753 to 12/31/9999
dm_double	5	number/float	RDBMS specific. Minimum of 1×10^{-129} to 1×10^{129}

7.12 Computed Attributes

dm_sysobjects have a set of attributes that are not stored as part of the object in the Docbase, but are computed on demand. These attributes are only accessible through the DFC and API (i.e., they are not accessible from DQL), and are primarily for internal use by the Content Server. However, they can also be valuable to developers. Table 7.3 lists the most common computed attributes and how to access them. For a detailed explanation of each attribute, see the *Documentum Content Server Object Reference Manual*. Note that other Docbase objects, such as dm_group and dm_policy, possess additional computed attributes not discussed here.

The table assumes an object named sObj has been instantiated as an IDfSysObject. A few of these attributes are repeating and, therefore, the DFC methods required to access them use an index to indicate which repeating value to retrieve. In these cases, the table will show the method name followed by (i) to indicate an index value is required. Chapter 8, *Putting It All Together in a Sample Application*, contains source code that demonstrates accessing and using these attributes.

Table 7.3—Computed Attributes

Computed Attribute Name	Accessor Method
_accessor_name	sObj.getAccessorName(i)
_accessor_permit	sObj.getAccessorPermit(i)
_accessor_xpermit	sObj.getAccessorXPermit(i)
_accessor_xpermit_names	sObj.getAccessorXPermitNames(i)
_acl_ref_valid	sObj.getAclRefValid()
_alias_set	sObj.getAliasSet()
_allow_change_location	sObj.getBoolean("_allow_change_ location")
_allow_change_permit	sObj.getBoolean("_allow_change_ permit")
_allow_change_state	sObj.getBoolean("_allow_change_ state")
_allow_execute_proc	sObj.getBoolean("_allow_execute_ proc")
_allow_change_owner	sObj.getBoolean("_allow_change_ owner")
_cached	sObj.getBoolean("_cached")
_changed	sObj.isDirty()
_componentID (if applicable)	sObj.getComponentId(i).getId()
_containID (if applicable)	sObj.getContainId(i).getId()
_content_buffer	(only applicable after a *getContent()* API method call)
_content_state	sObj.getContentState(i)
_count	sObj.getAttrCount()
_current_state	sObj.getCurrentState()
_docbase_id	sObj.getObjectId.getDocbaseId()
_dump	(contains same info the *dump()* API method provides)
_id	sObj.getObjectId.toString()
_isnew	sObj.isNew()
_isreplica	sObj.isReplica()
_lengths	dmAPIGet("get,c,<object id>,_lengths[i]")
_masterdocbase	sObj.getMasterDocbase()
_names	dmAPIGet("get,c,<object id>,_names[i]")
_permit	sObj.getPermit()
_policy_name	sObj.getPolicyName()

Computed Attribute Name	Accessor Method
_repeating	dmAPIGet("get,c,<object id>, _repeating[i]")
_status	sObj.getStatus()
_type_id	sObj.getString("_type_id")
_type_name	sObj.getTypeName()
_types	dmAPIGet("get,c,<object id>, _types[i]")
_typestring	dmAPIGet("get,c,<object id>, _typestring")
_values	dmAPIGet("get,c,<object id>, _values[i]")
_xpermit	sObj.getXPermit(IDfSession.getUser("").getUserName)
_xpermit_list	sObj.getXPermitList
_xpermit_names	sObj.getXPermitNames(IDfSession.getUser("").getUserName)

7.13 Format Types

Format type objects, `dm_format`, control the format of content in the Docbase (e.g., Microsoft Word, text, JPG.). By default, Documentum defines more than 270 formats. These formats are listed in Table 7.4. You can easily add more formats using the Documentum Administrator. See the *Documentum Content Server Administrator's Guide* for more information.

Table 7.4—Documentum Defined Format Objects

Object Name	Description	DOS Extension	MIME Type
123w	Lotus 1-2-3 r5	wk4	application/vnd.lotus-1-2-3
a-law	a-LAW Sound		
acad	AutoCAD Drawing	dwg	
aiff	AIFF Sound		audio/aiff
aiff-c	AIFF-C Sound		
amipro	AMI Professional	sam	

Object Name	Description	DOS Extension	MIME Type
as_applet	AppleScript application		
as_droplet	AppleScript droppable application		
as_script	AppleScript compiled script		
asp	Active Server Pages	asp	text/asp
atd	Auxiliary Tag Data	atd	text/plain
att	XMetaL Attribute Help Strings	att	text/plain
au	u-LAW sound		
audio	Audio File	au	audio/basic
avi	Video for Windows	avi	
binary	Binary Data		
bmp	Bit Mapped Image	bmp	image/bmp
image/bmp			
cals1	CALS 1 image	mil	
cals2	CALS 2 image	ov	
canvas	Canvas drawing	cvs	
cfm	Cold Fusion Template File (cfm)	cfm	
cfml	Cold Fusion Template File (cfml)	cfml	
cgi	Common Gateway Interface Program	cgi	application/cgi

Object Name	Description	DOS Extension	MIME Type
cgm	Computer Graphics Metafile	cgm	image/cgm
chemdraw	ChemDraw drawing		
class	Java Class File	class	java/*
com	COM.FORMAT		
crtext	Text Document (Windows)	txt	
css	Cascading Style Sheet Document	css	text/css
ctm	XMetaL Customization File	ctm	text/xml
daf	Documentum Annotation File	daf	
dca	DCA Revisible Form Text	rft	
dec	DEC - Compiled DTD	dec	application/x-epic-dec
dib	DIB image (Windows)	dib	
digital	Digital DX		
displaywrite	DisplayWrite		
dm_fulltext_copy	Copy for fulltext indexing		
dm_internal	Documentum Internal		
dm_print_copy	Copy for printing		
doc	Interleaf 3.x	doc	
dtd	DTD File	dtd	text/dtd

Object Name	Description	DOS Extension	MIME Type
dwf	AutoCAD Web Format	dwf	
dxf	AutoCAD DXF	dxf	
ebdic	EBCDIC		
elm	XML Supporting Document	elm	
enable	Enable		
ent	XML Entity File(ent)	ent	text/xml
eps	Encapsulated PostScript	eps	
excel	Excel 3.x worksheet	xls	application/vnd.ms-excel
excel2sheet	Excel 2.x worksheet	xls	application/vnd.ms-excel
excel4book	Excel 4.x workbook	xlw	application/vnd.ms-excel
excel4sheet	Excel 4.x worksheet	xls	application/vnd.ms-excel
excel5book	Excel workbook 5.0	xls	application/vnd.ms-excel
excel8book	Excel 97 / 2000 workbook	xls	application/vnd.ms-excel
excel8template	Excel 97 / 2000 template	xlt	application/vnd.ms-excel
filemaker2	FileMaker II		
filemakerpro	FileMaker Pro	fm	
filemakerpro3	FileMaker Pro 3.0	fp3	
filemakerpro4	FileMaker Pro 4.0	fp4	
finalform	Final Form text		
flash	Flash File	fla	application/x-flash

Object Name	Description	DOS Extension	MIME Type
fos	FOSI - Formatting Output Specification Instance	`fos`	
framework	FrameWork		
freehand1image	FreeHand 1.0 image		
freehand1template	FreeHand 1.0 template		
freehand2image	FreeHand 2.0 image		
freehand2template	FreeHand 2.0 template		
freehand3image	FreeHand 3.x image		
freelance	Freelance presentation	`pre`	application/vnd.lotus-freelance
fssd	SoundEdit sound		
fullwrite	FullWrite 1.1		
gem	GEM drawing		
gif	GIF image	`gif`	image/gif
hcom	Hcom Sound (MacOS)		
hdml	Handheld Device Markup Language Document	`hdml`	text/hdml
helix_express	Helix Express database		
hhf	XMetaL Form File	`hhf`	application/octet-stream
hpgl	HP Graphics Language		

Object Name	Description	DOS Extension	MIME Type
hpuxshrlib	HP-UX Shared Library	`sl`	
html	HTML Document	`htm`	text/html
hypercard	HyperCard stack		
i1	Interleaf Publisher 1.1		
i5	Interleaf Publisher 5.0		
iaf	Interleaf 5 ASCII Format		
ibmshrlib	IBM-AIX Shared Library	`so`	
iges	IGES drawing		
illustrator	Illustrator 3.0 image	`ai`	
illustrator1	Illustrator 1.x image		
illustrator5	Illustrator 5.x image	`ai`	
illustrator88	Illustrator 88 image		
image	Image		
imagemap	Image Map File	`map`	
ip	Interpress		
iw	Island Write		
jar	Java Archive File	`jar`	java/*
java	Java Source File	`java`	text/java
jhtml	Java within Hypertext Markup Language Document	`jhtml`	text/jhtml
jpeg	JPEG Image	`jpg`	image/jpeg

Object Name	Description	DOS Extension	MIME Type
js	JavaScript File	js	text/js
jsp	Java Server Pages	jsp	application/x-javascript
legacy	Legacy		
lotmanu	Lotus Manuscript 2.0	2.1	
lotus	1-2-3 r3.0		application/vnd.lotus-1-2-3
macdraw	MacDraw drawing		
macdrawp	MacDraw Pro drawing		
macp	MacPaint image		
macproject	MacProject 1.x		
macproject2	MacProject 2.x		
mactext	Text Document (MacOS)	txt	
macwrite	MacWrite 4.5-5.0		
macwrite2	MacWrite II		
macwritepro	MacWrite Pro		
maker	FrameMaker - internal format	fm	
maker51	FrameMaker 5.1 - internal format	fm	
maker55	FrameMaker 5.5 - internal format	fm	
man	UNIX man page		
mass11	MASS 11 8.x		
mbook	FrameMaker - book	bk	application/vnd.framemaker
mbook51	FrameMaker 5.1 book	bk	application/vnd.framemaker
mbook55	FrameMaker 5.5 book	bk	application/vnd.framemaker

Object Name	Description	DOS Extension	MIME Type
mcr	XMetaL Macro File	mcr	text/xml
mdoc	FrameMaker - document	fm	application/vnd.framemaker
mdoc51	FrameMaker 5.1 document	fm	application/vnd.framemaker
mdoc55	FrameMaker 5.5 document	fm	application/vnd.framemaker
mif	FrameMaker - MIF	mif	application/vnd.mif
mif51	FrameMaker 5.1 MIF	mif	application/vnd.mif
mif55	FrameMaker 5.5 MIF	mif	application/vnd.mif
mmdwt	Macromedia Template File	dwt	
mml	FrameMaker - MML		
mml51	FrameMaker 5.1 - MML		
mml55	FrameMaker 5.5 MML		
mmlbi	Macromedia Library File	lbi	
mod	MOD sound (Amiga)	mod	
mp3	MP3 File	mp3	audio/x-mpeg
mpeg	MPEG Video File	mpg	video/x-mpeg
ms_access	Access 1.x or 2.0 database	mdb	
ms_access7	Access 95 database	mdb	
ms_access8	Access 97 / 2000 database	mdb	

Object Name	Description	DOS Extension	MIME Type
msproject	MS Project - project	mpp	application/vnd.ms-project
msproject_calendar	MS Project - calendar	mpc	
msproject_view	MS Project - view	mpv	
msw	Word 4.x	doc	application/msword
msw3	Word 3.0-4.x	doc	application/msword
msw6	Word 6.0	doc	application/msword
msw6template	Word 6.x template	dot	application/msword
msw8	Word 97 / 2000 document	doc	application/msword
msw8template	Word 97 / 2000 template	dot	application/msword
mswm	Word 4.x	doc	application/msword
mswm1	Word 1.x (MacOS)		application/msword
msww	Word 1.x	doc	application/msword
multimate	MultiMate 4.x		
navydif	Navy DIF		
officewrite	OfficeWriter 4.0		
pagemaker	PageMaker 5.x publication	pm6	
pagemaker1pub	PageMaker 1.x publication		
pagemaker2pub	PageMaker 2.x publication		
pagemaker3pub	PageMaker 3.x publication		
pagemaker3template	PageMaker 3.x template		
pagemaker4pub	PageMaker 4.x publication		
pagemaker4template	PageMaker 4.x template		

Object Name	Description	DOS Extension	MIME Type
pagemaker5template	PageMaker 5.x template		
paradox	Paradox 3.5	`4.0`	
pbm	Portable Bitmap		
pcl	HP LaserJet series II	`pcl`	
pcx	PC Paint image (Windows)	`pcx`	
pdf	Acrobat PDF	`pdf`	application/pdf
pdftext	Acrobat PDF Text		
peachtext	PeachText 5000 v2.1		
pen	XML Entity File(pen)	`pen`	text/xml
persuasion	Persuasion		
photoshop	Photoshop 2.0 image		
photoshop3	Photoshop 2.5	`3.0 image`	
php	PHP Script File	`php`	text/php
php3	PHP within Hypertext Markup Language Document (php3)	`php3`	text/php3
phtml	PHP within Hypertext Markup Language Document (phtml)	`phtml`	text/phtml
pict	PICT image (MacOS)	`pct`	
png	PNG Image	`png`	image/png

Object Name	Description	DOS Extension	MIME Type
powerpoint	PowerPoint pre-3.0	ppt	application/vnd.ms-powerpoint
ppt8	PowerPoint 97 / 2000 presentation	ppt	application/vnd.ms-powerpoint
ppt8_template	PowerPoint 97 / 2000 template	pot	application/vnd.ms-powerpoint
ppt_mac3	PowerPoint 3.x (MacOS)	ppt	application/vnd.ms-powerpoint
ppt_mac4	PowerPoint 4.x (MacOS)	ppt	application/vnd.ms-powerpoint
ppt_win3	PowerPoint 3.x (Windows)	ppt	application/vnd.ms-powerpoint
ppt_win4	PowerPoint 4.x (Windows)	ppt	application/vnd.ms-powerpoint
ppt_win7	PowerPoint 7.0 (Windows)	ppt	application/vnd.ms-powerpoint
pro	PRO - Compiled DTD	pro	application/x-epic-pro
prowrite	Professional Write 1.0		
ps	PostScript	ps	application/postscript
ptcasm	Pro/Engineer Assembly	asm	
ptcdrw	Pro/Engineer Drawing	drw	
ptcprt	Pro/Engineer Part	prt	
ptd	PTD - Compiled DTD	ptd	application/x-epic-ptd
pub_html	Published HTML Document	htm	text/html
q&a	Q&A Write		
quark	Quark Express (MacOS)		

Object Name	Description	DOS Extension	MIME Type
quattropro	Quattro Pro 4.0		
quattroprow	Quattro Pro 1.0 (Windows)		
quicktime	QuickTime Movie	mov	video/quicktime
ra	RealAudio Clip File	ra	audio/vnd.rn-realaudio
ram	RealPlayer File (ram)	ram	audio/x-pn-realaudio
rapid	Rapid File		
ras	Sun Raster Image (RAS)	ras	
rls	XMetaL Compiled SGML DTD File	rls	application/octet-stream
rlx	XMetaL Compiled XML DTD File	rlx	application/octet-stream
rm	RealMedia File	rm	audio/vnd.rn-realmedia
rmm	RealPlayer File (rmm)	rmm	audio/x-pn-realaudio
rnx	RealPlayer File (rnx)	rnx	audio/vnd.rn-realplayer
rtf	Rich Text Format (RTF)	rtf	application/msword
rv	RealVideo Clip File	rv	audio/vnd.rn-realvideo
samna	Samna Word IV (Plus)		
scam	ScreenCam movie	scm	application/vnd.lotus-screencam
sgml	SGML text	sgm	text/sgml

Object Name	Description	DOS Extension	MIME Type
shtml	Server Parsed HTML Document (shtml)	shtml	text/shtml
snd	Macintosh Sound		
soc	OASIS Catalog	soc	text/plain
span	Kurzweil OCR/SPAN		
spl	Shockwave Flash File (spl)	spl	application/futuresplash
spml	Server Parsed HTML Document (spml)	spml	text/spml
ste	Scriptable Text Editor (MacOS)		
stm	Server Parsed HTML Document (stm)	stm	text/stm
sun	Sun Raster Image (Sun)	sun	
sunshrlib	Solaris Shared Library	so	
swf	Shockwave Flash File (swf)	swf	application/x-shockwave-flash
tbr	XMetaL Toolbar and Menu File	tbr	text/xml
teachtextro	Teach Text (read only)	txt	
tex	TeX Composition		
text	Text Document (Unix)	txt	text/plain
tiff	TIFF Image	tif	image/tiff
totalword	Total Word 1.2		

Object Name	Description	DOS Extension	MIME Type
troff	Troff		
u-law	u-LAW sound (au)	au	
unknown	Unknown		
ustn	MicroStation	dgn	application/x-microstation
vbbas	Visual Basic - source	bas	
vbfrm	Visual Basic - form	frm	
vbmak	Visual Basic - make	mak	
ventura	Ventura 2.0		
voc	VOC sound (Windows)	voc	
volkswrite	VolksWriter		
vrf	Virtual Resource File	vrf	
vsd1	Visio 1 drawing	vsd	application/vnd.visio
vsd2	Visio 2 drawing	vsd	application/vnd.visio
vsd3	Visio 3 drawing	vsd	application/vnd.visio
vsd4	Visio 4 drawing	vsd	application/vnd.visio
wangpc	Wang PC 3.0		
wave	Windows Sound	wav	audio/wav
win32shrlib	Windows Shared Library	dll	
winwrite	MS Write 3.0	wri	
wmf	Windows Metafile image	wmf	
wordstar	Wordstar		
wordstar2000	Wordstar 2000 3.0		
wp	WordPerfect 4.x (DOS)		

Object Name	Description	DOS Extension	MIME Type
wp5	WordPerfect 5.x	wpd	application/wordperfect5.1
wp6	WordPerfect 6.0	wpd	
wp7	WordPerfect 7.0	wpd	
wp8	WordPerfect 8.0	wpd	
wpmac	WordPerfect 2.x (MacOS)		
wpmac1	WordPerfect 1.x (MacOS)		
wpmac3	WordPerfect 3.x (MacOS)		
wps+	WPS-PLUS		
wpw	WordPerfect 5.1		
writeassit	IBM Writing Assistant 1.0		
writenow	WriteNow 3.0 (MacOS)		
wrl	VRML File	wrl	model/vrml
xbm	X Bitmap (Unix)		image/xbm
xml	XML Document	xml	text/xml
xsd	XML Schema	xsd	
xsl	XSL File	xsl	text/xsl
xwd	X-Windows screen dump (Unix)		
xywrite	XyWrite		
zip	Zip File	zip	application/x-zip-compressed
zip_html	Zipped HTML Files	zip	application/x-zip-compressed
zip_pub_html	Zipped & Published HTML Document	zip	application/x-zip-compressed

To determine which formats are defined in your Docbase, you can use the following query:

```
select name, description, dos_extension, mime_type from
    dm_format;
```

7.14 Object Permissions

Documentum provides seven levels of object permissions, or security, as described in Table 7.5. These permissions control user access to objects, and are hierarchical, meaning that each permission includes the access capabilities of the permission above it. For example, if a user possesses `Write` permission (6) on an object, he also possesses `Version`, `Relate`, `Read`, and `Browse` permission.

Docbase objects also possess extended permission that are expressed as strings, and are not hierarchical in nature. The extended permissions are described in Table 7.6.

Table 7.5—Documentum Base Object Permissions

Value	Permission Name	Description
1	None	No access. You don't even know these objects exist.
2	Browse	You can see the objects and read their attributes, but not their content.
3	Read	You can read attribute data and the content of these objects.
4	Relate	You can attach an annotation or workflow to these objects.
5	Version	You can create a new version of these objects.
6	Write	You can update these objects and save them as the same version.
7	Delete	You can destroy these objects.

Table 7.6—Documentum Extended Object Permissions

Permission Name	Description
Change State	You can change the document lifecycle state (business policy) of the object.
Change Permission	You can change the base permissions of the object.
Change Owner	You can change the owner of the object.
Execute Procedure	You can execute (i.e., run) the object, assuming it is an executable object (e.g., a procedure or workflow method). Users that have at least Browse (1) permission on the object automatically have Execute Procedure permission also.
Change Location	You can move an object from one folder to another. Users that have at least Browse (1) permission on the object automatically have Change Location permission also.

7.15 Registered Table Permissions

Documentum provides five levels of access for registered tables, as described in Table 7.7. These permissions apply to the underlying RDBMS tables and *not* the registered table objects (i.e., these permissions pertain to the world_table_permit, group_table_permit, and owner_table_ permit attributes). Unlike object permissions, registered table permissions are additive and not hierarchical. This means an access level does *not* assume the permissions of the levels above it. Rather, they are a summation of all granted permissions. For example, a user with Insert permission (4) does not have Update permission (2). To assign a user Insert and Update permission, the user must have an access level of 6 (4+2).

Table 7.7—Documentum Registered Table Permissions

Value	Permission Name	Description
0	None	No access.
1	Select	You can select data from these tables.
2	Update	You can update data in these tables.
4	Insert	You can insert new rows into these tables.
8	Delete	You can delete rows from these tables.

When working with registered tables, it is important to understand the difference between object permissions and table permissions. This difference was discussed in Chapter 3, *Working with Queries and Collections*.

7.16 Verity KeyView File Filters

The Verity full-text search engine embedded in the Content Server employs KeyView file filters to read a variety of common file formats. The file formats readable by the KeyView 7.0 file filters are listed in Table 7.8.

Table 7.8—KeyView 7.2 File Filters

Word Processing Formats		
Adobe Maker Interchange Format (MIF) 5.0, 5.5, 6.0, 7.0	Applix Words 4.2, 4.3, 4.4	ANSI Text 7 and 8-bit
ASCII Text 7 and 8-bit	Display Write 4.0	Folio Flat File 3.1
HTML 1.x, 2.x, 3.x	IBM DCA/RFT SC23-0758-1	JustSystems Ichitaro 8.0, 9.0, 10.0, 12.0
Lotus AMI Pro through 3.1	Lotus Word Pro 96 through Millennium Edition 9.6	Microsoft Word through 6.0
Microsoft Word for Macintosh 4.0 through 98	Microsoft Word Pad	Microsoft Works for Windows through 4.0
Microsoft Works for Windows through 6.0 (text only)	Microsoft Write 1.0 through 3.0	WordPerfect for DOS through 6.1
WordPerfect for Macintosh 1.02 through 3.1	WordPerfect for Windows 5.0, 6.0, 7.0, 8.0 and 10.0	Oasys 7.0 (text only)
WordPerfect for Linux 6.0	Unicode Text	XyWrite 4.12
Presentation Formats		
Adobe Portable Document Format (PDF) 1.1 through 1.4	Applix Presents 4.3, 4.4	Corel/Novell Presentations 7.0, 9.0, 10.0, 11.0 and 2002
Freelance for Windows through Millennium Edition 9.6	Microsoft PowerPoint for Windows 4.0 through 2002	Microsoft PowerPoint for Macintosh 98
Spreadsheet Formats		
Applix Spreadsheets 4.2, 4.3, 4.4	Comma Separated Values (CSV)	Quattro Pro for Windows through 8.0
Lotus 1-2-3 through 5.0	Lotus 1-2-3 for SmartSuite 96 and later	Lotus 1-2-3 Charts through 5.0
Microsoft Excel for Windows 3.0 through 2002	Microsoft Excel Charts 2.x through 7.0	Microsoft Excel for Macintosh 98
Microsoft Works Spreadsheet 1.0 through 4.0		

7.17 Menu Command State Flags

Menu command state flags are set on the **Behavior** tab of the Menu System Designer Tool, and used to control when menu options are enabled. The menu command state flags were first mentioned in Chapter 2, *Getting Started with Applications and Components*. Table 7.9 describes the command state flags.

Table 7.9—Menu Command State Flags

Flag	Explanation
DC_CSF_ALWAYS = DC_CSF_FIRST	Always.
DC_CSF_ANYTHING	Anything is selected.
DC_CSF_CHECKED_OUT_SELF	Selected item is checked out by the current user.
DC_CSF_CLIPBOARD	Clipboard contains data that can be pasted.
DC_CSF_CLIPBOARD_DIFFERENT_DOCBASE	Clipboard contains an object from a different Docbase.
DC_CSF_CLIPBOARD_SAME_DOCBASE	Clipboard contains an object from the same Docbase.
DC_CSF_EDIT	Selected item has content and is not checked out by someone else.
DC_CSF_FROZEN_ASSEMBLY	Selected item is associated with a frozen assembly.
DC_CSF_HAS_CONTENT	Selected item is a dm_sysobject with content.
DC_CSF_MAKE_PLAIN	Selected item may be made into a plain document.
DC_CSF_MAKE_VIRTUAL	Selected item may be made into a virtual document.
DC_CSF_NEVER	Never.
DC_CSF_NOT_CHECKED_OUT	Selected item is a document that is not checked out.
DC_CSF_UNFROZEN_ASSEMBLY	Selected item is associated with an unfrozen assembly.
DC_CSF_VIEW.	Selected item is available for viewing.
DC_CSF_VIRTUAL_DOCUMENT	Selected item is a virtual document.
C_SHELL_CSF_COMPLETED_UNACQUIRED_ROUTER = DC_SHELL_CSF_FIRST	Container or the selected item is a completed but unacquired router.

Flag	Explanation
DC_SHELL_CSF_CONNECTED	User is connected to any Docbase.
DC_SHELL_CSF_CONNECTED_DOCBASE	Container or selected item is a connected Docbase.
DC_SHELL_CSF_CONNECTED_LOGIN_ITEM	Container or selected item is a Docbase, the Inbox, or My Cabinet.
DC_SHELL_CSF_DELETE	Selected item can be deleted.
DC_SHELL_CSF_DOCBASE	Container or selected item is a Docbase (not necessarily connected).
DC_SHELL_CSF_DOCUMENT	Selected item is a document.
DC_SHELL_CSF_FOLDER	Container or selected item is a folder or cabinet.
DC_SHELL_CSF_INCOMPLETE_ROUTER	Container or selected item is an incomplete router.
DC_SHELL_CSF_INCOMPLETE_TASK	Container or selected item is an incomplete router or work item.
DC_SHELL_CSF_INCOMPLETE_WORK_ITEM.	Container or selected item is an incomplete work item.
DC_SHELL_CSF_LOCAL_COPY	Selected item is a Local Copy item in the Local Files container.
DC_SHELL_CSF_LOGIN_ITEM	Container or selected item is a Docbase, the Inbox or My Cabinet (not necessarily connected).
DC_SHELL_CSF_NON_RUNNING_ROUTER	Selected item is a non-running router.
DC_SHELL_CSF_SYSOBJECT	Selected item is a dm_sysobject.
DC_SHELL_CSF_UNACQUIRED_ROUTER	Container or selected item is an unacquired router.

Flag	Explanation
DC_SHELL_CSF_UNACQUIRED_TASK	Container or selected item is an unacquired router or work item.
DC_SHELL_CSF_UNLINK	Selected item is a dm_sysobject in a Docbase, cabinet or folder.
DC_VDM_CSF_ADD_CHILD = DC_VDM_CSF_FIRST	Selected item can have a child added to it in the virtual document structure.
DC_VDM_CSF_CLIPBOARD_DRAGDROP	Clipboard contains data that can be pasted or a drag-drop operation is occurring.
DC_VDM_CSF_COPY_BEHAVIOR	Selected item is not the root of the virtual document and not a component in an assembly.
DC_VDM_CSF_MDI_CHILD_OPEN MDI	Child window is open in the VDM editor.
DC_VDM_CSF_NOT_ASSEMBLY_ COMPONENT	Selected item is not a component in an assembly but can be the root.
DC_VDM_CSF_NOT_ASSEMBLY_ROOT	Selected item is not the root of an assembly.
DC_VDM_CSF_NOT_CDM_CHILD	Selected item is not a child of a compound document.
DC_VDM_CSF_NOT_CDM_PARENT	Selected item is not a parent of a compound document.
DC_VDM_CSF_NOT_ROOT	Selected item is not the root of the virtual document.
DC_VDM_CSF_PASTE_CLIPBOARD	Clipboard contains data that can be pasted and the target is not a compound document.
DC_VDM_CSF_PASTE_CLIPBOARD_ DRAGDROP	Clipboard contains data that can be pasted or a drag-drop operation is occurring and the target is not a compound document.

Flag	Explanation
DC_VDM_CSF_PASTE_SPECIAL	Selected item is available for the paste special operation.
DC_VDM_CSF_REMOVE	Selected item can be removed from the virtual document structure.
DC_VDM_CSF_USE_ASSEMBLY	Selected item is available for the use assembly operation.
DC_VDM_CSF_VDM_DIRTY	Virtual document has been changed.
DC_VDM_CSF_VDM_ROOT	Selected item is the root of the virtual document.

7.18 Uninstalling DocApps

DocApps are a terrific feature of Documentum, but if you ever mess one up and need to permanently remove it, you'll discover they are not easily uninstalled. The reason is, once a DocApp has been installed, there are potentially hundreds of other objects in the Docbase that could be using or referencing it or one of its components. Brute force deleting it could render your Docbase inoperable; therefore, the server will probably not let you simply delete it.

Although the Documentum Application Builder does not have an uninstall function for DocApps, there is a method for removing them. However, the safest way to remove a DocApp from a Docbase is to simply disable it by setting its ACL to one in which no one can access it.

The following steps[*] can be used to successfully remove a DocApp from a Docbase. *Use this procedure at your own risk!*

1. Using DQL, or whatever means works best for you, delete all the objects from the Docbase that are of types defined in the DocApp. For example, if you had an object type named `regional_doc`, you would want to delete all instances of `regional_doc` objects from the Docbase (this includes all versions and renditions). For example:

   ```
   delete regional_doc (all) objects;
   ```

---

[*] Based on Documentum Support Note #5908.

2. If any of the objects mentioned in step 1 have indexes on their attributes, these indexes need to be deleted. See `DROP_INDEX` in the *Documentum Content Server Fundamentals* manual for details on dropping indexes.
3. Because all `STRING` attributes are put in the full-text index automatically, the full-text index also needs to be cleared. This can be easily accomplished from the Documentum Administrator.
4. If necessary, uninstall any applicable workflow templates using the Workflow Manager.
5. Start Documentum Application Builder and open the DocApp.
6. Select objects (other than custom types), and click **Delete object from Docbase** in the **Edit** menu. For example, delete ACX forms, and lifecycles.
7. Delete custom types from the DocApp, by selecting them, right-clicking, and choosing **Remove selected object from DocApp/Type** from the context menu.
8. Checkin this version of the DocApp as the *same* version.
9. Close Documentum Application Builder.
10. Using the Documentum Desktop, navigate to the `/System/Applications/<DocApp Name>` folder where `<DocApp Name>` is the actual name of the DocApp.
11. Delete the DocApp virtual document (🌐), but not its children. The children could be in use by other DocApps.
12. If there are no other objects in this folder, or you are certain about the disposition of the objects that remain, you can delete the DocApp's folder.
13. Finally, delete the DocApp's alias set. You can do this with a simple DQL query:

    ```
    delete dm_alias_set object where object_name =
        '<DocApp Name>';
    ```

    where `<DocApp Name>` is the actual name of the DocApp.

The DocApp now is effectively deleted.

7.19 Server Error Files

All the error messages generated by the Content Server can be found in a set of text files on the server. These are the messages that appear in the DcReporter when exceptions occur, or are returned by the `getmessage()` API method. The files reside in the `%DM_HOME%\messages` directory and are listed in Table 7.10.

The files divide the error messages by "facility," such as ACL, group, or event. Their names are reasonably obvious. Each file is further divided by the severity of the error message. The five severity levels are:

- `FATAL`—an error the user has no control over.
- `ERROR`—an error due to something the user did.

- TRACE—messages output when tracing is in effect.
- WARNING—warning messages.
- INFORMATION—informational messages.

Each error message contains the following elements:

- Error String—composed of the error name in all caps, followed by the explanation.
- CAUSE—what caused the error.
- ACTION—contains what might be the most important part of the message: *how to remedy the error.* (This value is not output as part of the error message by the server.)
- PARAMETERS—an explanation of the values substituted into the Error String when it is output.

Table 7.10—Server Error Files

File Name	Purpose
dmacl.e	Errors messages returned by the DM_ACL facility (dmACL class).
dmapi.e	Errors messages returned by the DM_API facility (client API tracing).
dmassmbl.e	Errors messages returned by the DM_ASSEMBLY facility (dmAssembly class).
dmaudit.e	Errors messages returned by the DM_AUDITTRAIL facility.
dmbroker.e	Errors messages returned by the DM_DOCBROKER facility.
dmcab.e	Error messages returned by the DM_CABINET facility (dmCabinet).
dmccont.e	Error messages returned by the DM_CCONTENT facility (Common Content Area).
dmchtran.e	Error messages returned by the DM_CHARTRANS facility.
dmcntain.e	Error messages returned by the DM_CONTAINMENT facility (dmContainment class).
dmcompos.e	Error messages returned by the DM_COMPOSITE facility (dmComposite class).
dmcont.e	Error messages returned by the DM_CONTENT facility.
dmcrypto.e	Error messages returned by the DM_CRYPTO facility.
dmddict.e	Error messages returned by the DM_DATA_DICT facility (Data Dictionary).
dmdir.e	Error messages returned by the DM_DIRECTORY facility.
dmdoc.e	Error messages returned by the DM_DOCUMENT facility (dmDocument class).
dmdoccnf.e	Error messages returned by the DM_DCNFG facility (dmDocbaseConfig class).
dmdump.e	Error messages returned by the DM_DUMP facility (dmDump class).

File Name	Purpose
dmesign.e	Error messages returned by the DM_SIGN facility (Electronic Signature).
dmevent.e	Error messages returned by the DM_EVENT facility (dmInbox class).
dmexcept.e	Error messages returned by the DM_EXCEPTION facility.
dmexpr.e	Error messages returned by the DM_EXPRESSION facility.
dmfilter.e	Error messages returned by the DM_FILTER facility (dmFilter class).
dmfolder.e	Error messages returned by the DM_FOLDER facility (dmFolder class).
dmforgn.e	Error messages returned by the DM_FOREIGN facility (dmDocbaseIdMap class).
dmformat.e	Error messages returned by the DM_FORMAT facility.
dmftindx.e	Error messages returned by the DM_FT_INDEX facility (Full-text index management).
dmfull.e	Error messages returned by the DM_FULLTEXT facility.
dmgroup.e	Error messages returned by the DM_GROUP (dmGroup class).
dmiditr.e	Error messages returned by the DM_ITDR facility (SQL iterator).
dminbox.e	Error messages returned by the DM_INBOX facility (dmInbox class).
dminfo.e	Error messages returned by the DM_INFO facility.
dmintern.e	Error messages returned by the DM_INTERNAL facility.
dmload.e	Error messages returned by the DM_LOAD facility (dmLoad class).
dmlocale.e	Error messages returned by the DM_LOCALE facility (client local date format).
dmlocatn.e	Error messages returned by the DM_LOCATION facility.
dmmethod.e	Error messages returned by the DM_METHOD facility (dmNote class).
dmmtpt.e	Error messages returned by the DM_MTPT facility (mount point).
dmnote.e	Error messages returned by the DM_NOTE facility (dmNote class).
dmobject.e	Error messages returned by the DM_OBJECT facility (dmObject class).
dmoutdev.e	Error messages returned by the DM_OUTPUTDEVICE (output devices).
dmpart.e	Error messages returned by the DM_VERITY_COLL (fulltext partition management).

File Name	Purpose
dmplat.e	Error messages returned by the DM_PLATFORM facility.
dmpolicy.e	Error messages returned by the DM_POLICY facility (dmPolicy class).
dmpom.e	Error messages returned by the DM_OBJ_MGR (dmObjectManager class).
dmptm.e	Error messages returned by the DM_TYPE_MGR (dmTypeManager class).
dmquery.e	Error messages returned by the DM_QUERY facility.
dmquery2.e	Error messages returned by the DM_QUERY facility (continued due to limit of 256 messages per severity per facility).
dmrecov.e	Error messages returned by the DM_RECOVERY facility (recovery subsytem).
dmrelate.e	Error messages returned by the DM_RELATION (dmRelation class)
dmrelatp.e	Error messages returned by the DM_RELTYPE facility (dmRelation_type class).
dmrouter.e	Error messages returned by the DM_ROUTER facility (dmRouter class).
dmserver.e	Error messages returned by the DM_SERVER facility (generic server messages).
dmsess.e	Error messages returned by the DM_SESSION facility (dmSession class).
dmsql.e	Error messages returned by the SQL_TRACE facility.
dmsrvcnf.e	Error messages returned by the DM_SCNFG (dmServerConfig class).
dmstor.e	Error messages returned by the DM_STORAGE facility (storage errors).
dmsysobj.e	Error messages returned by theDM_SYSOBJECT facility (dmSysObject class).
dmupgmgr.e	Error messages returned by the DM_UPGRADE_MGR facility.
dmuser.e	Error messages returned by the DM_USER facility (dmUser and dmGroup classes).
dmvrsion.e	Error messages returned by the DM_VERSION facility.
dmwflow.e	Error messages returned by the DM_WORKFLOW facility (workflow errors).
dmxfrm.e	Error messages returned by the DM_XFRM facility (XML transformations).

Documentum provides an interactive utility to read these files: dm_error.bat. The dm_error.bat utility is found in the %DM_HOME%\bin directory. To use the utility, execute it from a command line with the following syntax form:

    dm_error <error_string>

where <error_string> is an error string returned by the Content Server.

For example:

    dm_error READONLY_ATTR

dm_error.bat responds with:

    dmacl.e:
    [DM_ACL_E_READONLY_ATTR]
            "The attribute '%s' of the ACL '%s' is read-only and
             not chngable."
    CAUSE: Try to change read-only attrs.

7.20 Anatomy Of The server.ini File

The server.ini file contains configuration information for a Docbase. Each Docbase has a configuration file located at %DOCUMENTUM%\dba\config\<Docbase Name>, where <Docbase Name> is the name of the Docbase. This file controls a variety of features that affect your Docbase, and is read every time the Docbase starts. The following discussion highlights some of the more commonly used features controlled by this file.

7.20.1 Enforce a Four Digit Year

The server will force the display and storage of four digit years if this option is enabled. By default, this option is disabled.

```
[SERVER_STARTUP]
enforce_four_digit_year = T
```

7.20.2 Client Session Timeout Period

The amount of time the server waits to hear from a client session before it disconnects the session is configurable. By default, the period is 5 minutes. The higher this value is, the longer the server will wait. This can be advantageous on a high-latency network; however, care should be taken when adjusting this value. If the value is too high, the server consumes valuable resources maintaining unnecessary sessions.

```
[SERVER_STARTUP]
client_session_timeout = 5
```

7.20.3 Concurrent Sessions

By default, the server is configured to handle 20 concurrent sessions. These sessions include not only user sessions, but sessions required by jobs, methods, and queries too. Care should be taken when adjusting this value. Too many concurrent sessions can degrade performance, but so can too few. The maximum concurrent sessions allowed is 1024.

```
[SERVER_STARTUP]
concurrent_sessions = 20
```

7.20.4 Login Ticket Timeout Period

A login ticket's lifetime is 5 minutes from the time it was generated. After that time period the ticket is invalid. This lifetime can be adjusted using this option.

```
[SERVER_STARTUP]
login_ticket_timeout = 5
```

7.20.5 Mail Notification

This option controls whether an email message is sent to a user when a workitem or message is queued to their inbox. This option is on by default.

```
[SERVER_STARTUP]
mail_notification = T
```

7.20.6 User Authentication Case

You can force the server to convert a user's name to upper or lowercase before authenticating them. Valid values for this option are: `upper`, `lower`, and `NULL`. The default is `NULL` meaning the server uses the user's name in whatever case it was entered.

```
[SERVER_STARTUP]
user_auth_case = NULL
```

7.20.7 Workflow Agent Sleep Interval

This option controls how frequently the workflow agent executes by indicating the sleep period between runs. The workflow agent executes the automatic activities in a workflow. The default sleep period is 60 seconds. A larger value represents a longer period of time between executions. Setting this value too high will unnecessarily prolong workflow activities. Setting this value too low can cause activities to collide.

```
[SERVER_STARTUP]
wf_sleep_interval = 60
```

7.21 Chapter Summary

This chapter contained an eclectic collection of useful information, and virtually no programming. Nonetheless, the topics covered here are topics frequently asked about on discussion groups or tech support forums. Most of the tables contained here can be found, or at least inferred, from the Documentum documentation or the Docbase itself. However, it is much easier to find and use them when they are all in a one location.

8

Putting It All Together In A Sample Application

In this final chapter, I will guide you through the construction of a simple, but useful, application based entirely on code, concepts, and techniques discussed in this book. The intent of this example is to demonstrate a few techniques within the context of a working program rather than as isolated code snippets. I think it's important to see how these concepts and techniques co-exist and interrelate.

I have limited the commentary in this chapter to portions of the code that are of particular interest, are different from those presented previously, or are new and need explanation. When a concept or technique is implemented in the code, I reference the applicable section of the book to show you the practical implementation of what you previously read. There is a cross-referenced summary at the end of the chapter containing all of the concepts and techniques used in this example, and the subroutines that implement them.

8.1 dmSpy

The name of the application you are about to build is *dmSpy*. *dmSpy* is a developer/admin tool that enables you to look under the hood of the Docbase to see the inner workings of your objects, i.e., *spy* on them. For a selected object, *dmSpy* will reveal all the object's attributes, computed attributes, and locations, including: the file system, the Docbase, virtual documents, and workflows. It also provides a DQL query facility where you can enter queries and have the results displayed in the tool.

To begin, create a new Visual Basic application as described in Chapter 2, *Getting Started with Applications and Components*.

- Name your project dmSpy.
- Add a form to the project and name it frmSpy.
- Add a module to the project and name it mainSpy.
- Copy the frm_ObjectSelector.frm file created in Chapter 6, *Working with Screen Controls*, into the dmSpy project directory, and add it to the project[*].
- Copy the DcSessionLock.cls file from the Documentum Desktop Component Source archive[**] to the dmSpy directory, and add it to the project.

Your dmSpy project should now consist of the files list in Table 8.1, and look like Figure 8.1.

Make sure your project references the following type libraries:

- Visual Basic for Applications
- Visual Basic Runtime Objects and Procedures
- Visual Basic Objects and Procedures
- OLE Automation
- Documentum Foundation Classes Type Library
- Documentum Login Manager Type Library
- Documentum Desktop Component Assistant Type Library
- Documentum Report Manager Type Library
- Documentum Desktop Utility Manager Type Library

---

[*] If your Object Selector dialog box acts erratically, double check the references and key values in the ImageList control. You may need to repair these references and values after you copy it to a new directory.

[**] You can download the Documentum Desktop Component Source archive from the Documentum Download Center (http://documentum.subscribenet.com).

Table 8.1—dmSpy File Descriptions

File Name	Name	Type	Purpose
dmSpy.vbp	dmSpy	Project	Contains all of the application's project information.
frmSpy.frm	frmSpy	Form	Contains the application's main form and all of the code to implement the functionality behind each screen control.
frm_ObjectSelector.frm	FrmObjectSelector	Form	The Object Selector form created in Chapter 6, *Working with Screen Controls*.
mainSpy.bas	mainSpy	Module	Contains the application's *Main()* subroutine.
DcSessionLock.cls	DcSessionLock	Class Module	Contains the Documentum-provided session locking class.

Figure 8.1—dmSpy Project in the Visual Basic Project Explorer

Add the following components to your project:

- Documentum Docbase-aware Controls
- Microsoft Windows Common Controls 6.0
- Microsoft Rich TextBox Control

8.1.1 The Form

This section discusses the graphical composition of the `frmSpy` form. The implementation of each control is described later in the chapter. The Object Selector form was discussed in Chapter 6, *Working with Screen Controls,* and the code for `DcSessionLock.cls` is proprietary Documentum code. These classes will not be discussed here.

The main interface for *dmSpy* is the `frmSpy` form, and looks like Figure 8.2. Table 8.2 describes each screen element.

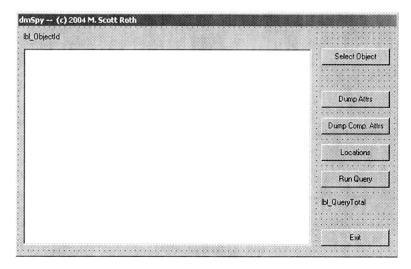

Figure 8.2—Designer View of frmSpy Form

Table 8.2—Form Elements

Name	Type	Caption	Comment
btn_SelectObject	Command Button	Select Object	This button opens the Object Selector form and allows the user to select an object. It could just as easily call the Documentum Open Dialog.
btn_Dump	Command Button	Dump Attrs.	This button displays all of the selected object's attributes.
btn_CompAttrDump	Command Button	Dump Comp. Attrs.	This button calculates and displays the selected object's computed attributes. The list of computed attributes and their access methods were discussed in Chapter 7, *Tips, Tools and Handy Information*.
btn_Location	Command Button	Locations	This button displays the selected object's locations. These locations include: the file system, Docbase paths, virtual documents, and workflows. These paths are obtained using queries discussed in Chapter 3, *Working with Queries and Collections*.

Name	Type	Caption	Comment
`btn_Query`	Command Button	**Run Query**	This button displays a simple input dialog to capture the user's DQL query. It then runs the query and displays the results in the RichTextBox control. This button uses collection-processing techniques discussed in Chapter 3, *Working with Queries and Collections*.
`btn_Exit`	Command Button	**Exit**	Quits dmSpy
`rtx_output`	RichText Box		This is the RichTextBox that holds the results generated by each button.
`lbl_QueryTotal`	Label		A label to hold the number of objects returned by a query. It is only visible when the **Run Query** button is clicked. The calculation of the size of the result set uses a technique discussed in Chapter 3, *Working with Queries and Collections*.
`lbl_ObjectId`	Label		Label to hold the selected object's Id. It is only visible when an object is selected.

8.1.2 The Code

In this section, I discuss the code in the `mainSpy.bas` and `frmSpy.frm` files. The `mainSpy.bas` file contains the startup logic necessary to login to the Docbase and display the main interface. The `frmSpy.frm` file contains the application's main interface, as well as implements the functionality behind each screen control.

8.1.2.1 The mainSpy.bas Module

The code in the `mainSpy.bas` file is based upon the skeleton code for a standalone Documentum application discussed in Chapter 2, *Getting Started with Applications and Components*. In addition, it contains the declaration of the `GetDesktopWindow()` Win32 API function, the `sleep()` subroutine, and the `lockSession()` function. The `GetDesktopWindow()` function is used throughout the application to provide the DcReporter object with a valid window handle. The `MAX_RESULTS` constant is used later by the `btn_Query_Click()` subroutine to determine if too many query results will be returned by the user's query.

Source Code A working example of this source code can be found in the "`Chapter8/dmSpy`" directory of the source code archive.

```
Option Explicit

' Win32API declares
Public Declare Function GetDesktopWindow Lib "user32" () As Long

' DCTM globals
Public loginMgr As New DcLoginManager
Public r As New DcReport
Public Const MAX_RESULTS = 250
```

The `Main()` subroutine consists primarily of the Login Manager code as discussed in Chapter 5, *Proven Solutions to Common Tasks*, and is essentially the same code found in the skeleton Documentum application code in Chapter 2, *Getting Started with Applications and Components*. The exception, of course, is the declaration of the `frm` variable as `frmSpy`.

```
Sub Main()
    Dim sessionId As String
    Dim frm As New frmSpy

    ' if no session, login
    If (sessionId = "") Then
        sessionId = loginMgr.Connect("", "", "", "", 0)
    End If

    ' if no session, error out
    If (sessionId = "") Then
        MsgBox "Could not Log In.", vbCritical, _
            "Could Not Log In"
        Set loginMgr = Nothing
```

```
        End
    End If

    ' pass sessionId to form
    frm.sessionId = sessionId

    ' show form
    frm.Show

    Set frm = Nothing

End Sub
```

The `sleep()` subroutine and the `lockSession()` function were discussed in Chapter 5, *Proven Solutions to Common Tasks*, and are here for convenience.

```
Sub sleep(t As Integer)
    Dim EndTime As Date

    EndTime = DateAdd("s", t, Now)
    Do Until Now > EndTime
        DoEvents
    Loop

End Sub


Function lockSession(session As IDfSession, context As String) _
                    As DcSessionLock

    Dim sessLock As New DcSessionLock
    Dim locked As Boolean

    locked = False

    ' Lock the session.  Keep trying until successful
    While (locked = False)
        locked = sessLock.GetLock(session, False, context)
```

```
        If (locked = False) Then
            sleep (1)
        End If
    Wend

    Set lockSession = sessLock

End Function
```

8.1.2.2 The frmSpy.frm Form

The `frmSpy.frm` file is where most of the application's logic and code reside. The form implements all of the logic behind each of its controls, with the exception of the Object Selector. The Object Selector is called from this form, but its logic and code are contained in the `frm_ObjectSelector.frm` file.

Like the skeleton code discussed in Chapter 2, *Getting Started with Applications and Components*, this form also begins by declaring a public `sessionId` variable, and private DFC client variables. The `sessionId` is passed into the form from the `Main()` subroutine and is used to instantiate local copies of the DFC client variables.

```
' frmSpy.frm
Option Explicit

Public sessionID As String

Private currentId As IDfId
Private cx As DfClientX
Private client As IDfClient
Private session As IDfSession
```

8.1.2.2.1   Form_Load()

The `Form_Load()` subroutine uses the same technique for instantiating DFC client objects as the skeleton code in Chapter 2, *Getting Started with Application and Components*. The remainder of the code initializes the various controls on the form and configures the UI.

```
Private Sub Form_Load()

    On Error GoTo HandleError
```

```
' set up dfc for form
If (session Is Nothing) Then
    Set cx = New DfClientX
    Set client = cx.getLocalClient
    Set session = client.findSession(sessionID)
End If

' enable buttons
Me.btn_Exit.Enabled = True
Me.btn_SelectObject.Enabled = True
Me.btn_Query.Enabled = True

' disable buttons
Me.btn_CompAttrDump.Enabled = False
Me.btn_Dump.Enabled = False
Me.btn_Location.Enabled = False

' hide query count label
Me.lbl_QueryTotal.Visible = False

' config rich text box
Me.rtx_Output.Font.Name = "Courier"
Me.rtx_Output.Font.Size = "10"
Me.rtx_Output.RightMargin = 100000
```

The subroutine then prints introductory and copyright information to the RichTextBox. It uses the *appendOutput()* subroutine to print this information. This subroutine is discussed in Section 8.1.2.2.8, *Miscellaneous Subroutines*, and simply formats and outputs a string to the RichTextBox.

```
' fill textbox with intro message
Call appendOutput("dmSpy Utility " & "version " & App.Major _
    & "." & App.Minor & "   (c) 2004 M. Scott Roth" _
    & vbCrLf, True)
Call appendOutput("Select an object from the Docbase by " _
    & "clicking "the ")
Call appendOutput("'Select Object' button on the right." _
    & vbCrLf)
Call appendOutput("Then select:" & vbCrLf)
```

```
    Call appendOutput("    1. 'Dump Attrs' to display all of " _
        & "the object's ")
    Call appendOutput("       attributes")
    Call appendOutput("    2. 'Dump Comp. Attrs' to display " _
        & "the object's ")
    Call appendOutput("       computed attributes")
    Call appendOutput("    3. 'Locations' to show the " _
        & "object's locations")
    Call appendOutput(vbCrLf & "Or, click the 'Run Query' " _
        & "button to execute a ")
    Call appendOutput("DQL query.")
```

The subroutine ends with error handling code. This is the same error handling code discussed in Chapter 5, *Proven Solutions to Common Tasks*, and is used repeatedly throughout this application. Note the use of the `GetDesktopWindow()` Win32 API call to obtain a handle to desktop window.

```
HandleError:

    If (Len(Err.Description) > 0) Then
        Dim e As IDfException
        Set e = cx.parseException(Err.Description)
        r.AddException e
        r.Display GetDesktopWindow(), DC_REPORT_OK_ONLY
    End If

End Sub
```

When the application runs and the user logs in, the `Form_Load()` subroutine displays the welcome screen as shown in Figure 8.3.

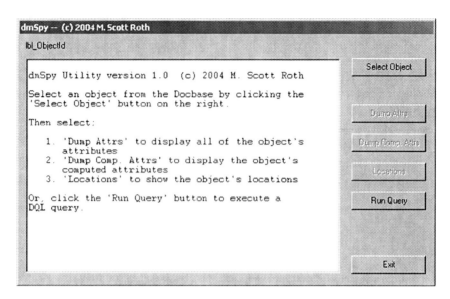

Figure 8.3—dmSpy Welcome Screen

8.1.2.2.2 Select Object Button

The first button on the form is the **Select Object** button. This button opens the Object Selector form. Its event handler is the `btn_SelectObject_Click()` subroutine. As you may recall, the Object Selector form was created to allow the user to navigate the Docbase and choose an object. Once an object is successfully chosen, its Id is stored in the `frmSpy`'s global IDfld variable, `currentId`. When an object is selected, additional buttons on the interface are enabled.

```
Private Sub btn_SelectObject_Click()
    Dim frmOS As New frm_ObjectSelector

    On Error GoTo HandleError

    ' hide query count label
    Me.lbl_QueryTotal.Visible = False

    frmOS.sessionID = sessionID
    frmOS.cabinet = "Temp"
    frmOS.Show vbModal
```

```
        ' get selected object
    If (Not frmOS.bCancel) Then
        Set currentId = cx.getId(frmOS.objectId)

        ' set object id label
        Me.lb_ObjectId.Caption = "Object Id:   " _
            & currentId.toString
        Me.lb_ObjectId.Visible = True

        ' enable buttons
        Me.btn_Dump.Enabled = True
        Me.btn_CompAttrDump.Enabled = True
        Me.btn_Location.Enabled = True

        ' default action is attr dump
        Call btn_Dump_Click
    Else
        Set currentId = Nothing
        Me.btn_Dump.Enabled = False
        Me.btn_CompAttrDump.Enabled = False
        Me.btn_Location.Enabled = False
        Me.lb_ObjectId.Visible = False

        ' if cancelled, go back to welcome message
        Call Form_Load

    End If

HandleError:

    Set frmOS = Nothing

    If (Len(Err.Description) > 0) Then
        Dim e As IDfException
        Set e = cx.parseException(Err.Description)
        r.AddException e
        r.Display GetDesktopWindow(), DC_REPORT_OK_ONLY
    End If

End Sub
```

The ObjectSelector form is shown in Figure 8.4.

After an object is selected, the application's default behavior is to dump the selected object's attributes by calling the `btn_Dump_Click()` subroutine.

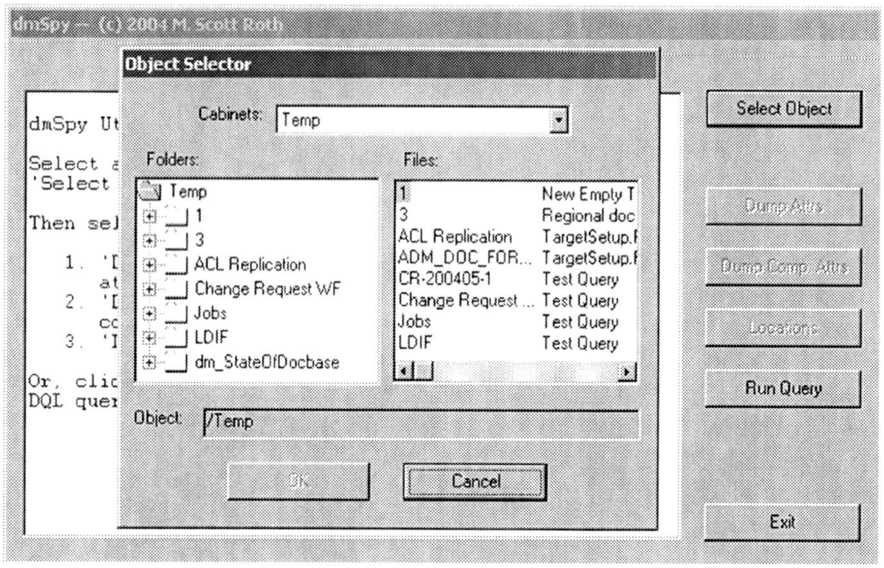

Figure 8.4—Object Selector Form

8.1.2.2.3 Dump Attrs Button

The **Dump Attrs** button is the default action for the form after an object is selected. The `btn_Dump_Click()` subroutine implements the event handler for this button. The subroutine simply dumps the selected object's attributes to the RichTextBox using the `IDfPersistentObject.dump()` method.

```
Private Sub btn_Dump_Click()
    Dim pObj As IDfPersistentObject
    Dim sLock As DcSessionLock

    On Error GoTo HandleError
```

```
    ' hide query count label
    Me.lbl_QueryTotal.Visible = False

    ' lock session
    Set sLock = lockSession(session, "Dump")

    ' fetch current object
    Set pObj = session.GetObject(currentId)

    ' dump it
    Me.rtx_Output.Text = ""
    Call appendOutput(pObj.dump, True)

HandleError:

    If (Not sLock Is Nothing) Then
        sLock.ReleaseLock
    End If

    If (Len(Err.Description) > 0) Then
        Dim e As IDfException
        Set e = cx.parseException(Err.Description)
        r.AddException e
        r.Display GetDesktopWindow(), DC_REPORT_OK_ONLY
    End If

End Sub
```

The result of clicking the **Dump Attrs** button is shown in Figure 8.5.

338   A Beginner's Guide to Developing Documentum® Desktop Applications

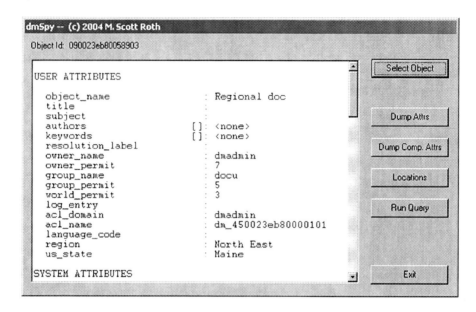

Figure 8.5—dmSpy Dump Attributes

8.1.2.2.4   Dump Comp. Attrs Button

The btn_CompAttrDump_Click() subroutine runs when the **Dump Comp. Attrs** button is clicked. This subroutine dumps all of the selected object's computed attributes to the RichTextBox. It accomplishes this using many different techniques; all of which were listed in Chapter 7, *Tips, Tools and Handy Information*.

This subroutine uses the formatOutput() subroutine to output information to the RichTextBox in a predefined format. Like appendOutput(), this subroutine is also defined at the end of the code listing, and simply formats and outputs strings to the RichTextBox.

```
Private Sub btn_CompAttrDump_Click()
    Dim sObj As IDfSysObject
    Dim i As Integer
    Dim tmp As String
    Dim sLock As DcSessionLock
```

```vb
' hide query count label
Me.lbl_QueryTotal.Visible = False

On Error GoTo HandleError

' lock the session
Set sLock = lockSession(session, "CompAttrDump")

' fetch current object
Set sObj = session.GetObject(currentId)

Call appendOutput("COMPUTED ATTRIBUTES" & vbCrLf, True)

' _accessor_name
For i = 0 To sObj.getAccessorCount - 1
    tmp = sObj.getAccessorName(i)
    If (i = 0) Then
        Call formatOutput("_accessor_name", tmp)
    Else
        Call formatOutput("", tmp)
    End If
Next i

' _accessor_permit
For i = 0 To sObj.getAccessorCount - 1
    tmp = sObj.getAccessorPermit(i)
    If (i = 0) Then
        Call formatOutput("_accessor_permit", tmp)
    Else
        Call formatOutput("", tmp)
    End If
Next i

' _accessor_xpermit
For i = 0 To sObj.getAccessorCount - 1
    tmp = sObj.getAccessorXPermit(i)
    If (i = 0) Then
        Call formatOutput("_accessor_xpermit", tmp)
    Else
```

```
                Call formatOutput("", tmp)
        End If
    Next i

    ' _accessor_xpermitnames
    For i = 0 To sObj.getAccessorCount - 1
        tmp = sObj.getAccessorXPermitNames(i)
        If (i = 0) Then
            Call formatOutput("_accessor_xpermitnames", tmp)
        Else
            Call formatOutput("", tmp)
        End If
    Next i

    ' _acl_ref_valid
    Call formatOutput("_acl_ref_valid", sObj.getAclRefValid)

    ' _alias_set
    Call formatOutput("_alias_set", sObj.getAliasSet)

    ' _allow_change_location
    Call formatOutput("_allow_change_location", _
        sObj.getBoolean("_allow_change_location"))

    ' _allow_change_permit
    Call formatOutput("_allow_change_permit", _
        sObj.getBoolean("_allow_change_permit"))

    ' _allow_change_state
    Call formatOutput("_allow_change_state", _
        sObj.getBoolean("_allow_change_state"))

    ' _allow_execute_proc
    Call formatOutput("_allow_execute_proc", _
        sObj.getBoolean("_allow_execute_proc"))

    ' _allow_change_owner
    Call formatOutput("_allow_change_owner", _
        sObj.getBoolean("_allow_change_owner"))
```

```
' _cached
Call formatOutput("_cached", sObj.getBoolean("_cached"))

' _changed
Call formatOutput("_changed", sObj.isDirty)

' _componentID
If (sObj.isVirtualDocument) Then
    For i = 0 To sObj.getComponentIdCount - 1
        If (i = 0) Then
            Call formatOutput("_componentID", _
                sObj.getComponentId(i).toString)
        Else
            Call formatOutput("", _
                sObj.getComponentId(i).toString)
        End If
    Next i
End If

' _containID
If (sObj.isVirtualDocument) Then
    For i = 0 To sObj.getComponentIdCount - 1
        If (i = 0) Then
            Call formatOutput("_containID", _
                sObj.getContainId(i).toString)
        Else
            Call formatOutput("", _
                sObj.getContainId(i).toString)
        End If
    Next i
End If

' _content_state
For i = 0 To sObj.getContentStateCount - 1
    If (i = 0) Then
        Call formatOutput("_content_state", _
            sObj.getContentState(i))
    Else
        Call formatOutput("", sObj.getContentState(i))
```

```
      End If
Next i

    ' _count
    Call formatOutput("_count", sObj.getAttrCount)

    ' _current_state
    Call formatOutput("_current_state", sObj.getCurrentState)

    ' _docbase_id
    Call formatOutput("_docbase_id", _
        sObj.getObjectId.getDocbaseId)

    ' _id
    Call formatOutput("_id", sObj.getObjectId.toString)

    ' _isnew
    Call formatOutput("_isnew", sObj.isNew)

    ' _isreplica
    Call formatOutput("_isreplica", sObj.isReplica)

    ' _masterdocbase
    Call formatOutput("_masterdocbase", sObj.getMasterDocbase)

    ' _permit
    Call formatOutput("_permit", sObj.getPermit)

    ' _policy_name
    Call formatOutput("_policy_name", sObj.getPolicyName)

    ' _status
    Call formatOutput("_status", sObj.getStatus)

    ' _type_id
    Call formatOutput("_type_id", sObj.getString("_type_id"))
```

```
    ' _type_name
    Call formatOutput("_type_name", sObj.getTypeName)
    ' _xpermit
    Call formatOutput("_xpermit", _
        sObj.getXPermit(session.getUser("").getUserName))

    ' _xpermit_list
    Call formatOutput("_xpermit_list", sObj.getXPermitList)

    ' _xpermit_names
    Call formatOutput("_xpermit_names", _
        sObj.getXPermitNames(session.getUser("").getUserName))

HandleError:

    If (Not sLock Is Nothing) Then
        sLock.ReleaseLock
    End If

    If (Len(Err.Description) > 0) Then
        Dim e As IDfException
        Set e = cx.parseException(Err.Description)
        r.AddException e
        r.Display GetDesktopWindow(), DC_REPORT_OK_ONLY
    End If

End Sub
```

The result of clicking the **Dump Comp. Attrs** button is shown in Figure 8.6.

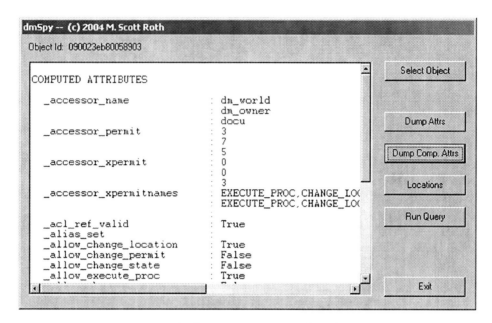

Figure 8.6—dmSpy Dump Computed Attributes

8.1.2.2.5 Locations Button

The `btn_Location_Click()` subroutine runs whenever the **Locations** button is clicked. This subroutine uses queries discussed in Chapter 3, *Working with Queries and Collections*, to determine all of the selected object's locations.

```
Private Sub btn_Location_Click()
    Dim sObj As IDfSysObject
    Dim tmp As String
    Dim i As Integer
    Dim fObj As IDfFolder
    Dim q As IDfQuery
    Dim col As IDfCollection
    Dim sLock As DcSessionLock

    ' hide query count label
    Me.lbl_QueryTotal.Visible = False

    On Error GoTo HandleError
```

```
' lock session
Set sLock = lockSession(session, "Location")

' fetch current object
Set sObj = session.GetObject(currentId)

Call appendOutput("LOCATIONS" & vbCrLf, True)

'
' get path on file system
' some objects don't have content (i.e., dm_folder)
'
If (sObj.getContentSize > 1) Then
    tmp = sObj.getPath(0)
    If (tmp = "") Then
        Call formatOutput("file system location", _
            "Content not stored on file system")
    Else
        Call formatOutput("file system location", tmp)
    End If
End If

'
' get path in docbase
' if its not in a folder it must be at the root level
'
If (sObj.getFolderIdCount = 0) Then
    Call formatOutput("docbase location", "/")
Else
    For i = 0 To sObj.getFolderIdCount - 1
        Set fObj = session.GetObject(sObj.getFolderId(i))
        Call formatOutput("docbase location", _
            fObj.getFolderPath(0))
    Next i
End If

'
' get virtual document participation
'
```

```
Set q = cx.getQuery
q.setDQL ("select parent_id from dmr_containment where " _
    & "component_id = '" & sObj.getChronicleId.toString _
    & "'")

Set col = q.execute(session, DFCLib.IDfQuery_DF_READ_QUERY)

i = 0
While (col.Next = True)
    tmp = col.getString("parent_id")

    If (i > 0) Then
        Call formatOutput("", tmp)
    Else
        Call formatOutput("virtual document", tmp)
    End If
    i = i + 1
Wend
col.Close

'
' get workflow participation
'
q.setDQL ("select distinct r_workflow_id from dmi_package " _
    & " where any r_component_id = '" _
    & sObj.getObjectId.toString & "'")

Set col = q.execute(session, DFCLib.IDfQuery_DF_READ_QUERY)

i = 1
While (col.Next = True)
    If (i = 1) Then
        Call formatOutput("workflow", _
            col.getString("r_workflow_id"))
    Else
        Call formatOutput("", col.getString("r_workflow_id"))
    End If
    i = i + 1
Wend
col.Close
```

```
HandleError:

    If (Not sLock Is Nothing) Then
        sLock.ReleaseLock
    End If

    If (Len(Err.Description) > 0) Then
        Dim e As IDfException
        Set e = cx.parseException(Err.Description)
        r.AddException e
        r.Display GetDesktopWindow(), DC_REPORT_OK_ONLY
    End If

    If (Not col Is Nothing) Then
        If (col.getState <> DF_CLOSED_STATE) Then
            col.Close
        End If
    End If

End Sub
```

The result of clicking the **Locations** button is shown in Figure 8.7.

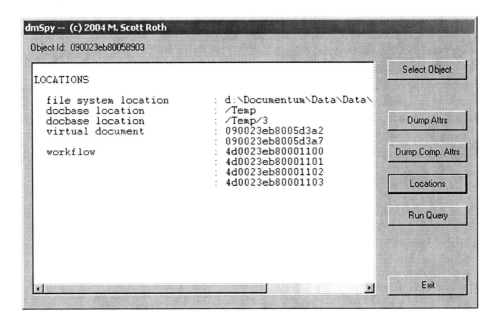

Figure 8.7—dmSpy Locations

8.1.2.2.6 **Run Query** Button

The `btn_Query_Click()` subroutine runs when the **Run Query** button is clicked. It is the most involved subroutine in the application, but when you break it down, you will see it contains nothing difficult. At its core, the `btn_Query_Click()` subroutine uses the collection-processing technique discussed in Chapter 3, *Working with Queries and Collections.*

To get the DQL string from the user, *dmSpy* uses a simple Visual Basic `InputBox` as shown in Figure 8.8; nothing fancy.

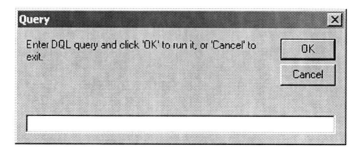

Figure 8.8—Query Input Box

After the DQL string is obtained, three checks are made.

1. If the string is blank, the subroutine exits. This will happen if the user clicks **Cancel** on the `InputBox`.
2. Ensure that the first six letters of the DQL string spell the word `SELECT`. The *dmSpy* application will only process DQL queries of the `SELECT` nature. If the DQL string doesn't start with the word `SELECT`, exit the subroutine.
3. If the query will return more than `MAX_RESULTS` rows, exit the subroutine. The row count is obtained using a collection counting technique discussed in Chapter 3, *Working with Queries and Collections.* I chose 250 as an arbitrary upper limit for `MAX_RESULTS`; feel free to change it.

```
Private Sub btn_Query_Click()
    Dim dql As String
    Dim q As IDfQuery
    Dim col As IDfCollection
    Dim attr As IDfAttr
    Dim numCols As Integer
    Dim colName As String
```

```
    Dim colValue As String
    Dim tmp As String
    Dim i As Integer
    Dim j As Integer
    Dim sLock As DcSessionLock
    Dim cnt As Integer
    Dim results() As String
    Dim resultsSize() As Integer

    On Error GoTo HandleError

    ' get dql string
    dql = InputBox("Enter DQL query and click 'OK' to run it, " _
        & "or 'Cancel' to exit.", "Query")

    '
    ' check if cancel clicked
    '
    If (dql = "") Then
        ' hide query count label
        Me.lbl_QueryTotal.Visible = False
        Exit Sub
    End If

    '
    ' check for SELECT
    '
    If (LCase(Left(dql, 6)) <> "select") Then
        MsgBox "The dmSpy query processor can only handle " _
            & "SELECT queries.  Please enter a new query.", _
            vbCritical, "Wrong Query Type"
        Me.lbl_QueryTotal.Visible = False
        Exit Sub
    End If

    ' disable non-applicable buttons
    Me.btn_CompAttrDump.Enabled = False
    Me.btn_Dump.Enabled = False
    Me.btn_Location.Enabled = False
```

```
' clear the current object
Set currentId = Nothing

' hide object id label
Me.lb_ObjectId.Visible = False

'
' show query total
'
cnt = QueryCount(dql)
If (cnt < MAX_RESULTS) Then
    Me.lbl_QueryTotal.Caption = "Result Count: " & cnt
    Me.lbl_QueryTotal.Visible = True
Else
    MsgBox "Your query will return " & cnt & " objects, " _
        & "which is more than the " & MAX_RESULTS _
        & " limit. Please refine your query.", _
        vbCritical, "Limit Exceeded"
    Me.lbl_QueryTotal.Visible = False
    Exit Sub
End If
```

The *QueryCount ()* function returns the number of rows the query will return. It is discussed in more detail in Section 8.1.2.2.8, *Miscellaneous Subroutines*. If the query passes the three tests, it is executed.

```
' user feedback
Screen.MousePointer = vbHourglass

' lock session
Set sLock = lockSession(session, "Query")

' run query
Set q = cx.getQuery
q.setDQL (dql)
Set col = q.execute(session, DF_READ_QUERY)
```

The collection is processed using the technique described in Chapter 3, *Working with Queries and Collections*. The major difference between what was described there, and what is implemented here, is the use of arrays to hold the values extracted from the collection. To make the display of the query results more aesthetically pleasing, the collection rows and columns are captured in a two-dimensional array (`results`), and the length of the longest value in each column is recorded in another array (`resultsSize`). After the arrays are fully loaded, their contents are output to the RichTextBox in easy-to-read columns.

```
' output query
Call appendOutput("QUERY" & vbCrLf, True)
Call appendOutput(q.getDQL & vbCrLf & vbCrLf)

'
' work with collection
' get number of attrs in collection
numCols = col.getAttrCount

' resize result arrays
ReDim results(cnt, numCols)
ReDim resultsSize(numCols)

' get column names from attrs in collection
For i = 1 To numCols
    colName = col.GetAttr(i - 1).getName

    ' put colName in array
    results(0, i) = colName

    ' capture column width
    If (Len(colName) > resultsSize(i)) Then
        resultsSize(i) = Len(colName)
    End If
Next i

'
' iterate over collection and process each row
'
j = 1
While (col.Next = True)

    ' process each column in a row
```

```
        For i = 1 To numCols
            Set attr = col.GetAttr(i - 1)
            
            ' get value in column
            Select Case attr.getDataType
                Case DF_BOOLEAN
                    colValue = col.getBoolean(attr.getName)
                Case DF_DOUBLE
                    colValue = col.getDouble(attr.getName)
                Case DF_ID
                    colValue = col.getId(attr.getName).toString
                Case DF_INTEGER
                    colValue = col.getInt(attr.getName)
                Case DF_STRING
                    colValue = col.getString(attr.getName)
                Case DF_TIME
                    colValue = col.getTime(attr.getName).toString
            End Select
            
            ' put colValue in array
            results(j, i) = colValue
            
            ' capture column width
            If (Len(colValue) > resultsSize(i)) Then
                resultsSize(i) = Len(colValue)
            End If
        Next i
        
        ' increment row in results array
        j = j + 1
Wend
col.Close

Call appendOutput("QUERY RESULTS" & vbCrLf)

' output columns with padding
For j = 0 To cnt
    tmp = ""
    For i = 1 To numCols
```

```
                    tmp = tmp & "| " & results(j, i) _
                         & Space(resultsSize(i) - _
                         Len(results(j, i)))
            Next i
            tmp = tmp & " |"
            Call appendOutput(tmp)
        Next j

HandleError:

    ' user feedback
    Screen.MousePointer = vbDefault

    If (Not sLock Is Nothing) Then
        sLock.ReleaseLock
    End If

    If (Len(Err.Description) > 0) Then
        Dim e As IDfException
        Set e = cx.parseException(Err.Description)
        r.AddException e
        r.Display GetDesktopWindow(), DC_REPORT_OK_ONLY
    End If

    If (Not col Is Nothing) Then
        If (col.getState <> DF_CLOSED_STATE) Then
            col.Close
        End If
    End If

End Sub
```

Typical query output is shown in Figure 8.9.

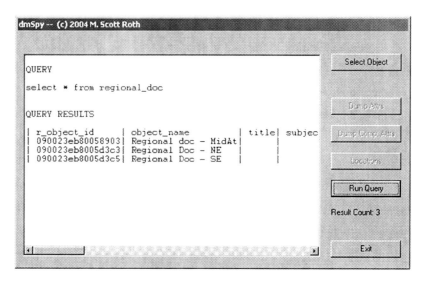

Figure 8.9—dmSpy Query Results

8.1.2.2.7 Exit Button

The `btn_Exit_Click()` subroutine is the simplest in the application. It runs when the Exit button is clicked and simply disconnects the session and unloads the `frmSpy` form.

```
Private Sub btn_Exit_Click()

'disconnect session
session.disconnect

'close form
Unload Me

End Sub
```

8.1.2.2.8 Miscellaneous Subroutines

Three subroutines have been mentioned but not yet discussed, they are: `appendOutput()`, `formatOutput()`, and `QueryCount()`. The `appendOutput()` and `formatOutput()` subroutines format the data output to the RichTextBox. The `appendOutput()` subroutine appends `str` to the text already in the RichTextBox, unless the `blnClear` Boolean argument is passed. If `blnClear` is set to `True`, the RichTextBox is cleared, and `str` is add as its only content.

```
Sub appendOutput(str As String, Optional blnClear As Boolean)

    If (blnClear = True) Then
        Me.rtx_Output.Text = ""
    End If

    Me.rtx_Output.Text = Me.rtx_Output.Text & vbCrLf & str

End Sub
```

The *formatOutput()* subroutine prints `strLeft` and `strRight` to the RichTextBox in two padded columns using the *appendOutput()* subroutine.

```
Sub formatOutput(strLeft As String, strRight As String)
    Dim tmp As String

    tmp = "   " & strLeft & Space(27 - Len(strLeft)) & ": " _
            & strRight

    appendOutput (tmp)

End Sub
```

The final function in the application, *QueryCount()*, calculates the number of rows the query will return. This subroutine employs the second collection sizing technique described in Chapter 3, *Working with Queries and Collections*, to calculate the number of rows that will be returned by the query.

```
Function QueryCount(dql As String) As Integer
    Dim q As IDfQuery
    Dim col As IDfCollection
    Dim sLock As DcSessionLock
    Dim i As Integer
    Dim c As Integer
    Dim countDQL As String

    On Error GoTo HandleError
```

```vb
        c = -1
        
        ' build count DQL string
        i = InStr(1, LCase(dql), "from", vbTextCompare)
        countDQL = "select count(*) " & Right(dql, Len(dql) - i + 1)
        
        Set q = cx.getQuery
        q.setDQL (countDQL)
        
        ' lock session
        Set sLock = lockSession(session, "Query Count")
        
        Set col = q.execute(session, DF_READ_QUERY)
        
        ' process collection
        col.Next
            c = col.getInt("count(*)")
        col.Close

HandleError:

    If (Not sLock Is Nothing) Then
        sLock.ReleaseLock
    End If
    
    If (Len(Err.Description) > 0) Then
        Dim e As IDfException
        Set e = cx.parseException(Err.Description)
        r.AddException e
        r.Display GetDesktopWindow(), DC_REPORT_OK_ONLY
    End If
    
    If (Not col Is Nothing) Then
        If (col.getState <> DF_CLOSED_STATE) Then
            col.Close
        End If
    End If
    
    ' return result
    QueryCount = c
    
End Function
```

There are two important things to note about this subroutine. The first is the parser that replaces the `SELECT` clause with the `COUNT(*)` clause is not foolproof. It can be tricked and will break the application. The second important thing to note is that to calculate the number of rows, the query is executed. This can be an expensive operation depending upon the query. A better solution to limit the number of rows returned by the user's query could be to use the `RETURN_TOP` DQL hint. However, this option will not inform you of the actual number of rows returned. See the *Documentum Content Server DQL Reference Manual* for more information regarding DQL hints.

8.1.3 Using dmSpy

Now that you've written *dmSpy*, compile it by choosing **Make dmSpy.exe**...from the **File** menu in the Visual Basic IDE. Now, run it. After logging in, you should be greeted by the welcome screen where you can choose an object to spy on, or enter a query.

8.2 Chapter Summary

This chapter presented *dmSpy*, a real-world application, and not a bad little tool for only 500 lines of code! It is a good demonstration of ways to apply many of the techniques developed and discussed in this book. In fact, it should be clear that aside from the design of the UI, most of the "meat" in this application was cut and pasted from previous chapters in this book. That, of course, was the idea! The techniques discussed in this book are proven techniques. Why re-invent them each time you need them?

Table 8.3 summarizes the techniques used in this application.

Table 8.3—of Techniques Used in dmSpy

Technique (Chapter)	dmSpy Subroutine Name
Application skeleton code (Chapter 2, *Getting Started with Applications and Components*)	`dmSpy Project, Main(), Form_Load()`
Login manager (Chapter 5, *Proven Solutions to Common Tasks*)	`Main()`
`sleep()` function (Chapter 5, *Proven Solutions to Common Tasks*)	`lockSession()`
`lockSession()` function (Chapter 5, *Proven Solutions to Common Tasks*)	Numerous, (e.g., `btn_Dump_Click()`)
Session Id passing (Chapter 5, *Proven Solutions to Common Tasks*)	`Main(), btn_SelectObject_Click()`
Local DFC client variables (Chapter 5, *Proven Solutions to Common Tasks*)	`Form_Load()`
Error handling (Chapter 5, *Proven Solutions to Common Tasks*)	Numerous, (e.g., `btn_Dump_Click()`)
Accessing computed attributes (Chapter 7, *Tips, Tools and Handy Information*)	`btn_CompAttrDump_click()`
Finding object locations on the file system, in the Docbase, in virtual documents, and in workflows (Chapter 3, *Working with Queries and Collections*)	`btn_Location_Click()`
Collection processing pattern (Chapter 3, *Working with Queries and Collections*)	`btn_Query_Click()`
Calculating collection size (Chapter 3, *Working with Queries and Collections*)	`btn_Query_Click()`
The Object Selector form (Chapter 6, *Working with Screen Controls*)	`frm_ObjectSelector.frm` file

Afterword

As a fellow programmer, I know and appreciate the value of leveraging someone else's work, and I am delighted you have chosen to leverage mine. I believe—and I hope you agree—this book fills an important void in our community. It sits in the gap between what Documentum offers out-of-the-box and in training courses, and what others have pain-stakingly mastered over time. My hope is that it will enable many beginning developers to quickly master the basics of writing Documentum Desktop applications, and become productive, respected members of this community.

As I stated earlier, this book largely grew out of my own experiences and research. Though I vetted this book with experts in the industry and Documentum, you may have even better ideas or disagree with mine. Please contact me; I'd love to hear from you and get your thoughts. The easiest way to reach me is through my website, `www.dm-book.com`. Thank you for taking the time to read this book, it was a labor of love for me to write. I hope you found it helpful.

Before closing, I want to acknowledge and thank the many people in my life that have made this book possible. Because I have a "day job", this book was completed primarily in my "spare time" (read: late at night and weekends). Therefore, it had no budget—monetarily or otherwise—and its existence wouldn't be possible without the help and support of these wonderful people. These people have all given graciously of their time, talents and energy to help me complete this book.

At the top of this list are Rachael and Kristin, my wife and daughter, to whom this book is dedicated. They have tolerated me working on this manuscript in some form or fashion for a *very* long time. Without their love, encouragement and understanding, I would have given up on this project long ago. I love them both dearly, and thank God for the blessings they are to me.

I thank Scott Effler who has been a wonderful and enlightening colleague for many years. It is a pleasure to work with someone as knowledgeable and capable as Scott, and I am sincerely grateful for the many challenges and ideas he has presented me over the years. Scott's reviews of this manuscript have been extremely helpful.

I also owe a huge thanks to Michael Trafton of the Blue Fish Development Group (keepers of the `dm_developer` website) for his thorough technical review of this manuscript. Mike has been invaluable in assuring the quality of the technical information in this book.

Dan Biggins of Zen Technology was also a key reviewer of this manuscript, and I thank Dan for all of his efforts as well.

I thank Stacey Page, my boss at SAIC, for her continued interest and support. Stacey was instrumental in helping me navigate the legality and practicality of this project with the corporation. Thanks also to Tina Nassif-Shinn in the SAIC contracts department, and Faye Hammersley in the SAIC legal department for their work in tracking down contracts, and clearing the legal way for me to publish this book.

Thanks to Steve Moline who has always been an enthusiastic supporter, a great project manager, and a fun and admirable guy.

Many thanks to Sharon Allison for the "binding" and proofreading jobs she did while assembling various drafts of this book.

Thanks to my Mom and Dad, who have always been tremendous role models in my life, and instilled in me the confidence and discipline to pursue a project like this.

Finally, I want to reiterate my thanks to God the Father for the many blessing He has bestowed on my family and me. *Soli Deo Gloria!*

[SOLI DEO GLORIA]
Proverbs 3:5-6

"Scott Roth provides an invaluable resource to the Documentum community. The first book of its kind, *A Beginner's Guide to Developing Documentum Desktop Applications* teaches developers tricks that can take years to learn the hard way. Where was this book when I first started?"
—Michael Trafton, Chief Architect, Blue Fish Development Group

"*A Beginner's Guide to Developing Documentum Desktop Applications* is the missing piece in the puzzle for a Documentum developer. The answers to those well kept Documentum secrets are unlocked inside."
—Scott Effler, Business Solution Architect, SAIC

In this book, Scott Roth, an accomplished Documentum application developer, has produced an invaluable reference of practical tips, techniques, and best practices for developing Documentum Desktop applications. The material and examples in this book range from an explanation of the application/component framework, to the details of using query techniques and screen controls. Along the way Mr. Roth reveals numerous best practices and proven solutions. This book is a must-have for Documentum developers.

INDEX

A

a_full_text, 72, 96-97, 232
ACX, 44-47, 316
apiExec(), 278-280
apiGet(), 278-281
apiSet(), 278, 280-281
apply(), 66, 78, 108, 171, 173-174
audit trail, 177-179
auditing, 3, 145, 176

B

batch_hint_size, 285-286
Binary Compatibility, 29-30, 53-54

C

cache map, 69
cache_queries, 69, 284, 286
cached query, 68-71
casting, 11-12, 14
client_cache_size, 285
client_session_timeout, 321
COM, 2-3, 5, 12, 15, 24-25, 29-31, 37, 41, 52-54, 129, 153, 165-166, 182, 193, 255, 263, 324, 359
Command State Flag, 49, 51-52
Computed Attribute, 292
concurrent_sessions, 321
conditional value assistance, 227-229, 233, 250-253, 277, 284
ConnectFlag, 147, 149-150

D

DART, 25, 41-42, 48, 55, 157
Db-Documentum, xviii
DcAbstractItem, 41
DcComponentDispatcher, 25, 157-160
DcCustomOnLoadingCode(), 53
DcCustomOnSavingCode(), 53
DcCustomOnUnloadingCode(), 53
DcFind, 41, 44
DcFindTarget, 57-58
DcItems, 40-41, 159
DcLoginManager, 9, 11, 21, 32, 38, 147, 149-150, 207-208, 212-213, 329
DcProgressMonitor, 140, 142
DcRegistryKey, 182-183, 185-186
DcReport, 5, 9, 36, 40, 159-161, 198, 201, 223, 265, 329
DcRunQuery, 9
DcSessionLock, 153-155, 218, 263, 267, 269-270, 273, 324, 326, 330, 336, 338, 344, 349, 355
deep copy, 120-121, 134
deep delete, 117, 120-121, 133-134
DFC, 0-2, 5-14, 16, 22-23, 33, 35-36, 40, 43, 57-58, 64, 67, 85, 100, 110-111, 115, 129-130, 144-146, 150-153, 160, 162, 165, 167-171, 174, 176, 182, 194, 197, 201, 207-208, 212-213, 218-219, 231-

232, 237-238, 248, 264-265, 278, 280, 291-292, 331-332
DFCLib, 8, 219, 265-266, 346
DfClient, 55
DfClientX, 4-5, 8, 10, 12, 22, 32-33, 35-36, 40, 64, 132, 146, 150-153, 165, 170-171, 183, 207-208, 212-213, 219, 231, 238, 248, 265-266, 331-332
DfwAttrCombo, 234
DfwAttributeLabel, 232-233
DfwAttrList, 234
DfwAvailableDocbasesCombo, 235
DfwCheckBox, 235
DfwComboBox, 233, 250
DfwConnectedDocbasesCombo, 234
DfwFormatsCombo, 234
DfwFormatsList, 234
DfwGroupsCombo, 234
DfwGroupsList, 234
DfwListBox, 233
DfwOperatorCombo, 234
DfwOTCombo, 235
DfwOTList, 235
DfwRepeating, 235
DfwTextBox, 233, 235, 237
DfwUsersCombo, 235
DfwUsersList, 235
dm_activity, 101-103
dm_audittrail, 177-180
dm_dbo, 97-99
dm_DMClean, 107, 204
dm_DMFileScan, 107
dm_document, 8, 11-14, 57, 59-60, 62-64, 72-73, 82, 84-87, 90, 92, 94-95, 106-107, 111-116, 119, 165, 168-169, 207, 228, 236, 238-239, 242, 254, 259-260, 282, 287, 291
dm_dump_record, 204-208, 210-211, 214
dm_folder, 88-90, 106-108, 118, 122-123, 133, 196, 198-199, 206-207, 258, 269, 271, 345
dm_FulltextMgr, 72, 96
dm_persistentobject, 7
dm_process, 101-102
dm_registered, 98-99
dm_sysobject, 7-8, 11, 88, 90, 95-97, 100, 103, 105-108, 117, 122, 201, 222, 273-274, 279-281, 291

dm_workflow, 101-103
dmAPIExec(). 278-280
dmAPIGet(), 278-281
dmAPISet(), 278, 280-281
DMCL, 5-7, 69, 83, 153, 162, 167-168, 284-286
DMCL cache, 153, 284
dmcl.ini, 69, 83, 162, 167-168, 284-286
dmi_package, 101-104, 346
dmi_workitem, 101-103
dmMkDir(), 122
dmSpy, 3, 5, 323-326, 329, 332, 334, 338, 344, 347-349, 354, 357-358
DocApp, 24-25, 30, 36, 41-47, 50-51, 55, 228, 315-316
Docbase Browser, 235-236, 240, 254-256, 260, 268, 277
Docbase cache, 284
Docbase-aware controls, 3, 226, 234-237, 240, 245-246, 248, 254, 256, 260-261, 263, 277, 326
DocBroker, 69, 168, 283-285
Documentum API, 66, 162, 207, 212, 215, 278, 280, 291
Documentum Component Dispatcher, 19, 25, 30, 33, 41-42
Documentum Desktop Component Source, 31, 36-37, 52, 129, 153, 182, 255, 263, 324
Documentum Docbase Browser, 235, 254-255
Documentum Foundation Classes, xix, 1, 5, 64, 324
Documentum Open Dialog, 235, 237, 239, 241-244, 261, 277
Documentum Validation Event Dispatcher, 227-228
Documentum Validation Widgets, 228
Documentum Widget Logic, 228
DRL, 190-194
Dump, 3, 145, 204-216, 225, 282, 332-333, 335-338, 343-344, 349
dump_operation, 204-207, 209-211
dump_parameter, 206, 209

E

effective_date, 68, 70
e-mail, 190, 192-194, 321
error trapping, 3, 5, 68, 160, 162, 198, 200, 218, 261

G

getRegSubKeyList(), 186
global component, 44, 46, 48, 51

I

i_chronicle_id, 100, 105, 115, 191
iAPI, 173, 213, 278-279, 283
IDcComponent, 24-25, 31-35, 40-41
IDcComponent_DeInit, 24-25, 31-32, 35
IDcComponent_Init, 24-25, 31-35, 41
IDcComponent_Run, 24-25, 31, 33-35
IDfACL, 8
IDfActivity, 8
IDfAttr, 92, 178, 223, 348
IDfAttrLine, 59, 61-62
IDfCancelCheckoutOperation, 137
IDfCheckedOutObject, 183-185
IDfCheckinOperation, 12, 138
IDfCheckoutOperation, 135-137, 140, 142
IDfClient, 4-5, 10, 22, 32, 35-36, 40, 146, 150-153, 174, 208, 212, 218, 248, 265, 331
IDfCollection, 12, 61, 64-65, 67, 70, 82-89, 91-93, 109, 115-118, 121, 167, 178, 196, 202, 216, 220, 223, 249, 256-257, 269-270, 273, 344, 348, 355
IDfCopyOperation, 134
IDfDeleteOperation, 133-134
IDfDocbaseMap, 9
IDfDocument, 8, 13-14
IDfException, 160-161, 201, 223, 267, 270, 272, 274, 333, 335, 337, 343, 347, 353, 356
IDfExportOperation, 131
IDfFile, 9
IDfFolder, 113, 120-121, 124, 194-196, 198, 344
IDfFormat, 125-128
IDfGroup, 8
IDfId, 12, 84, 113, 120-121, 202, 331, 334
IDfImportOperation, 131
IDfList, 185-188, 195-196, 251-252
IDfLoginInfo, 10-11, 146-147
IDfMoveOperation, 131
IDfOperation, 8, 12, 111, 129-131, 133, 136, 139, 141, 143-144

IDfOperationMonitor, 139-140, 142
IDfPersistentObject, 7, 11, 13-14, 84, 117-118, 178, 208, 213, 336
IDfProcess, 8
IDfProperties, 142, 252-253
IDfQuery, 8, 12, 57, 64-65, 67, 69-70, 82-84, 86-89, 92, 108, 115-117, 121, 165-166, 178, 196, 202, 216, 220, 249, 256-257, 268, 270, 273, 344, 346, 348, 355
IDfQueryLocation, 59, 61-62
IDfQueryMgr, 57-62, 108, 216
IDfRegistry, 182-183
IDfSession, 4, 8, 11, 22, 32, 35-36, 40, 55, 65, 68-69, 84, 113, 146, 150-155, 198, 201, 208, 212, 219, 248, 265, 279-281, 330-331
IDfSysObject, 7-8, 11, 13-14, 59, 62, 111-115, 120-121, 123, 125-129, 132-135, 137-138, 140, 142, 153, 155, 191, 193-196, 201-202, 229, 231, 248, 250, 253, 292, 338, 344
IDfTime, 202
IDfTypedObject, 59, 62, 83-84
IDfUser, 8
IDfValidationOperation, 131
IDfValidator, 250-253
IDfValueAssistance, 250-253
IDfViewedObject, 184
IDfVirtualDocument, 9
IDfWorkflow, 8
IDfWorkItem, 8
IDfXMLTransformOperation, 131
iDQL, 67-68, 279
Inbox, 103-104, 201-203, 321
include_content, 204, 206, 209
Interactive Message Tester, 282
IUnknown, 25

J

Java, 5, 12-14, 165-166

L

library services, 3, 110, 183
Load, 3, 10, 15-16, 22, 28, 36, 40, 50-52, 145, 152-

153, 193, 204, 211-216, 218-219, 225, 231-232, 237-238, 248-251, 255-256, 265-269, 331, 333, 335
local_path, 285
lockSession(), 154-156, 275
logging in, 3, 145-147, 357
Login Manager, 19, 21, 30, 33, 39, 147-151, 156, 207, 212, 235, 324, 329

M

mail_notification, 321
Menu System Designer Tool, 48-52, 55, 312
MenuSystem.ini, 48
Microsoft Outlook, 192-193

N

Notification, 104, 201-203, 321

O

Object Permission, xvii, 309-310
Open Dialog, 235-239, 241-244, 261, 277
operation monitor, 139-141, 143-144, 180, 182

P

Package & Deployment Wizard, 23, 43-44, 54
Perl, 0
preload.exe, 211, 213
Progress Sentinel, 180-182, 210
project group, 36-37, 55

Q

Query Manager, 57-59, 61-62, 64, 108-109

R

r_object_id, 52, 59-62, 64, 82-90, 94-98, 100-103, 105-108, 114-115, 117-118, 122, 165, 167-169, 179, 191, 196, 198, 203, 216, 219-220, 236, 238-239, 254, 256, 258-259, 264, 268-269, 271, 273-274, 282, 286-287
recursive, 88-89, 91, 109, 117-119, 121
registered table, 68, 93, 97-99, 204, 310
Registered Table Permission, 98, 310
registry, 3, 125-127, 136-139, 144, 182-189, 225
ReleaseLock(), 153
revert(), 215

S

Samson, 283
screen controls, xvii, 1-3, 217, 226, 234, 245, 263, 277, 284, 324, 326, 363
SEARCH DOCUMENT CONTAINS, 71-73, 94-95
SEARCH TOPIC, 72-73, 94-96
server.ini, 320
session locking, 5, 151, 153, 218, 223, 261
sleep(), 61, 155-157, 275
SmartList, 63

T

test harness, 36-39, 41-42
trace_file, 154-155, 167-169, 171, 174-176, 286
trace_level, 85, 163, 165, 167-172, 174, 286
tracing, xi-xii, 3, 83, 85, 154, 162-165, 167-174, 176, 283, 286, 317
type-specific component, 46, 51

U

Unlock, 105-106, 151, 153
Unregister, 98
use_compression, 286
user_auth_case, 322

V

validation controls, xiii, 3, 226-234, 236-237, 245-246, 248, 251, 253-254, 260-261, 277
Verity Query Language, 72
virtual document, xi, 6, 93, 100, 136, 139, 316, 345-346
VQL, 72-73, 81

W

wf_sleep_interval, 322
Workflow, 6, 24, 88, 93, 101-104, 201, 204, 260, 316, 322, 346
WorkSpace, v, 48, 107, 282
www.dmdeveloper.com, xviii

0-595-33968-9

Printed in the United States
104870LV00005B/25-26/A